In this volume, the author describes Pascal's pilgrimage from anguish to joy. He suggests that the sources of Pascal's anguish are uncertainty about his own personal identity, uncertainty about his relationship to his sister, Jacqueline, and uncertainty about his relationship to God. In Part One, the author describes Pascal's search in quest of his identity. He analyzes Pascal's discovery of his true self, and Pascal's pilgrimage toward an ever-deepening joy in an experience of ultimate authority and certainty.

In Part Two, the author deals with insights, drawn from Pascal, which throw light on the nature of doubt and certainty, the question of identity, and the epistemological issue of authority. In addition, Part Two analyzes Pascal's understanding of the hiddenness of God and the nature of joy, violence and ethics.

PASCAL'S ANGUISH
AND JOY

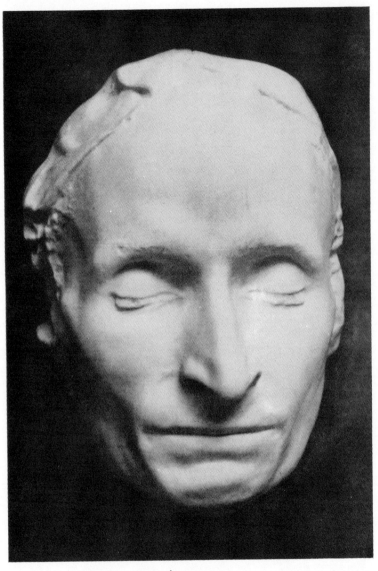

PASCAL'S DEATH MASK
From the cast in the Library of Newnham College, Cambridge

PASCAL'S ANGUISH
AND JOY

by

CHARLES S. MACKENZIE, Ph.D.

President
Grove City College
Grove City
Pennsylvania

PHILOSOPHICAL LIBRARY
New York

Manufactured in the United States of America

Dedicated
to

my wife

Florence

who has made such a difference
in my life

TABLE OF CONTENTS

Foreword ix

Chapter

One — "Genius in the Making" (1635-1637) 3
Two — "The Rivals" (1636-1639) 17
Three — "Renewal for the Church" 37
Four — "Rouen" (1639-1647) 47
Five — "Paris" (1647-1649) 63
Six — "The Last Reunion" (1649-1653) 83
Seven — "Sampling the World" (1653-1654) 107
Eight — "The Approach of the Storm" (1655-1658) 133
Nine — "The Final Contest" (1658-1661) 159
Ten — "The Last Conversion" (1662) 179
Eleven — "The Vindication of Christianity" 187
Twelve — "Pascal and the Anatomy of Doubt" 205
Thirteen — "Pascal and the Absence of God" 213
Fourteen — "Pascal and Joy" 223
Fifteen — "Pascal and a New Morality" 235
Sixteen — "Pascal and Violence" 245
Seventeen — "Pascal and Authority" 255
Bibliography 261
Footnotes 265

113060

FOREWORD

BLAISE PASCAL was one of the ranking geniuses of all time. After three centuries, his stature is undiminished. He stood at the crossroads where science and religion, nature and grace, doubt and faith intersect. What he said at the dawning of the modern era has great cogency for today's thinking men and women.

Central to all his thought was the question of faith and doubt, certitude and scepticism. Throughout his brief life, he anguished over the question of his own identity, which finally was resolved only when he was convinced of the identity of Jesus Christ as his Lord. Born June 19, 1623 into a gifted family, he was in constant competition with his beloved younger sister Jacqueline who helped to shape his life and destiny. As a mature young man he faced an identity crisis. Was he first a scientist, an amateur theologian or a "darling" of the royal court? Unsure of himself, he was unsure of God and his ultimate destiny. Then a vibrant, dynamic encounter with Jesus Christ settled the issue for him. Henceforth, he was primarily God's man filled with certitude and faith and joy.

This volume seeks first to outline and to interpret his life, his feelings and his thought, showing something of the influences which shaped both his faith and his doubt. It attaches special significance to the interaction between Blaise and his sister Jacqueline. It describes his quest for an abiding faith. He had faith in reason, but then he doubted reason. He had faith in science, but then he discovered science had its limitations. He had faith in the Roman Catholic Church, but then he questioned the Church. His pilgrimage into certitude and unshakable faith is the subject of chapters one through ten.

Secondly, chapters eleven through seventeen describe something of what he said to sceptics and what he says to us moderns as we, in an age of violence, journey from doubt and anguish toward faith and certitude.

Throughout this study of Pascal, references to his "Pensées" will be followed by two numbers in parentheses. The first is the number assigned by Lafuma. The second is that assigned by Brunschvicg. The author favors the ordering of Lafuma since it is closer to that intended by Pascal himself. In addition, whenever a reference is made to the "Oeuvres," it refers to Léon Brunschvicg's monumental work listed in the Appendix.

This volume has been written in the hope that it will be of assistance to others in their journey from the anguish of doubt to the joy of faith. Wherein it succeeds, it is due to the greatness of Pascal's life and thought. Wherein it falls short, it is due to the shortcomings of the writer.

C. S. MacKenzie
Grove City College

PASCAL'S ANGUISH
AND JOY

CHAPTER ONE

"GENIUS IN THE MAKING" (1635-1637)

THE YOUNG genius was hunched over on the tiled floor of the playroom. The only sounds in the small room were his labored breathing and the scratching of his charcoal pencil on the polished tiles. Outside could be heard the occasional, muted sound of carriage wheels crunching along Rue Brisemiche in Paris.

The lad who one day would be the talk of France shifted his frail body excitedly and with rapid strokes of the charcoal continued to trace triangles and circles on the chilly floor tiles. "These three 'bars'," thought the twelve-year-old, "intersect to form a triangle. The sum of the angles of the triangle ought to equal half of a 'round'." His charcoal traced a line when he said "bar," and drew a circle when he said "round." He had not yet been taught to call "bars" lines or "rounds" circles.

He paused in his scribbling. Out of the corner of his eye, he saw the boots and breeches of someone towering over him. Startled, he turned to find his father standing behind him. Etienne Pascal had entered the room quietly and had been watching his young son for some time.

Forty-seven-year-old Etienne Pascal was devoted to his son. He loved his daughters, capable Gilberte and fragile Jacqueline. But he had fastened all his hopes on the future of his son, Blaise.

Ever since the stormy night, nine years earlier, when Etienne's wife, tender Antoinette, had died in the large house in muddy

Clermont, the grief-stricken Etienne had devoted himself unstintingly to his children. Etienne had loved Clermont, with its 9,000 inhabitants, in Central France. He felt a part of the rugged, provincial countryside of Auvergne. He loved the jagged, green hills and the dirty, brown villages.

Etienne's father, Martin Pascal[1], had had great hopes for his oldest son. So he sent him to Paris to study law. When Etienne returned to Clermont in 1610, his star rose slowly. First, he had become a member of the lowest court set up to settle tax disputes. Then, 14 years later, he had become Deputy President of the Court of Aids at Montferrand, near Clermont. This made him one of the notables of the province. In 1616, he married twenty-year-old Antoinette Begon.

Then tragedy struck in 1626. When she was only thirty years old, his beloved Antoinette had died, leaving him with three small children. When Antoinette died, Gilberte, who would become the little mother to the family, was only six years old. Blaise was three. Jacqueline was only one year old. Etienne now was forced to become both mother and father to his children.

For five years he struggled to fulfill his roles both as a leading citizen of Clermont and as a devoted parent to his children. But it was too much for Etienne to handle alone. So, the lonely father made a momentous decision. He and his family left Clermont to move to Paris. Perhaps he felt that he had risen as high as he could in the provinces. Certainly, he was anxious to place his precocious young son in the intellectual stream which had its fountainhead in seventeenth-century Paris.

Thus, January 1632 found the Pascals moving into the Rue de la Tissanderie on the edge of the Marais district in Paris. Many luxurious mansions of the nouveau riche, mostly financiers and nobility, were being built there. After a taste of the exhilarating atmosphere of Paris, Etienne finally decided to cross his Rubicon and sell both his sprawling home on Clermont's Rue des Gras and his post as President of the Court of Aids to his brother Blaise. When he returned to Paris, he proceeded to invest his wealth[2] in bonds of Paris' Hôtel de Ville (City Hall), feeling that "municipal bonds" were as solid an investment as one could make.

A step up the social ladder also seemed in order. So, in 1634, after a pleasant sojourn in the comfortable house on Rue de la Tissanderie, he moved his family across the River Seine to a more elaborate house on the Rue de la Condé in the aristocratic Faubourg Saint-Germain, a wealthy suburb where some of the best-known leaders of Paris society had addresses. The Pascals' new home was almost next door to the Luxembourg Palace. In fact the Rue de la Condé ran right into the vast palace where Marie de Medici, the queen mother, had held court.

The splendor of the Luxembourg Palace, set amidst the flaming color of acres of gardens, was the pride of the neighborhood. When Etienne and his children walked to the head of the street, they were able to drink in the cold beauty of the stone palace that Jacques Debrosse had designed for Marie de Medici after the death of her husband, King Henry IV. Debrosse had laid out swirling acres of colorful flowers and greenery. In the palace Rubens had painted a series of pictures on the life of the vainglorious Queen mother, Marie. The Pascal girls were enchanted with the beautiful palace, its parks, its gardens and its famous fountains. And then, across from their house was the Condé mansion which was a meeting place for many fashionable and cultured groups. How excited the children became as famous men and women came and went at the house across the street.

Etienne, the man from the provinces, was surrounded by incredible wealth and opulence which made his own affluence pale in comparison. Yet Etienne was not abashed. He was first and foremost a man of the intellect. The realm of the mind mattered more to him than all the royal court with its lackeys and trappings.

5

But as Etienne checked his accounts, he realized later in 1634 that the luxury of an address in the Faubourg Saint-Germain was too expensive for his income. So he arranged to cancel his lease. Then he began the search for a new house. The right bank of the Seine seemed desirable since his friend the scholarly Father Mersenne lived there at the monastery of the Friars Minor in the Place Royale. So he sought a house in the area around the City Hall.

Etienne's intellectual stimulation in Faubourg Saint-Germain had been found mainly among poets at the exciting salon of the glamorous Madame Sainctot. But in 1635, Father Mersenne, who was well known for his extensive correspondence with Descartes in Holland and Fermat in Toulouse, had invited Etienne to join him, Mydorges, Roberval, Desargues and others in founding an academy of scientists.[3] This was flattering indeed for Etienne who was already enjoying something of a reputation in science. He had been recognized by Cardinal Richelieu in 1634, when the Cardinal named him to be one of five commissioned to investigate the work of Sieur Morin, who claimed to have perfected a method for determining longitudes. Now it was quite natural that Etienne should seek a residence near Mersenne.

Etienne soon learned of a house on Rue Brisemiche under the shadow of the Church of Saint-Merri. It was a beautiful house, smaller than most of the mansions in the area but quite large enough for Etienne. It was owned by Denis Baron, a Councilor of the King, who lived close by. The attractive two-story house was soon to be vacated by the family of Monsieur Dupuy, a public official.

Accordingly, on April 30th, 1635, Etienne climbed the steps of Baron's house and in the presence of the notary Bonot signed a five year lease at an annual rent of 525 livres. On the 24th of June, the Pascals and their servants moved in.

Rue Brisemiche had once been a side street where prostitutes and ruffians consorted. But in 1635 it had become a posh area. Antoine Arnauld, the famous lawyer, lived on nearby Rue Simon-le-Franc. Just a stone's throw away, the Pascals could see the side wall of the palatial residence of the fashionable Hennequin family. Wealthy Marie Hennequin had married titled Henri Gouffier. They had an 8-year-old son, Artus, and a 2-year-old daughter, Charlotte, when the Pascals became their neighbors. The day they moved in, Blaise little realized what a part Artus, the young Duke de Roannez, would play in his later life.

Etienne would return to the Rue de Condé from time to time to attend the meetings that would be started in 1638 by the avant garde Abbé Bourdelot in the Condé mansion. But in 1635, he succumbed to a magnetic pull to the right bank where much of the intellectual action was and where expenses were not so great.

Their new home in the Saint-Merri district was a sharp contrast to the aristocratic atmosphere near the Luxembourg Palace. Artisans of all sorts gave the Saint-Merri neighborhood its character. Haberdashers sold hats, furs and perfumes. The hairdressers of the most fashionable ladies of Paris had their establishments here. Jewelers, bankers and entertainers lived in its narrow streets. The Church of Saint-Merri was just a stone's throw from the Pascals' new home. Saint-Merri's flamboyant Gothic architecture was cramped by the three and four-story homes which crowded in upon it.

Into this atmosphere, Etienne brought his three children. Here, near Father Mersenne, he was sure he would find the intellectual stimulation he craved for himself and for his children.

It was here that Etienne discovered his twelve-year-old son pondering over the circles and triangles of geometry which were sketched in charcoal on the playroom floor[4]. As Etienne stood in silence watching the lad, he could remember that sometime earlier Blaise had looked up from dinner in their simple but comfortable dining room and, with his boyish head turned quizzically, had asked, "What is geometry, father?"

Etienne had peered intently across the table at the lad and

had slowly answered that it was "the method of making correct figures and of discovering the proportions which they bear to each other." Then he had changed the conversation, for it was his plan not to educate his son in mathematics until he was fifteen or sixteen years of age.

Now as Etienne stood watching dark-haired Blaise kneeling on the floor, he inquired "What is it that you are doing?" Blaise responded in his high voice that he had discovered that the sum of the angles of a triangle is equal to two right angles, 180 degrees, or "half a round." "Mon Dieu," Etienne thought, "without anyone's assistance, he is on the verge of discovering the thirty-second theorem of the first book of Euclid."

Quivering with excitement, the amazed Etienne turned on his heels and made his way down the stairs. Sometime later he seized his hat and cloak and went out into the crowded street. He had to find his friend, Le Pailleur. He wanted to share this news with someone who could rejoice with him. All his own love of mathematics, all his hopes that his son might attain the heights of greatness which he himself would never climb, made him feel like shouting the news to one and all.

When Etienne located his friend, Jacques Le Pailleur, he stood stock still in front of him as one transfixed. Etienne had met Jacques Le Pailleur many years before when they had been fellow students in Paris. Recently, he had rediscovered Le Pailleur among the group that met at Madame Sainctot's salon to discuss poetry and other cultural matters. He and Le Pailleur had taken immediately to discussing the mathematics of the time.

As Etienne recounted his son's discovery to his friend, he remembered the care he had taken to prevent Blaise from studying mathematics. He was afraid of distracting him from other subjects which he considered necessary as a proper foundation for his son's education. He could recollect, however, Blaise's dawning interest in science. When they had lived at Faubourg Saint-Germain, Blaise had surprised them one night at dinner.

Someone accidentally struck a dish with a knife. Blaise noticed the hum which the vibrations of the plate gave. But he also noticed that with a touch of one's hand, one could silence the vibrations. Young Pascal was not satisfied with the explanation Etienne had given him when he asked, "Why?" Therefore, he sought to discover the reasons for himself. Blaise had conducted experiment after experiment using glasses and plates and metal and wood. Then he assembled his data and wrote a very acceptable treatise on sound. Etienne was well aware of his son's precocity.

Etienne had always felt a very special responsibility for Blaise. He was a sickly infant. When he was only a year old, the family had nearly lost him. When Etienne discovered that a certain woman had cast an evil spell upon him, he frightened her into transferring the spell to a black cat which promptly died. With the aid of a special poultice, Blaise soon recovered. But Etienne had always felt a very special concern for him.

After his mother died, Etienne had determined to give Blaise the best possible education. He had always sought to hold his son above his tasks so that he would be able to put forth his best effort. He had encouraged Blaise to observe everything most carefully and to search out reasons for everything that happened.[5]

It had been his strategy to involve Blaise with Latin the very year his son had discovered geometry. He purposely kept mathematics from his little son, hoping to introduce him to it when he became fifteen or sixteen. Etienne, himself, had found such satisfaction in mathematics that he was afraid Blaise would become intoxicated with this pure science and neglect his other studies. But now he had discovered geometry on his own. Etienne was overjoyed, yet alarmed at his son's precocity. He asked Le Pailleur, "What am I to do, my friend?" In his slow, deliberate manner, Le Pailleur advised Etienne that since a hungry man dies without food, this new interest in Blaise should be nurtured as if it were a precious flower. Le Pailleur advised Etienne to water this interest, to nurture it, to feed it, to encourage it.

9

He urged his friend to give Blaise all the books on mathematics he was willing to read and to answer all his questions. He pointed out that his was a gift that had to be developed.

On a day soon after his conversation with Le Pailleur, Etienne called his son into the sun-drenched study of their home. Spread out on a table by the window were books and papers. Then and there the mind of Blaise Pascal began an exploration into the mysteries of mathematics. Day after day, father and son read and discussed Euclid, Pythagoras, Galileo and eventually Descartes. Blaise's high voice grew as excited as Columbus discovering America when he discovered the thrill of pondering a problem and then finding the answer by his own reasoning powers. It often was difficult for father and son to tear themselves away to answer the summons of Miss Louise, the heavy-set housekeeper as she called them to lunch.

Louise Default, the faithful housekeeper whom Etienne had engaged when he first came to Paris, probably shook her head woefully at the long hours father and son spent over their books. She must have wondered whether her young charge was being ruined by his father. She would have preferred that he spend more time with children his own age. She was delighted when Blaise was invited to the Roannez mansion across the street. Young Artus Gouffier to whom would go the title "Duke de Roannez," was more than four years younger than Blaise. When Artus first escorted Blaise into his home, Blaise was impressed by the great hall with its gilded chandeliers and its vivid tapestries of "The Adoration of Three Kings," "Herodias," and "The Four Seasons." But when Blaise went with Artus up the winding stairs to the young Duke's room in the attic of the old Hennequin mansion, he was startled by the severity of his rich neighbor's room. The windows had no curtains. A small inexpensive Bergamo tapestry hung on the large wall. Artus' high-poster bed was made of walnut. His lackey's low-poster bed was drab. The room contained three chairs covered with leather, two small tables and four chests. The room was heated by a fireplace in which stood a pair of andirons surmounted by twin balls of copper. Artus' room must have seemed plain and cold to young Pascal.

Blaise showed little desire to be with the Roannez children. After all, when one is going on thirteen, he feels infinitely superior to an eight-year-old. So for the time being, Artus and Blaise remained just neighborhood acquaintances.

As Blaise entered his teen years, he was intoxicated by mathematics. When he went with his family to mass at the neighborhood church, Saint-Merri, he could lose himself in studying the proportions of the soaring Gothic arches or in measuring the angles of the stained glass windows in the choir. Not that he lacked religious interest. To the contrary, through the years Etienne had seen to it that the catechism was a frequent topic of discussion. Sunday afternoons, after church, they would often sit and discuss Christianity.

It was the Sunday custom for Etienne to open the Bible, to read a passage and then to discuss the Catholic doctrine which could be inferred from the passage. As Blaise's questioning mind grew in its power to reason, Etienne secured a copy of "The Catechism of the Council of Trent" from his friend, Father Mersenne. The Catechism had been prepared for the instruction of the clergy, but Etienne's love of excellence may have prompted him to reason, "What is good for the clergy will be good for my son." So Etienne read and reread the Catechism to arm himself for the questions he knew would come.

One day, his high forehead furrowed, Blaise asked his father, "If reason can unlock so many mysteries for us in mathematics, what then is the need for faith?"

Etienne slowly and thoughtfully explained that some things are known only by faith. Some things are known only by reason. God has constructed the universe so that objects of faith can be understood only by faith and objects of reason can be discovered only by reason. We must learn to distinguish when to use reason and when to rely on faith. In the back of his mind,

Etienne could remember that a similar distinction had been made in Paragraph One of the Catechism.

Etienne continued to explain that there are various levels of reality. Each level of reality has its appropriate method and key. To understand spiritual realities, one must utilize faith.[6] About that time, Etienne decided that Blaise was ready to probe the higher levels of the mind and so he determined to take his son with him to the meetings of the Academy where Father Mersenne was a master at relating science to religion.

On a Thursday, Etienne and Blaise made their way to the Place Royale, and climbed the steps of the Hôtel de Minimes, the Monastery of the Friars Minor, where Father Mersenne lived. The wide-eyed youth was awed to come face to face with the short, serious priest whose eyes sparkled like sunlight shining through the clouds when he was pleased. The grey mingled with black in Mersenne's small, pointed beard. His tiny mustache was neatly groomed. His black cowl thrown back over his shoulders formed a frame for a kindly face dominated by a high, expansive forehead. Blaise had heard his father quote Mersenne often. As the thirteen-year-old bowed to meet Mersenne, others also were arriving at the Friary. There was Professor Gilles Personne de Roberval. Blaise was certain that this stern-faced scholar did not like him. The distinguished Professor of Science at the College of France reminded him of a man who had eaten too much and was in great discomfort. Later, Blaise would discover that Roberval was abrupt with everyone. The great Roberval actually was quite fond of the Pascals. That very year Roberval and Etienne had collaborated on a letter to Fermat of Toulouse in which they not only gave their viewpoint on gravity but also defined their view of the scientific method. Others arriving were the lawyer Carcavi, their family friend Le Pailleur, and the lens maker, Judge Mydorge. Then a slender young man entered the high-ceilinged salon. He was Pierre Petit, who entered with Gerard Desargues. Petit was an engineer, who was soon to be put in charge of French fortifications along the English Channel. Perhaps, because of his own youthfulness, Petit instantly warmed to the teenager sitting in the corner, Desargues also greeted Blaise warmly. In the course of the Thursday afternoons that were to follow, Desargues, when he was not detained by business in Lyons where he was the city architect, would often whisper words of clarification to the lad when the discussion would become difficult to follow. Desargues was a gentleman who was constantly thinking of others. His workmen at Lyons esteemed him for his thoughtfulness and for his careful explanations of the scientific principles underlying their work.

Thursday after Thursday, Blaise sat in the drawing room absorbed in the discussions of these savants. At first, he simply listened and asked an occasional question. Later, he began to interject his own observations.

He was particularly impressed with the elderly Mersenne. He watched the priest carefully as his eyes sparkled when he pressed a point in the discussions or as he disputed the irreverence of the Abbé Bourdelot, whose use of reason to undercut Christian dogma was to him a scandal.

One Thursday in 1636, Mersenne placed before the Academy members his latest book, which bore the title "Universal Harmony." He said, "This contains much of what I have been trying to say in our meetings. Namely, that religion and science are two aspects of the one body of truth." That had led to an exciting series of discussions as Mersenne's friends picked apart the work of their host. Yet they always seemed to concur with him that there was no necessary conflict between true science and true religion.

After such sessions, as Blaise and Etienne strolled homeward through the busy streets, they must have shared one with the other their questions and conclusions. Undoubtedly they would enter the house engaged in vigorous discussion which often carried over into the evening dinner hour. The faithful housekeeper, Louise, may have shaken her head sadly when father and son would scarcely notice the meals she prepared.

13

On a Thursday in 1637 as the Pascals entered the somber meeting place of the Academy, they saw a look of suppressed excitement on Father Mersenne's face. As the meeting began, Mersenne, his eyes flashing, announced, that that very week he had received from his friend Réné Descartes in Holland, a copy of his latest work. Descartes had given it the wordy title, "PLAN OF A UNIVERSAL SCIENCE THAT CAN RAISE OUR NATURE TO ITS HIGHEST DEGREE OF PERFECTION: IN PARTICULAR, DIOPTRIC, METEORS AND GEOMETRY, IN WHICH THE MOST CURIOUS MATTERS THE AUTHOR COULD SELECT ARE EXPLAINED IN SUCH A MANNER THAT EVEN THOSE WHO HAVE NOT STUDIED CAN UNDERSTAND THEM." The circle of scholars, hearing this lengthy title, must have looked at one another with amused smiles. Descartes needed to practice in his titles the simplicity he espoused in his book.

The next several meetings of the Academy were given to discussing this latest work of Descartes. Blaise learned, as he listened, that the forty-one-year-old Descartes was a strange blending of the mystical and the scientific. Descartes had studied mathematics and philosophy under the Jesuits at the College de la Fleche. He had traveled extensively as a soldier. He had lived in Paris for a short while but now was residing in Holland. When the Vatican's Holy Office had condemned the views of Galileo, which were also his own views, Descartes had been strangely silent. But now, at last, he had spelled out many of his convictions in this new book.

The members of the group rapidly passed over the first section, "A Discourse on Method." After all, Descartes' emphasis on questioning and doubting, his emphasis on experience and experimentation, was not new to that group. Blaise must have found great satisfaction in knowing that for a long while his older friends had been practicing the openness of mind which the great Descartes was espousing.

But when it came to the section on Dioptrics and optical

phenomena, it was a different matter. Roberval and Etienne labelled it confused. They said it did not appeal sufficiently to experience. Mersenne may have chided the two good-naturedly, wondering if their criticism had anything to do with their alliance with Fermat in his recent controversy with Réné Descartes. It seemed to him that his friend Réné used God merely to establish the reliability of man's knowledge of himself and of the world. This led to an intense discussion of God and his relationship to the world.

When Blaise went down the steps of the Friary late that afternoon, a dislike for Descartes had been born in his heart. Later that dislike would be fanned into a flame which would be fed both by jealousy and by imperious desire to rescue God from a man who seemed bent on imprisoning Deity in human thought processes. The young mind of genius was preparing to challenge the intellectual giants of the age.

CHAPTER TWO

"THE RIVALS" (1636-1639)

PARIS has always been an exciting place to live. In 1636, gay street fairs, the Carnival and crowded theaters gave the city an atmosphere of gaiety which enthralled the young people of France. One day as the family sat together, Etienne happily announced that he was planning to take his children to the Theater Marais to see a play that had had standing room only for weeks. Mondory, whom he had known ever since they had lived in Clermont, was playing a leading role.

Jacqueline, sitting beside her father, glowed with excitement as her father spoke. What eleven-year-old wouldn't be excited! She and Gilberte had often accompanied the Sainctot girls, Anne and Catherine, to the noisy fairs and colorful carnival. But now she was going to see Corneille's new play, "Le Cid."

Later she secured her own copy of "Le Cid." In the privacy of her room, she read and reread the play. She read it through, musing on the more meaningful lines. In her childish voice she read it aloud. As she came to the dinner table, she would often quote long portions of the play. Her pretty, little face must have shone in the candlelight as she excitedly recited the lines Corneille had written.

Placid Gilberte must have trembled with emotion to see her tiny sister as intense about Corneille as Blaise was about Euclid or Descartes. But then, Gilberte had often felt overwhelmed by the precocity of her younger sister. She could remember that even when Jacqueline had first begun to speak, she showed signs of unusual brightness and intelligence. She had learned to associate words and things so quickly.

Etienne had assigned Gilberte the task of teaching her younger sister to read. But when Jacqueline began to read, she had rebelled at first. Then came a turning point on a certain day in the house on Rue de la Tissanderie. Gilberte was reading poetry aloud to Jacqueline. The seven-year-old seemed entranced by the verses. She said, "If you want me to read, teach me out of a versebook. Then I will say my lesson as often as you like." So, patient Gilberte had struggled until late at night to compose verses of instruction. How Jacqueline responded! Indeed, by the time she was eight years of age, Jacqueline was composing her own poetry. Now, as Gilberte saw her eleven-year-old sister enchanted by Corneille's latest play, she should not have been surprised. Nevertheless, she was startled at the quickness and ease with which her sister memorized and "felt" the play.

For Jacqueline, the days must have dragged on slowly. Then came the hour when Etienne and his three children stood shivering in the autumn chill as the long line outside the Theater Marais moved towards the doors. Blaise shifted from one foot to another patiently. Gilberte stood quietly, trying to appear quite grown up. Tiny Jacqueline, however, squeezed her father's hand tightly. Her eyes were as large as saucers as she breathlessly watched the elegant ladies and their escorts arriving at the theater. When they finally were inside, amidst the ornate splendor of the theater, she sat up straight, taking in all the scenes, identifying with each character on stage, laughing and weeping alternately with Chimene and Rodrigue. It was a moving experience for Jacqueline to see Chimene seek the death of the man she loved on a point of honor.

That night when the house on Rue Brisemiche was hushed, she probably lay in her bed going over the lines of the play again and again. Undoubtedly, she imagined herself on stage. The eyes of hundreds were on her. She held her fantasy audience spellbound. Thus, an actress in embryo fell asleep.

Not long afterwards, Etienne announced to the family that soon he must return to the mountains of Auvergne for a visit.

Gilberte was excited. Family ties meant a great deal to the "little mother." She was eager to return to visit her birthplace and to be with relatives she had not seen for a long while. Blaise was non-committal. He would miss the Thursday discussions at Father Mersenne's but he would have more time both to read some of the books he loved and to discuss them with his father. Jacqueline, however, was in tears. To leave Paris and the atmosphere of the theater was tragic for the moppet who used her dolls to portray characters of her creation on the stage which was her bed.

Nevertheless, on a chill fall day, as leaves were spreading a tapestry of orange and gold across the French countryside, Etienne, Gilberte and Blaise left by carriage for Clermont. Jacqueline was not with them, though. She was on the other side of Paris happily ensconced in the home of Madame Sainctot whose daughters, Anne and Catherine, had persuaded their mother to invite coquettish Jacqueline to stay with them while her family went down to Clermont.

Jacqueline was in her glory at Madame Sainctot's. The Sainctot girls had a great deal of freedom. Their father, who had been the Treasurer of France at Tours, was dead. The beautiful Madame Sainctot and her brother, the poet D'Alibray, were preoccupied with her salon where she entertained many of the famous actors and poets of Paris.

In this atmosphere, Jacqueline, Anne and Catherine spent hours each day closeted together. The servants may have wondered at the low murmur of childish voices that came hour after hour from the room upstairs. As is the case with young girls, the mumble of voices was probably broken by giggles and then by torrents of laughter which floated through the house. Then one day, everyone learned what had been going on in the room upstairs. The girls had been composing a five-act play.

On a frosty, autumn day, they presented their play to a select audience of adults. In the tapestried drawing room, they put

19

on their play twice in one week, each time eliciting the "oohs" and the "aahs" which heralded it to be a success. What a thrill surged through Jacqueline as she realized that she was not only an actress but also a playwright.

Several weeks later, Etienne was back in Paris. His family was reunited in their home on snow-covered Rue Brisemiche. Winter eased over into spring, summer and fall. As 1638 dawned, Blaise was soon to be a gangly fifteen-year-old, still intoxicated with his mathematics and science. Gilberte was becoming an attractive, affectionate eighteen year-old. Jacqueline was just entering her teens.

In the nearly three years that the Pascals had lived on Rue Brisemiche, they had come to have several noteworthy acquaintances. Among them were the members of the Roannez family whose ducal palace stood on the nearby corner where the Rue Taillepain and the Rue du Cloitre-Saint-Merri intersected. The Roannez children, Artus and Charlotte, were not too different in age from Blaise and Jacqueline. Their mother was the shy Marie d'Hennequin, daughter of the fabulously wealthy president of Parliament. Their grandfather, Duke Louis, was a dissolute old man who scandalized the neighborhood with his risque reputation. The Roannez children used to wave to the Pascals when they met at church, but because of their different stations in life, theirs was kept just a nodding acquaintanceship.

It was different, however, with Monsieur and Madame de Morangis who also lived nearby. Monsieur de Morangis was Antoine Barillon of the powerful Barillon family. He was not only a Counsellor of State, he was also an administrative counsellor of their parish church, Saint Merri. This aristocratic couple had become enamoured with the gaiety, the precocity and the sweetness of Jacqueline, who often went to visit in their home.

About that time, Parisians were rejoicing in the news that their Queen, Anne of Austria, was pregnant. Every loyal Frenchman's heart rejoiced to know that the future of the monarchy was assured. The Pascal household was no exception.

One day Jacqueline, curled up by the window in her room, penned a sonnet in honor of the occasion. When she had finished it, she ran down the street to Madame de Morangis' house. As the gracious lady sat in her sitting room, listening to Jacqueline read her verses, she put down her embroidery, took the child in her arms and declared, "Ma petite, Her Majesty must hear these verses."

So it was that a few days later Jacqueline, dressed in her finest apparel, rode through the streets with Madame de Morangis to St. Germain, the royal palace. Jacqueline could not help but be impressed as she was ushered toward the royal apartment by an elegant young page dressed in velvet with lace trimming. At the entrance to the Queen's apartment was a large reception room. The pale blue walls, trimmed in white and gold; the deep blue drapes with gold tassels; the huge, crystal chandelier at the center of the room, all formed a backdrop of royal splendor. Ladies-in-waiting lounged about the room. Pages and squires scurried about. The scent of perfume filled the air.

As Madame de Morangis and her young charge entered the room, from near the window a strikingly beautiful, tall, young lady turned and swiftly crossed to greet them. She was the talk of Paris. Madame de Morangis presented the twelve-year-old to Mademoiselle de Montpensier, the King's niece. She was popularly known as the "Grande Mademoiselle" because of her height. In the struggles for power at the royal court, she was most effective in advancing the cause of her father, the Duke of Orleans. Mademoiselle, in turn, introduced diminutive Jacqueline to others in the crowded reception room. Meanwhile, Madame de Morangis learned that it would be awhile before the Queen could see them.

So she said to her friends, "Jacqueline has composed some amazing verses in honor of our Queen. You must hear them." Then turning to Jacqueline, she said, "Will you do us the honor?"

Jacqueline, always eager for an audience, folded her hands in front of her and softly began:

"Let us rejoice, since our Princess
Has our desires so richly blessed.
For by this pregnancy so long denied
Our disappointment and misfortunes have all died.

Our hearts at this stroke of fate o'erflow with joy,
Knowing that our enemies will all be destroyed.
For a Dauphin will take our woes as his own
And by him all evil designs be o'erthrown.

O France, your vows to Divinity repay,
By this dear Dauphin so longtime desired,
Will our hopes be fulfilled and our souls inspired.

Great God! To you I fondly appeal,
In your protection, our Queen conceal.
Since to preserve her, is to preserve France."

When she had finished, a wave of applause swept over the
room. It seemed incredible that this twelve-year-old had composed such thoughtful sentiments. Indeed, the Grande Mademoiselle, as if to test the child's ability, said, "You make verses
so well, make some for me."

Within Jacqueline's tiny body was a strong will which rose
courageously to any challenge. So she replied, "It will bring me
great joy to do as you bid me."

Then, she went to a table by the window where she worked
with bowed head, writing and scratching out. Then she returned,
bowed to Mademoiselle and when she had received a nod in
return began:

22

"It is our noble princess' will
That Thou my Muse, exert Thy skill
To celebrate her charms today:
Hopeless our task! — The only way
To praise her well is to avow
The simple truth — we know not how."

Again applause filled the room, this time led by the flattered Mademoiselle. But one last time Mademoiselle put her to the test, saying, "Now make one for Madame de Hautefort." Madame de Hautefort, another lady-in-waiting, blushed but appeared pleased.

Again, Jacqueline withdrew to compose her verse. And again she returned to read to the crowd gathered about Mademoiselle:

"O marvel not, bright masterpiece of earth,
At the prompt tribute by your charms called forth.
Your glance, that roves the world around
In every clime hath captives found.
That ray which charms my youthful heart,
May well arouse my fancy's art."

This time the room rocked with the ovation that was given Jacqueline.

But then the door to the Queen's apartment opened, a servant beckoned and Madame de Morangis and Jacqueline were on their way to see the Queen.

The Queen, Anne of Austria, was a beautiful woman in her mid-thirties. Her complexion was like honey and cream. Her eyes were warm and friendly. Her lovely hair was long and silken. She vibrated with health and strength. When she was pleased, her full lips rounded into a gentle smile. She usually awakened at ten or eleven o'clock, received a few visitors and then breakfasted.

As Jacqueline entered the Queen's apartment, she kept her eyes downcast in an appropriately demure manner. Then she stood before the great lady. She found herself thinking how modestly her Queen dressed, without gold or silver jewelry, without rouge upon her lovely face.

Jacqueline bowed in a low curtsy. Madame de Morangis explained to the sovereign about Jacqueline's verses in honor of the Queen's pregnancy. A smile of amusement played about the Queen's face as Jacqueline began to recite. But the Queen's look of amusement gave way to an air of puzzlement. When Jacqueline was finished, the Queen said softly, "But she is so young. It is impossible that she could have composed these verses."

Madame de Morangis quickly responded, "That is what the others outside thought, your Majesty. But when they asked her to write verses in honor of both Mademoiselle and of Madame de Hautefort, she produced these without hesitation." With that she held out to the Queen the papers on which Jacqueline had scratched her epigrams in the waiting salon. The Queen glanced at them and then burst into a broad, sunshiny smile. She beckoned the child to her, gave her a quick hug and said, "You must come back to see me often, my little one."

As in a dream, Jacqueline was then led out of the royal apartment, back to the waiting room and a while later she rode home in triumph.

During the days that followed, Jacqueline often accompanied Madame de Morangis to St. Germain. She became a favorite of the ladies-in-waiting. Once she was even allowed to assist Mademoiselle in waiting on the Queen as she dined on cutlets, sausages and bread-porridge in her apartment. What a world of splendor this opened up to the youngest Pascal.

24

Meanwhile, a storm was gathering on the horizon. In spite of the prosperity under Richelieu's rule, taxes had to be increased both to pay the armies fighting on German soil and to finance the continuing struggle with Spain in the Low Countries. Duke Bernhard of SaxeWeimar was winning the day in Alsace for King Louis XIII but he had to be supplied generous amounts of French money. In addition, in the Lowlands the victorious French generals, who were slowly capturing one after another of the towns in Artois from the Spanish forces, were in need of funds. Consequently, early in March 1638, Cardinal Richelieu imposed a stiff tax on the dividends of Paris' Hôtel de Ville. On some bonds, no interest was to be paid at all.

When word reached Etienne, who depended so heavily for his income on dividends from the Hôtel de Ville, he put his head in hands and wept. "Mon Dieu," he cried, "I am ruined."

On March 21st, a number of the 400 investors affected gathered at the City Hall to make their protest. Etienne was among the leaders of the protest before the powerful Chancellor Séguier. The argument grew heated. Violence and even rebellion was threatened against a regime that would not honor its promises. Amidst threats and shouting, the white-faced, angry Chancellor Séguier withdrew from the council hall followed by his excited assistants.

The Hôtel de Ville had been the scene of much clamor since it was built in 1553. Its front entrances, its high turrets, its host of windows looked out on the dreaded Place de Grève where France's kings had enemies of the throne executed. As Etienne and the other enraged investors streamed down the steps after their stormy interview with the Chancellor of France, they were brave on the outside but some may have wondered if their violent meeting might lead them to an appointment with the executioner in the Place de Grève.

Later in the day, when Séguier in his robes of office, stood before the imperious Cardinal Richelieu and reported on the protest meeting, Richelieu, without a moment's hesitation, raised his hand to halt the Chancellor's flow of words and immediately gave the command that the ringleaders of the protest group be arrested and imprisoned.

Meanwhile, Etienne had hurriedly entered his house. Louise, the housekeeper, could see that something was amiss. Etienne, after directing Louise to pack his clothes, gathered the children together and hastily recounted what had happened. After reassuring the children that he would return soon, he told them that he must travel to Auvergne to remain there until the Chancellor's temper had cooled. Then with a tearful embrace for each child, with a hasty word to Louise to care well for the children and with an assurance that Madame Sainctot would be in constant touch with them, he went down the stairs and was gone. That evening, the house seemed strangely quiet except for the muffled sobs which came from frightened children fearful for their father's life. For long they had been motherless. Now for awhile they must be fatherless.

The days lenghtened into weeks and the weeks into months. Blaise buried his head in his books as if to escape the fears he had for his father. Gilberte busied herself helping Louise care for the house. The warm summer days found Jacqueline playing with her dolls, acting out plays which she created for them.

Occasionally, she would curl up by the open window of her room and draft some verses for the Queen that she now did not dare to approach. The verses came easily. Soon she had a collection of poems which she dedicated to the Queen, hopeful that her efforts might atone for her father's imprudence. Madame de Morangis arranged to have them printed under the title "Verses of the Little Pascal." It was hoped that they might cause the Queen to intervene on behalf of Etienne. But the Queen was not ready to challenge an action of the Cardinal who held France in his iron grasp.

The hot summer days found the Pascal children praying fervently for their father's return. The messages they had received from him indicated that he was safe but that it was not yet wise for him to return to the city that was honeycombed with Richelieu's agents.

One Sunday in August, after they had returned from mass at Saint-Merri, Jacqueline read to her brother and sister her latest poem which showed the prayerful direction of her thoughts. In her soft voice she read:

"Lord of the Universe
If the strong chains of verse
Round my delighted soul their links entwine.
Here let me own
The gift is thine alone
And come, great God, from no desert of mine.

Yea, Lord, how many long
For the sweet power of song,
Which Thou hast placed in my young, feeble hear
Thy bounties string my lyre,
And, with celestial fire,
To my dull soul a hidden light impart.

O Lord of thankless mind
Will not acquittal find
In Thy pure presence. Therefore it is just
That, touched with godlike flame,
I should Thy love proclaim,
And chant the glories of Thy name august.

As waterfall, and rills,
And streams wind past the hills
In steady progress toward their parent sea,
Thus Lord my simple lays,

Heedless of this world's praise,
Find their way home, O Source Divine to Thee."

Gilberte, as always, was enraptured by her sister's verses. Blaise was strangely silent. Later as he made his way upstairs to his room, the fifteen-year-old had justification to wonder, "Heedless of this world's praise indeed!" His little sister was very proud of her accomplishments.

But soon Jacqueline was to be humbled. As the fall days grew shorter and the nights colder, dreaded smallpox attacked her slight frame.

While she lay on her bed shivering and trembling from the disease, a messenger was racing over the roads to Clermont carrying the dark news to Etienne. Within a few days, Etienne had made his way back to Paris, through the door of the house on Rue Brisemiche and was sitting in Jacqueline's darkened room, holding her hand and praying. Friends urged him to come away before Richelieu's spies learned that he was back. But Etienne could not be persuaded. Night and day he stayed by her side, watching the doctor, supervising the nurse who bathed her thin body. He slept in fits and starts. Then, finally, the crisis was over and she was on the mend. Then, and only then, did the tormented father leave her side to resume his hiding.

It took a long time for Jacqueline to regain her strength. During the days of recuperation, Gilberte and Blaise wondered how she would react when she discovered that smallpox had marked her pretty little face with "pits." They didn't have to wait long. When they discovered her latest verse, they knew that she had seen herself in the mirror. After the initial shock, and after a few tears, she had penned the words:

"These I accept, my sovereign Lord!
As token seals that Thy blest hand
Would guard henceforth my innocence."

28

Later she revealed how deep was her acceptance of her scars in a poem entitled, "Thanking God for Recovery from the Smallpóx:"

"Ruler of earth and skies
Bid Thou my hymn arise
As from an angel's tongue;
I sound no mortal's praise,
To Thee my voice I raise,
And at Thine altars chant my grateful song.

Thou from Thy throne above,
Hast looked, in sovereign love,
On a poor earth-worm's trail;
Thy hand my fever broke,
And shielded from death's stroke
A racked and restless frame, than glass more frail.

All men, great God may see
Thy pure benignity
To one so weak and worn;
Without Thy loving aid
Thus wonderfully displayed,
My life had faded in its April morn.

When in the mirror, I
scars of mine illness spy,
Those hollow marks attest
The heart rejoicing truth,
That I am thine, in sooth,
For Thou dost chasten whom Thou lovest best.

I take them for a brand
That, Master, Thy kind hand
Would on my forehead have,
Mine innocence to show: —
And shall I murmur? No.
While Thy rod comforts me, I will not grieve.

But Lord, my work is vain,
No human heart or strain
To praise Thee hath the skill.
To tell Thy bounties here
That charm the eye and ear,
Passes my power, but cannot pass my will."

As 1639 dawned, Jacqueline's friends, the De Morangis, realized that if Etienne was to be absolved, it was necessary to go beyond the King and Queen to appeal to the all-powerful Richelieu. But how to get to the Cardinal? This was the unanswered question.

Then a strange set of circumstances took place. Richelieu's niece, who had been a neighbor of the Pascals when they lived in the Faubourg Saint-Germain, was trying to get together a children's play to amuse the Cardinal and some of his guests. Richelieu delighted in the theater and had tried his own hand at writing tragedies. He had let fall the remark that he would be amused to see a tragedy acted out by children. His niece, the Duchess d'Aiguillon, over-hearing his remark, set to work to honor his request. She turned to Madame Sainctot for help. Madame Sainctot saw this as an opportunity to help Etienne and so she suggested that in addition to one of her daughters that Jacqueline also be part of the cast.

Thus one day an elegant carriage entered Rue Brisemiche and drew up in front of the Pascal house. A messenger extended the Duchess' invitation to Jacqueline. Gilberte was present and haughtily replied, "The Cardinal has not been kind enough to us, to make us take any pains to give him pleasure." When Gilberte's message was carried back to the Duchess, who was accustomed to healing rifts caused by her uncle, she gently replied to the teen-aged head of the house that through Jacqueline the Cardinal might be persuaded to pardon her father. With this argument, Gilberte was won over, but only after securing the advice of the De Morangis.

Within a few days, the famous actor Mondory began rehearsing the children in Scudéry's play "L'Amour Tryrannique." Mondory gave special attention to Jacqueline's portrayal of Cassandra. How she toiled over her lines. She spent long hours before her mirror, practicing facial expressions and gestures.

Then came the all-important night. At seven o'clock a distinguished throng was assembled at the Cardinal's new residence, behind the Louvre. The newly built Palais-Cardinal, designed for Richelieu by the famous Mercier, was becoming known for its art collection, its echoing galleries, its formal gardens, as well as for its famous inhabitant. In the theater of the Palace, Jacqueline and the other children peered from the wings at the crowd that was gathering beneath the great candelabra. Then the Cardinal entered!

Mondory went to welcome Richelieu and to offer a word of explanation about the play. The lean, intense Cardinal was relaxed and in a jovial mood. So Mondory took occasion to mention the littlest Pascal and to offer a good word for her missing father. Then he retired. Most of the candelabra were extinguished, the curtain was lifted and the play began.

As the children moved across the stage, reciting their lines of passion and intrigue with utter seriousness, the Cardinal and his guests were moved with admiration mingled with tenderness to see little people performing as adults.

31

Then the curtain fell and the theater rang with applause. The youthful cast stepped down from the stage. Jacqueline was watching for Madame Sainctot who was supposed to lead her to the Duchess d'Aiguillon who was then to present her to the Cardinal. But Madame Sainctot was nowhere in sight. To Jacqueline's dismay, the Cardinal was rising, ready to leave the theater. In panic, the littlest Pascal, tears flooding her eyes, rushed to the side of the great Richelieu. When he saw her standing before him, he exclaimed, "There is the little Pascal." Then, noting her tears he sat down again, drew her close and said in a gentle voice, "Why are you crying?"

With trembling voice, Jacqueline replied,

"Deem it not strange, Thou Prince without a peer,
If I have failed to hold thine eye and ear;
My trembling frame seems palsied with dismay,
And trouble steals my very voice away.
If thou wouldest have me win thy gracious smile,
Call back a banished father from exile.

Of clemency oft proved this boon I crave,
From perils vast the innocent to save.
Thus wilt thou set soul, voice and gesture free
To task their utmost skill in pleasing thee."

Startled into utter seriousness, Richelieu made answer, "I grant you all that you ask. Write your father telling him that he may return in safety."

Just then Madame d'Aiguillon approached her uncle and whispered in his ear, "Really uncle, you ought to do something for that man. I have heard much said of him. He is an honest and learned man. It is too bad that his talents are not used. He has a son who, though only fifteen years old, is a learned mathematician."

The Cardinal interrupted her to say again to Jacqueline that she should send for her father and that he could return in safety.

Jacqueline, noting the Cardinal's good humor, then added, "My Lord, I have still another favor to ask of your eminence."

"Ask what you like, little one, and I will grant it," he responded.

"I entreat your eminence," she said, "to allow my father the honor of paying his respects to you on his return, so that he may himself thank you for the kindness you have done us all today."

The Cardinal smiled and said, "Not only granted, but it is just what I wish. Tell him that he need have no apprehension in coming and let him bring his whole family with him." Glancing at Gilberte and Blaise standing nearby, he commented on what pleasure it gave him to restore the father to this charming family. Then he arose and made his way through the fawning crowd, out of the theater to his own apartment

The cast and their admirers made their way down a long hall to another room in the palace where they saw a long table, presided over by huge silver candelabra and graced with fresh fruits, dried fruits and tarty lemonade. As the young actors and actresses enjoyed the refreshment, Blaise and Gilberte sat at the edge of the room, barely able to contain their excitement that their father could return home.

The next day, April 4th, Jacqueline sat at the desk in her room and wrote her father the glad news in a long letter. She energetically wrote, "When I saw him (the Cardinal) in such a good temper I asked whether he would allow you to make your reverence to him. He said you would be welcome and added, 'Tell your father that when he comes back he must come and see me', and repeated this several times. Then as Madame d'Aiguillon left, my sister saluted her, and she asked where my brother was, saying she wanted to see him. My sister brought Blaise to her and she paid him many compliments on his science. Then we were taken to a room where a wonderful feast was spread for us." She brought her letter to a close, penning the words, "I feel extremely happy to have helped to bring about something which must give you satisfaction. That has always been the intense desire of your very humble and very obedient daughter and servant." The stilted language of the letter, so characteristic of the age, could scarcely convey the pride and joy which Jacqueline felt as she sealed the letter and sent it on its way.

Shortly thereafter, Etienne arrived back at the house on Rue Brisemiche. As his family gathered about him in his study, there were tears of joy. Laughter punctuated long periods of intense seriousness as the Pascals recounted to each other the experiences of the months that were now past. Then they turned their thoughts and plans to Etienne's meeting with the Cardinal.

Just a short distance west of Paris lies the Village of Rueil. Etienne was told that the Cardinal was in seclusion there. As he rode the narrow road to Rueil, Etienne noted that the grass was turning green and that song birds were reappearing in the trees overhead. Spring was about to break forth upon the tranquil French countryside.

When Etienne entered the Cardinal's country residence, his heart sank as the Cardinal's secretary told him that he would be admitted only if he brought his family with him.

So the next day Etienne again rode the road to Rueil. This time he was accompanied by Jacqueline, Blaise and Gilberte. Their presence quickly gained him an audience with the most powerful man in France. Richelieu was gracious, as he could be when he desired. He said, "It gives me great gratification to reunite your family. These children need tender care. Watch over them carefully. I intend to make something great of them." Then with a caress for Jacqueline, a pat on the shoulder for Gilberte and a smile for Blaise, he dismissed them. But not until he had instructed his squire to give the Pascals a tour of Rueil and to entertain them generously.

As Etienne and his children walked through the gardens and the park at Rueil before returning to Paris, Jacqueline's young heart was singing. They were a family reunited and she had accomplished it.

CHAPTER THREE

RENEWAL FOR THE CHURCH

ABOUT twenty-five miles southwest of Paris, in the wooded valley of the Chevreuse, amidst marshy fields and meandering streams, was the abbey of Port-Royal. This tiny community of the Cistercian order was founded in the year 1204 by a woman of wealth, Mathilde de Garlande, as an act of thanksgiving for the safe return of her crusader husband. The abbey lay in a spot which had originally been called Porrois, a name derived from the French "Porra," a hole filled with brushwood and stagnant water. In 1600, the abbey had fallen into disrepair and disrepute. It was in truth "a hole filled with brushwood and stagnant water." Discipline was almost non-existent. With the exception of seven or eight occasions when nuns had made their professions, nearly thirty years had passed since a sermon had been preached at the abbey. In 1600, the nuns made their communion only once a month. Masquerades were held frequently at the abbey. The Bernardine monk who was the Confessor didn't understand the Lord's Prayer and didn't know a word of the Catechism. His chief exercise was hunting. Port-Royal was dead spiritually!

There amidst the dampness of the Chevreuse valley, there intercepted by springs and a broad canal, were the grounds of Port-Royal. The soaring church faced the southeast. The cloister was south of the Church. Four-storied buildings ranged about the grassy area south of the Church. Directly opposite the main entrance to the Church was the simple refrectory. A little distance east of the Church, on the edge of the woods, was "The Solitude," an outdoor place dominated by a large cross.

There, in that semi-circle dug into the side of the hill, the mother superior in years to come would gather her nuns around her on stone benches for prayers.

As the sixteenth century drew to its close, a distinguished lawyer of Paris, Antoine Arnauld, took an interest in Port-Royal. Arnauld, after Jesuits had attempted to assassinate King Henry IV in 1594, had spoken before the French Parliament against the suspect Jesuit order. His eloquence helped to bring about the expulsion of the Jesuits shortly afterwards. He was well-known and well-to-do when he turned his attention to Port-Royal.

He had fathered some twenty children but only ten of them had lived. He thought it fitting for a man with his religious "connections" to have some of his children "in religion." So he arranged for seven-and-a-half-year-old Jacqueline Arnauld to be made titular co-adjutor of the desolate convent of Port-Royal. Accordingly, in 1599, she was invested and given the name Angélique. Her younger sister, five-and-a-half-year-old Jeanne, entered the novitiate at the Benedictine abbey of Saint-Cyr in 1600 and was given the name Agnes.

Angélique's (Jacqueline's) function at Port-Royal was considered to be purely honorary since her senior colleague, though advanced in years, seemed to be in good health. Agnes' (Jeanne's) responsibilities were to be assumed by a proxy until she reached twenty.

But Angélique's abbess died unexpectedly! After some tricky negotiations in which eleven-year-old Angélique was reported to be twenty, approval of her appointment as abbess was secured from Rome. She was installed in her office on July 5, 1602.

Angélique was bright and perceptive. But life at Port-Royal was dull and dreary. She soon grew weary of life at the abbey. She struggled to keep her spirit alive by entertaining visitors, walking beside the brooks and under the linden trees, and by reading secular writings of the times.

But by the time she was fifteen, she could stand it no longer.

Her dream was to run away from the damp Chevreuse valley to her Huguenot aunts at La Rochelle. Those Protestant relatives would surely welcome a runaway nun.

Then sickness struck. Her father had her transported carefully to Paris for treatment. At the Arnauld's fashionable mansion in Paris, Angélique's heart ached as she saw again the rich life of her sophisticated aunts and uncles and as she realized that they represented a world she could not enter. The siren call to life in the world sounded loudly in her soul. But her strong-willed father muted that call by forcing her to sign, without giving her time even to read it, a statement renewing her vows. So Angélique returned to the dismal Chevreuse valley where she pined all winter, hating her lot. Not even the frequent visits of her devout younger sister, Agnes, seemed to help.

As Lent 1608 approached, her teen-age restlessness was acute. Her reading had become limited to a book of Meditations which she had been given. Her only "excitement" was the arrival of a Capuchin monk, Father Basil, who asked the opportunity to preach to the little community. At least this would be something different, so the captive young abbess gave her consent.

The shadows lengthened toward evening on the appointed day. The monk stood in the chapel before the curious gaze of the assembled nuns. He spoke of the coming of the Son of God to be born of a young woman in a lowly manger. Young Angélique was spellbound. This monk of questionable character was opening a new world to her. Later she declared, "During this sermon, God touched me so that from that moment I felt happier to be a nun than I had felt unhappy to be one before." A personal awareness of God's love began to dawn within her soul.

The months which followed saw the young abbess struggling to understand what this new experience meant for her life and for her community. It now seemed crystal clear to her that Port-Royal needed a spiritual renovation. But her nuns showed little sympathy with a reform movement.

Another sermon, on All Saint's Day 1608, stabbed into her soul. She was at war with herself. Should she do what she felt to be right in the eyes of God or should she accede to the anti-reformation mood of her nuns? The inner torment of her soul left her listless and weak of body.

When the Lenten season 1609 arrived, the Prioress of the abbey approached Angélique to say that the nuns were so concerned about her inner turmoil that they wished the reform to begin at once if only it would restore her to health. Immediately, the reform of Port-Royal was undertaken. Agnes came from Saint-Cyr to assist her sister.

The nuns now were to own all things in common. The community was closed off from the world. Spiritual discipline was reinstituted. A spiritual revolution was in the making.

Antoine Arnauld knew nothing of all this. But he soon learned! On September 25, 1609, he, his wife, their oldest son and daughter and a younger daughter, journeyed from Paris through the falling leaves of autumn to visit Angélique, Agnes and another daughter, Marie-Claire, at Port-Royal.

As the carriage pulled up near the outer gate, Antoine stepped out of the carriage, walked the little distance to the convent, and knocked at the wicket gate. The little inspection window opened to reveal the face of seventeen-year-old Angélique. Two strong-willed Arnaulds were face to face through the window. Antoine insisted upon entering. Angélique explained her reformation policies and refused him admission. Antoine, his wife and son were furious. The other two daughters sat silently in the carriage, frightened by all the commotion.

Antoine insisted that Angélique hand over her two younger sisters to him. Agnes and Marie-Claire came out by a side door; but still Antoine did not get in.

Indignant, he was about to mount the coach to return to Paris when Agnes persuaded him to enter a little side parlor which had been set aside to receive outsiders. Through the grille dividing the room, Antoine pleaded with Angélique to remember all that he had done for her. After all, he was her father. With all the techniques of the master lawyer, he appealed to her not to ruin herself with these ridiculous disciplines and austerities.

Suddenly the room began to spin for Angélique. Everything went black for her and she fell over in a faint.[1] It had been too much for her to hear her own father trying to dissuade her from doing what she felt God wanted her to do.

Antoine, fearful for his daughter prostrate before him, changed his tune. When Angélique recovered, the whole family talked with her, still through the grille. They agreed that henceforth the women of the family might enter freely but that the men might only visit the grounds, not the cloister.

As the Arnaulds returned to Paris, Angélique had won the victory, a victory which made her such a heroine to her community that she now was able to impose an even stricter rule of poverty upon her nuns. Port-Royal was no longer the Arnauld's country place. It had become a religious community.

As the years flitted by, Port-Royal became widely known for its piety and spiritual discipline. It became a model for other convents to follow. Mother Angélique was called upon to help reform other abbeys like the disordered abbey of Maubuisson. Her work at Maubuisson attracted the attention of Monsieur de Saint-Cyran and St. Francis de Sales. Indeed, upon her return to Port-Royal from Maubuisson, she persuaded De Sales to visit her abbey. Her nuns were captivated and inspired by his gentle, affectionate spirit as he walked among them.

In 1626, Angélique's mother, now a widow and desirous of taking the veil, persuaded the community of eighty to move to Paris from their damp and unhealthy valley where fifteen had died in the last two years. They left only a chaplain to serve the church at Port-Royal in the Fields. The new Port-Royal in Paris occupied an estate in the rural section of Paris' Faubourg St. Jacques. In 1627, a papal bull placed the Port-Royal community under the Archbishop of Paris.

Then a strange succession of events occurred. Angélique resigned as abbess at Port-Royal to be made superior of the New Institute of the Holy Sacrament, an elegant new convent near the Louvre. Her sister Agnes was elected abbess of Port-Royal. Eventually Angélique returned to Port-Royal. But she brought a new influence to bear upon the transplanted community of Port-Royal. For while Angélique was superior at the Institute, her devotional booklet, the "Secret Chaplet", had been criticized by the Bishop of Sens. It was defended publicly by Saint-Cyran. Subsequently, Saint-Cyran had been appointed director of the Institute in 1634. Thus an alliance of destiny was forged which resulted in Saint-Cyran's following Angélique back to Port-Royal where he became the Spiritual Director in 1636.

Saint-Cyran's name was Jean du Vergier de Hauranne. He had been born of a noble family in Bayonne in 1581. He studied at the Sorbonne and Louvain where he attracted much attention by his intellectual brilliance. Along the line, he struck up a profound friendship with Cornelius Jansen. Both of these young men were vitally concerned over the spiritual deadness of the Church. They had spent the better portion of five years at De Hauranne's home in Bayonne where they studied together the sources of the Christian faith, particularly St. Augustine. Their passion was to discover the doctrines which had given Christianity its original vitality.

When they parted, Jansen returned to Louvain where he was appointed Principal of the new college of Holland in 1617. Later he would be consecrated Bishop of Ypres. On the other hand, De Hauranne was made abbot of Saint-Cyran in 1620. It was at Saint-Cyran that he met his first Arnauld, d'Andilly, the eldest son of Antoine.

Through the years, letters continued to be exchanged between Saint-Cyran and Jansen. Their dream was to reinstate the Biblical doctrine of grace. Together they agreed on an outline for the book entitled, "Augustinus," which Jansen would write. They dreamt of finding a religious community where their dreams of renewal could be translated into practical reality. Port-Royal was to be that community.

One of Saint-Cyran's innovations at Port-Royal was the formation of a group of solitaries. These men occupied Port-

42

Royal in the Fields. The Arnaulds were the nucleus of this group. In 1637 the grandson of Antoine, thirty-year-old Antoine le Maitre, retired from the legal profession where he was making a brilliant name for himself. Antoine built a little hermitage on the edge of the empty convent grounds. Soon he was joined by his youngest brother Isaac who later would enter the priesthood, changing his name to De Saci. One by one others joined them in their simple and austere life in the Chevreuse valley. There they drained the marshes. There they instructed the children of the region. There one day they would be joined by Blaise Pascal.

But first, in 1638, Cornelius Jansen died. Two years later his masterpiece, "The Augustinus," was published at Louvain. It was a massive study in Latin of the teachings of Augustine on grace. In 1641, it was published at Paris and in 1643 at Rouen.

The "Augustinus" described by Saint-Cyran as "*the* book of devotion of these latter days" consisted of three volumes. In the first volume, Jansen analyzed the Pelagian heresy. In the second volume, he described Adam's state of innocence and the state of man after the Fall. The introduction to the second volume discussed the limitations of human reason. The third volume dealt with the grace of Christ and delineated the errors of the Semi-Pelagians in comparison to contemporary groups such as the Jesuits.

When Jansen's massive work appeared, Saint-Cyran was in prison at Vincennes. Richelieu had never liked Saint-Cyran. He declared, "He is a Basque. His entrails are on fire and they send into his head vapours which he mistakes for inspirations." Cardinal Richelieu and many in the religious establishment were bitterly resentful of Saint-Cyran's criticisms of the worldly, secularized church of the age. Saint-Cyran had even been so bold as to say, "God has shown me that there has not been a real church for more than five or six hundred years." The prophet has always made his contemporaries feel uncomfortable. Thus Richelieu in his discomfort sent Saint-Cyran to prison

43

without a trial and without any explanation except words spoken to a friend, "If Luther and Calvin had been clapped into jail the moment they started dogmatizing, the nations would have been saved a great deal of trouble." In addition, the theologically inflexible Richelieu also maintained that attrition or sorrow for sin out of fear of eternal punishment was sufficient for absolution. He resented Saint-Cyran's contentions that contrition or penitence prompted by the love of God was necessary.

Five years later, after Richelieu's death, Saint-Cyran was released from prison. Though he died a short time later, in 1643, he succeeded in tying the destiny of Port-Royal firmly to that of Jansen's "Augustinus." Though an Arnauld would become Port-Royal's chief exponent of the "Augustinus," Saint-Cyran had conditioned Port-Royal to receive it. When the "Augustinus" was published in 1640, it was like a delayed action bomb waiting to explode into the life of France and into the life of the Pascal family.

The "Augustinus" quickly became a topic of conversation in ecclesiastical circles at Paris. Some were persuaded by its ring of truth. Others were repulsed by what seemed to border on heresy. Father Havert, a canon of Notre Dame, preached several sermons against the doctrine of the book. Saint-Cyran prodded Antoine Arnauld to defend the doctrine.

The discussion of Jansen was not confined to Paris, however. It was being discussed in Rouen also. Father Maignart, the priest of the Church of the Holy Cross in Saint Owen in Rouen was a friend of Saint-Cyran. Jean Guillebert, the new pastor at Rouville, a suburb of Rouen, had also been touched and convinced both by Jansen's message and Saint-Cyran's spirit. While he had been pursuing his studies at the Sorbonne, he had placed himself under the spiritual direction of Saint-Cyran. Guillebert, too, was convinced that the Biblical and Augustinian message of grace needed to be proclaimed once again. He was convinced that the grace of God could change men's lives. He saw how the crowds flocked to hear his preaching in the church at Rouville. He even saw members of the Parliament at Rouen hiring lodging in Rouville on Saturdays in order to be present to hear his preaching on Sundays. He knew that the message of grace met human need and transformed men. He knew that the message of grace was bringing spiritual revival to Rouen. He had witnessed the transformation of hundreds, but the conversions of the two Deschamps brothers had been especially thrilling. One brother was De la Bouteillerie. The other was Deslandes. From childhood days, the two brothers had set broken bones, had studied anatomy and had played with medicine as an amusement. Their fiery dispositions made them ready to draw their swords on any point of honor. But then the preaching of Guillebert touched their hearts giving them a new love and new motivations. Under Guillebert's influence, each built a hospital. Deslandes built a hospital with 10 beds. His brother built one with 20. Their ministry of healing became known throughout greater Rouen. Their faith was known as a faith that worked. They were devout students of the Bible. They were Jansenists. Though they probably had never been to Port-Royal, they would help the Pascal's to journey there. They would be waiting to meet the Pascals at the next turn of the road.

CHAPTER FOUR

ROUEN (1639-1647)

AVRANCHES was a picturesque but poor little town on the coast of Normandy. Its inhabitants loved to look out across the golden sands of the bay to turreted, beautiful Mont-St-Michel perched on the heights of the great rock Monte Tombe. They were grateful that centuries before, their Bishop Aubert had responded to a mystic vision of St. Michael by building a chapel in his honor on Monte Tombe presiding over the waters of the bay.

The peasants of Avranches were poor. Taxes were heavy. During the summer of 1639, a government administrator from the town of Coutances arrived in Avranches. Word was whispered through the town that he had come to levy a new tax, a salt tax. This was the last straw. The peasants did more than grumble on street corners this time. They drafted an ecclesiastic whom they had nick-named Jean "Va-nu-pieds,' John the "Barefooted," to be their leader. Soon there were 20,000 peasants or "va-nu-pieds" massed behind him. Their revolt spread quickly to Caen, Falaise, Bayeux and Rouen. In August, an edict controlling the manufacture of dyes caused riots, killing and looting to rock the city of Rouen. The residents of that ancient city on the upper reaches of the Seine earlier had refused to accept the new taxes that Richelieu had imposed to finance his wars. Now the powder keg exploded causing the Administrator, Claude de Paris, to leave the city in haste. All of Normandy was in revolt but Rouen had become the storm center of the rebellion.

Richelieu, in Paris, was determined to bring peace to Normandy. The Calvinistic Field Marshal Gassion was assigned

4000 troops with which to put down the rebellion. His intructions were "besides chastising individuals, you must raze the walls of the towns to the ground." Claude de Paris was to be the Commissioner to Rouen with oversight of the military forces. But Richelieu also needed a commissioner to oversee the reorganization of the finances of the area. The tax office in Rouen had been gutted and destroyed by the rioters. Etienne Pascal had made a good impression in his meeting with Richelieu. So, in September 1639, Richelieu once again demonstrated his ability to size up men by appointing Etienne to be "His Majesty's Deputy Commissioner in Upper Normandy for the levying of taxes and duties."

Thus Etienne set out across the snow and ice-covered roads toward Rouen. He went first to Gisors about 58 kilometers southeast of Rouen on the Epte River. There he met with Claude de Paris. Together they coordinated their plans. They agreed on a plan to levy fines and taxes upon Rouen and its environs. Then they journeyed to Gaillion near where the River Epte meets the Seine as it meanders toward the sea.

At Gaillion, on the top of a rise, in the turreted Chateau de Gaillion they met with Chancellor Séguier to discuss strategy. Then the three of them advanced to join Field Marshal Gassion as he approached the shattered city of Rouen.

On January 2nd, 1640, two thousand troops entered the riot-torn city. The populace looked on sullenly. And well they might, for they would be forced to submit to humiliating cruelty from the troops, to provide lodging for them and to pay a fine of 1,085,000 livres. Joan of Arc's proud city was bitter in its brokenness.

Feelings were still runing high in Rouen when Etienne moved his children into their house on Rue des Murs-Saint-Owen behind the walls of the Church of Saint Owen. Here, surrounded by the homes of magistrates and officials, the Pascals would live for seven years. The antiquity of Rouen's Gothic edifices with their gables and turrets may have made Jacqueline wonder if anything had changed since Joan of Arc had been burned alive there over two hundred years earlier.

Etienne quickly settled down to work. He had to reorganize tax procedures, to appoint officials, to reassess the eighteen townships of the area. This was a seemingly hopeless task since most of the tax records had been destroyed in the uprising. It was also a thankless task since Richelieu's agents were despised. One voice was raised accusing Etienne of "watching Rouen like a vampire, imposing new taxes on it without interruption." Nevertheless, Etienne labored night and day, traveling among the 1,798 parishes to estimate the taxable resources of each one. His scrupulous honesty led him to issue orders that none of his employees was to accept gifts or "kick-backs". These orders were strictly enforced. Indeed, he discharged his own secretary for accepting a single louis d'or. Eventually his integrity would be recognized by the gift of a purse of silver coins which would be especially minted and awarded him by a grateful city. But in the meantime, his was an onerous and difficult task.

Overcome by the immensity of his assignment, Etienne asked the young lawyer Florin Perier in Clermont to come to Rouen to help him. Thus Florin, a cousin of the Pascal children, joined Etienne's staff. What a time of reunion there was as Florin brought the Pascals news of mutual friends and relatives in faraway Clermont.

Blaise, now seventeen years old, also was drafted to help his father. He assisted Etienne in compiling the long tax lists. He also made occasional business trips to Clermont and Paris for his father. It certainly must have delighted his heart to return to Paris to see Father Mersenne and other members of the Academy. They were anxious to talk with him about his "Essay on Conic Sections," which had been published in 1640. During 1639, Blaise had toiled and sweated over this essay. In it he had described the properties of conic sections. He had described a hexagon inscribed within a conic section as a "mystic hexagram." He had gone beyond the projective geometry espoused by Desargues to discover the lemma which would become known as the Pascal Theorem. This stated that a hexagon inscribed in a conic section has this property, that the meeting points on opposite sides will always be in a straight line. He deduced all the properties of conic sections from this one theorem. A summary of this essay had been published as a placard, in poster form, in 1640.

When Blaise made his occasional trips to Paris for his father, he seized on the opportunities to talk with his friends of the Academy. It is possible that his friend Mersenne may have helped him to discern the method he had followed in his study of conic sections. Mersenne may have pointed out the way in which Blaise had considered the properties of a complex figure to be modifications of a simpler figure. Others may have highlighted for him the sense of participation whereby the properties of simpler figures participated in the properties of more complicated figures. An ascending scale made up of different orders of reality is dimly discernible in this startling essay of 1640.[1] We can imagine his friends gathered in Mersenne's drawing room as they pondered the young Pascal's ability to wed ideas with physical reality. They could see his genius shining through the essay.

Meanwhile in Rouen, the drudgery of Etienne's new office was relieved by frequent visits from the Pascals' old friend Mondory, who introduced them to their neighbor, Pierre Corneille, the author of the smash hit "Le Cid" which they had seen on the Paris stage.

As Corneille and his gentle new bride, Marie, were entertained in the Pascals' home Etienne and his guests probed some of the deeper meanings and motifs in Corneille's plays. The thirty-year-old Corneille was the talk of France. He was a very ordinary man. His speech sounded quite common though it only disguised his astounding creative abilities. Once when Jacqueline was chatting with her idol, Corneille, the writer, in almost monotonous tones, urged Jacqueline to develop her literary gifts. He insisted, "You should compete in the Palinods." He went on to explain that the Palinods was a poetry competition which had been initiated in the fifteenth century. The perpetual theme was the Immaculate Conception of the Virgin Mary. Corneille, himself, had won the competition seven years earlier.

Jacqueline, at fourteen years of age, was experiencing a difficult adolescence. Her pock-marked face made her terribly self-conscious. Thus she declined most of the invitations from the ladies of Rouen for her to recite poetry at their teas and soirées. She preferred to remain in the seclusion of her room where she played with her dolls which posed no threat to her.

However, the challenge of the Palinods excited her, particularly since its theme was religious. She set to work to compose verses which she would dedicate to the glory of the Immaculate Conception of Mary. Day in and day out she read the Bible. She thought. She wrote and rewrote. She prayed for inspiration. Gradually the idea of comparing the Virgin to the Ark of the Philistines took shape in her mind. Carefully she sought for just the right words to express her thoughts. One day she read some of her verses to the family.

"Execrable inventors of a false belief,
Whose hypocritical breast contains a heart of gall,
Cast your feeble eyes on the Ark of the Covenant
And you will see that it resembles the Queen of Heaven."

As usual, Gilberte and Etienne were lavish in their praise. Blaise, too, was impressed with his rival's efforts. Thus Jacqueline entered her lines in the competition.

When December 8, 1640 arrived, a large crowd gathered in the Grande Place, at the center of Rouen, to celebrate the Festival of the Conception of the Virgin. Gay music filled the crisp, cold air. Trumpets blared, drums rolled. And then the winners of the Palinods were announced. A silver rose was to be awarded for the best poem of three eight-lined stanzas with a four-lined envoy. A silver castle was to be given for the best stanzas. When the judges declared that the silver medallion went to Jacqueline Pascal, the first of her sex ever to win the prize, the crowd roared with delight.

But Jacqueline was nowhere to be found. She conveniently had gone out of town lest she be called to display her disfigurement before the throng. Fortunately Pierre Corneille was present to receive the award in her behalf. Corneille accepted the prize, addressing a hastily improvised greeting to the President of Puis who was presiding over the festivities. He said:

> "Prince, I shall take care to thank you on behalf of a young muse who is absent. Both her age and sex are grounds which encourage us to raise to heaven her a-borning glory which is still growing."

The crowd exploded with applause. Later some of the throng paraded through the streets with trumpets and drums sounding to deliver the prize to her door. Jacqueline could chalk up another triumph.

As 1641 dawned, the Pascals' relationship with Corneille deepened. Corneille's conviction that the real subject of drama ought not to be the events but the feelings they produce in the minds of the characters was rubbing off on Jacqueline. As she listened to the actor Mondory read portions of Corneille's newest works, "Cinna" and "Polyeucte," she was captivated. She knew that she had found her master. Henceforth, she consciously imitated Corneille.

In the meantime, romance had blossomed between Gilberte, now a well-formed, attractive young woman of twenty-one and Florin Perier, the young Auvergnat lawyer. A major event on the social calendar of Rouen was the simple wedding of Gilberte and her cousin Florin on June 15th, 1641. Shortly afterwards, they returned to Clermont to establish their home among the hills of Auvergne.

All the while, Blaise had been struggling to assist his father with the endless tax accounts. For one period of four months, except for half a dozen times, Etienne did not climb into bed until two o'clock in the morning. The fertile mind of young Blaise sought some way to assist his weary father. He lay awake nights trying to think of an easier way to add the long columns of figures. Then one night he sat bolt upright in bed. He jumped out of bed, lit a lamp and began to sketch a machine which could add numbers at the touch of a finger! As the night watch cried out in the early morning hours, Blaise was hunched over his desk scribbling his ideas on paper.

The next day the young Pascal left the house, made his way through the narrow streets of Rouen to the shop of one of the clockmakers in the city. When Blaise had entered the shop, the nineteen-year-old sat before the artisan explaining what he wanted the clockmaker to manufacture. Blaise spoke rapidly, describing the wheels and cylinders that he needed to manufacture his "arithmetic machine."

This was the beginning of many such conferences. One by one the clock-maker made the parts Blaise required. Time after time, Blaise would enter the artisan's shop protesting that a wheel was not the proper size or that two gears did not mesh properly. At home, Blaise complained of the difficulty he was having. The workmen were incompetent. The clockmaker was stupid. Several times Blaise nearly gave up in frustration.[2]

Nevertheless, piece by piece the calculating machine was being assembled. Model after model was made. A novel piece of machinery called a "jumper" was developed. The Pascal home was cluttered with scores of models made of wood, ivory, ebony and copper. Finally, in 1645, after years of toil, Blaise had one which worked to his satisfaction. It was portable, about the size of a 14 by 5 by 3 inch glove box. This model was to be sent to Chancellor Séguier. The Chancellor in Paris had earlier heard reports of the machine Blaise was creating and had commented favorably upon the effort. As Blaise explained to his father, "Sending this to the Chancellor will establish my right to a patent. It will advertise that the machine is available for purchase. And it will assure Monsieur Séguier of our good intentions, in case he harbors any antagonism over your disagreements in the past." So the model was sent to Paris. The Chancellor was intrigued with it and had it placed in a special cabinet with other rare and unusual gifts that had been given him. Shortly afterwards, Blaise penned the Chancellor a Dedicatory letter. As he sat at his desk, he wrote:

To
His Lordship
the
Chancellor

"Sir:
If the public derives any benefit from the invention which I have made . . . . it will be under greater obligation to your Highness than to my slight efforts."

Blaise paused, pursed his lips, decided to point out how difficult a task he had accomplished and wrote: "Since I lacked the skill to manipulate metal and a hammer as I do pen and compass, and since the artisans had more knowledge and practice in their art than in the sciences on which it is based, I saw myself reduced to giving up my whole enterprise, which brought only a great deal of weariness without any degree of success. But, Sir, your Highness kept up my courage, which was waning, and did me the favor of speaking of the simple draft which my friends had presented to you in terms which led me to see it quite differently from what it had previously appeared to me."

Feverishly Blaise continued writing, a frail stripling excited about the attention his invention might secure and thrilled that the spotlight of glory was fixed upon him again. This invention would enable him to compete with Jacqueline for their father's attention.

"Sir, when I reflect that this same tongue, which daily pronounces oracles on the throne of Justice, has deigned to praise the first attempt of a man of twenty years, that you have deemed it worthy of being the subject of your conversation more than once, and to see it placed in your cabinet among so many other rare and precious things with which it is filled, I am covered with glory, and I find no words to show my gratitude to Your Highness and my joy to everybody."

So the Dedicatory Letter, along with instructions on the use of his machine, was sent to Paris.

A promotional campaign was tried. Roberval gave demonstrations of the machine in his home in Paris. An advertising leaflet was prepared. Blaise journeyed to Paris to give lecture-demonstrations in the salon of the Duchesse d'Aiguillon. However, the unusual machine did not sell. It was expensive (100 livres). The mechanism was continually getting out of order as parts came loose and gears wore down. Only Blaise or one of his workmen could repair it. Though his invention was not making him rich, it nevertheless was spreading his fame. To Blaise that perhaps was enough. From time to time in the next few years Blaise would continue to perfect his machine, but his invention was essentially completed.

But the strain both of assisting his father in his work and of struggling through the manufacture of numerous models of his adding machine had taken its toll. Since late in 1641, Blaise had begun to suffer intense headaches, burning in his abdomen, cramps and chills. The days when he had to remain in bed became more and more frequent. Etienne held many whispered conferences with Jacqueline. Their concern for Blaise's health weighed heavily upon them. Nevertheless, between his bouts with pain, Blaise continued both his experiments and his assistance of his father.

One frigid day in January 1646, a messenger pounded on the door of the house on Rue des Murs-Saint-Ouen. When he was admitted, he told Etienne of a duel that was about to take place and pleaded that only he could prevent it.

Hastily Etienne donned his boots, his hat and wrapping his warm cape about him went out into the chill winter winds. As he hurried along, he stepped on a patch of ice, stumbled and fell. For a moment, he lay motionless and stunned on the frozen ground. When he tried to rise, excruciating pain made him cry out. When Blaise and Jacqueline saw their father carried back into the house, they were distraught. A doctor was quickly summoned. His diagnosis was that Etienne had dislocated his hip and would need skilled care and attention.

Adrien and Jean Deschamps, devout men who practiced medicine and surgery, were summoned. The two brothers spent many hours ministering to Etienne's needs as he lay restlessly in his bedroom on the second floor. Their medical proficiency and their personal strength of character impressed the Pascals' deeply. In turn the Deschamps were impressed by the famous young Pascals — so impressed they dreamt of winning them to their Jansenist view of the Christian faith.

Often, during the three months of Etienne's recuperation, after attending to their patient's needs, the brothers would sit in the drawing room with the famous young Pascals. As they sat by the fire, they shared with Blaise and Jacqueline how Jean Guillebert, the pastor at Rouville had touched their lives. They discussed freely the Jansenist doctrine of Saint-Cyran. They told how Guillebert had been stirred by his contacts with Saint-Cyran and how, in turn, he was stirring all of Rouen with the message of the grace of God.

Blaise and Jacqueline looked forward to the visits of the Deschamps. They were men of great ability and strength and dedication to the power of the love of God working within them. Blaise was fascinated by these newly found heroes. They claimed that, by himself, man is helpless. Man's helplessness is demonstrated in man's physical sufferings and limitations. Blaise, troubled by his own piercing pains, found this easy to believe. He pondered seriously the logic that sin has made all

56

men powerless. Slowly he came to agree with the Deschamps that only the power and grace of God can shatter the debilitating hold sin has on humanity. Blaise and Jacqueline, like moths to a flame, were attracted to the higher life they saw incarnated in the Deschamps brothers.

Blaise was the first to be won over to the Jansenist viewpoint.[3] He soon won Jacqueline to his side. Then, the two of them, sitting by the edge of their father's bed, convinced quiet Etienne of these truths. When his three months' recuperation was complete, Etienne was a convinced Jansenist. Late in 1646 when Gilberte and her family came for a long visit to Rouen, she, too, was persuaded.

Thus, the whole Pascal family became Jansenist in their thinking. In the months that followed, they read Jansen's "The Augustinus." They devoured Augustine's letters, sermons and essays. They read and discussed Arnauld d'Andilly's "Discourse on the Reformation of the Inner Man." Family life was transformed for the Pascals. The social whirl, vanity in one's dress, extravagances of any sort were replaced by the simple life. Indeed Jacqueline began to live like a nun, or like one of Corneille's stoic heroines. They enjoyed discussing theology and the Fathers of the Church at dinner. The Bible became an all-important source of authority to them. Piety, prayer, and Bible reading attained a new priority. Jansenism had won distinguished converts.

But Blaise's scientific pursuits, though temporarily interrupted, continued on. His interest was stimulated greatly by the arrival in Rouen that summer of their old friend Pierre Petit from Mersenne's Academy in Paris. He was on his way north to the seaport of Dieppe. A dozen years earlier a warship, the "Senegalais," had sunk at the entrance to the harbor when a sailor had lit his pipe too near the powder and had blown up the ship. There had been 40,000 crowns on board. Now Jean Pradine from Marseilles had invented a diving rig with an underwater light. He claimed he could stay under water for six hours. Pradine was at work searching for the wreckage of the ship. Petit was eager to see his invention as well as to examine the fortifications of Dieppe. The Pascals were curious about this invention of Pradine.

Petit, as he sat chatting by the hour with the Pascals, also brought news of a phenomenon that had caught the attention of many savants throughout Europe. Torricelli in Italy had devised a fascinating experiment two years earlier. When a long tube filled with mercury is upended in a tub, the column of mercury falls leaving an empty space at the upper end of the tube. As Petit described the experiment, Etienne exclaimed, "The space must be a void." But Petit responded that learned doctors insist that nature will not allow an empty space, a nothingness, a vacuum to exist, for the heavens would collapse inward upon the earth to fill that void. So they argued far into the night. The next day Petit continued on to Dieppe.

In October 1646, when Petit had returned to Rouen from his inspection tour, the discussion was continued. Petit and the Pascals agreed to attempt the experiment. So they went to where the Rue de Prés and the Rue de la Pie-aux-Anglais intersected. There in one of the finest glass factories in Europe they had a glass tube four feet long and the width of the little finger blown. It was sealed at one end. Then they purchased 50 livres worth of quicksilver. In the courtyard of the glassworks, Petit carefully filled the slender glass tube with mercury. Then, while the others gently held the middle and one end, he covered the open end of the tube with his finger, slowly and breathlessly upended the tube, lowered the open end into a bowl filled with mercury and removed his finger. The mercury descended part way in the tube and stopped. Petit measuring the height of the column of mercury declared, "Eighteen inches".

Blaise expostulated, "Imbeciles I suppose will say that the empty space above the mercury is really air which penetrated through the pores of the glass."

Petit replied, "But why then didn't all the mercury fall into the bowl if air entered the tube through the pores?" That night the discussion in the Pascal house didn't end until the wee hours of the morning.

As the days went by, they conducted experiment after experiment. Each time, they noted the height of the mercury was constant. Again, in January and February of 1647 Blaise conducted several experiments at the glassworks before fascinated crowds of up to 500 citizens. Tubes of various diameters and shapes were used to demonstrate that the void was not determined by cubic content. One of Pascal's more spectacular experiments involved two glass tubes 46 feet long. He executed this experiment down at the wharves. The two glass tubes were bound to ships' masts for support. As crowds lined the quai, he filled one tube with water and the other with wine. The water fell to a level of 34 French feet about the tub's level. The wine stood higher in its tube. This quashed the argument that the wine released vapors into the upper end of the tube for if this were true the volatile wine would have released more vapors than the water and would have been pushed lower in the tube than the water.

Blaise was assiduously taking notes on all these experiments and was giving birth to the science of pneumatics. His studies of air pressure were to become foundation stones for a new science.

Meanwhile, in addition to perfecting his adding machine and in addition to his experiments with the void, Blaise continued his exploration into theology. During the winter of 1646-1647 he found an opportunity to exercise his zeal for theology.

An elderly Capuchin, Dr. Jacques Forton, known as Saint-Ange, had recently come to Rouen applying for a parish. He caused quite a stir in the city by his claim to be able to demonstrate many theological doctrines, among them the Incarnation and the Trinity, by reason alone. He declared he did not need recourse to authorities such as the Bible or the Church to establish these doctrines. On February 1st and again on February 5th, 1647, Blaise and two young friends sat in discussions with the scholarly priest. His companions in this theological exchange were the young mathematician, Adrien Auzoult and the son of a municipal magistrate, Raoul Halle. At the tense meeting on February 5th, they also brought to the meeting at Monsieur Courtin's home Sieur Cornier de Sainte Helene, Doctor of the Sorbonne. At this meeting, Saint-Ange startled his critics by saying that the Bible was obscure on the age of the earth. He dismayed them further by stating that the Virgin Mary had offered her obedience and death to God for the redemption of the world as truly as did Christ. They were also shocked to hear this man, set adrift from Biblical authority, declare that the body of Jesus Christ was not formed of the blood of the Virgin Mary but from a special substance specially created for this purpose. Jesus Christ was of a different substance from other men. This and other novel theological views thoroughly scandalized the three zealots who regarded Biblical authority as determinative.[4]

Therefore, the threesome, inspired by Saint-Cyran's demand for a reformation of the nation's clergy, made their way to the Archbishop's residence to register their protest. There they were told that Monseigneur de Harlay was at his chateau de Gaillion recovering from illness and fatigue but that Bishop Coadjutor Camus, a gentle, sweet-tempered man would see them. Camus heard the three young men graciously and assured them that he would look into the situation. This he did. But being content with the reassurance given him by Saint-Ange, he let the matter drop.

The youthful amateurs in theology, however, were not content. When the Archbishop returned, they made their charges to him demanding a retraction of 12 doubtful propositions Saint-Ange had espoused.

The vexed Monseigneur de Harlay examined Saint-Ange, compelled him to sign a statement repudiating the errors ascribed to him and instructed his Coadjutor to assign him to the church at Crosville.

Nevertheless, the young inquisitors won out. Saint-Ange had

been given a heretical reputation so he sought reassignment to Sartrouville where his reputation followed him and his views again were called in question. He finally left for Paris where he died under the ominous pall of heresy.

The emotions of this crusade, coupled with the strain of perfecting his calculating machine and of conducting his experiments on the void, left Blaise exhausted. He suffered intense headaches and awful pains in the abdomen. His medicines had to be warmed and fed him drop by drop. To warm his icy feet, cloths soaked in brandy had to be applied to them. For a short time, he was paralyzed from the waist down.[5] He prescribed for himself horseback riding through the Norman countryside, tennis and other exercises which provided temporary relief. But his infirmities returned. Finally, in the summer of 1647, Etienne sent his son and Jacqueline to Paris in search of expert medical help. Then he began preparation to resign his government post and to join his children in Paris.

CHAPTER FIVE

PARIS (1647-1649)

WHEN Jacqueline assisted Blaise up the steps to their Paris home on Rue Brisemiche, he was a very sick young man. The warm spring breezes of 1647 were bringing little children and romantic young couples out into the streets. Paris was coming to life with the return of the warm weather. Yet Blaise felt himself close to death. The best doctors of Paris were consulted. Some diagnosed his illness as a syphilletic infection. Others thought it was cancer. The only thing on which they agreed was that he had over-extended himself and that he must forego any prolonged intellectual exertion. Some have wondered if a deep sense of guilt over his fervid attack on Saint-Ange didn't have something to do with the depression which accompanied his illness.

The neighborhood had changed little outwardly during the Pascals' sojourn in Rouen. The talk was that Monsieur de Morangis was about to be appointed the royal director of finances but little else was new. Yet Jacqueline and Blaise could sense an excitement, a spiritual ferment taking place. The neighborhood church, St. Merri, had two new priests, Father Duhamel and Father Barré. Duhamel had been influenced by the Abbé Saint-Cyran. Encouraged by the Arnaulds, and especially by Monsieur d'Andilly, who lived nearby at the intersection of Rue de la Verrerie and Rue du Renard, these priests had made St. Merri a center of Jansenist influence. Each Sunday afternoon at four they had arranged for Matthieu Feydeau, a doctor of the Sorbonne, to hold catechism classes which parents attended with their children. Many in the neighborhood had been touched. Among them was Denis Baron, the Pascals' landlord and Charlotte Gouffier, the fourteen-year-old sister of the young duke Roannez. Baron had been deeply stirred by the message of grace. Charlotte had also become interested and enthusiastic. Artus Gouffier, the twenty-year-old duke of Roannez, seemed only midly interested, however, in the fervor being generated at Saint Merri. Though he supported the Church generously, he was preoccupied with the worldly responsibilities which had fallen upon him as he came of age in the summer of 1647. On the sixteenth of July, his mother turned over much of her wealth to him. Young Artus had to manage his own wealth as well as hers. As he surveyed his holdings which were valued at many millions of livres, he also had to balance them against huge debts.

Artus, however was delighted that his twenty-four-year-old friend Blaise had returned to Paris. That summer the two young men sat in Pascal's house hour after hour discussing the scientific discoveries that were exciting men throughout Europe. But then their conversations ceased for awhile. Blaise suffered a physical relapse and Artus was off on trips to inspect his holdings.

As summer eased over into autumn, Blaise was being pressed by his friend Father Mersenne to see the famous Descartes, who had requested an interview. In mid-September Blaise had written Mersenne requesting a clarification of Descartes' views on the "vacuum". Mersenne's reply was difficult to read since the aging priest recently had an artery in his right arm cut during a "bleeding". In his reply, Mersenne again indicated that Descartes wished to see Pascal and his adding machine. Yet Blaise felt too weak to see Descartes.

Then on Sunday evening, September 22nd, two visitors were admitted to the Pascal residence. They were Monsieur Habert and Monsieur de Montigny. They asked for Monsieur Pascal. When Louise Delault replied that Blaise was at Church, M. de

Montigny said his intimate friend Réné Descartes would like an appointment to see Blaise the next day. With that Jacqueline was summoned. M. de Montigny announced that Descartes would like to come to see Blaise at nine o'clock the next morning. Jacqueline was inwardly torn. She knew how difficult it was for Blaise to make any exertion before noon. Yet she did not want to decline the honor of a call by the great Descartes. So the date was set for ten-thirty the next morning.

When Blaise returned from Church, he was restrained in his excitement. After having his feet bled, he retired early. That night as he lay on his bed, he wearily anticipated the great man's coming and then fell into a fitful sleep. The next morning promptly at half-past ten, Descartes and his entourage, M. Habert, M. de Montigny, a young priest, de Montigny's son, three little boys and Roberval were gathered in the Pascals' drawing room. The 51-year-old Descartes had been engaged for several years in violent controversy over his philosophy. That very year Revius, the theologian at the University of Leyden, had accused him of blasphemy, a crime punishable by law. Descartes, nevertheless, on this trip to Paris had been honored by Cardinal Mazarin, who granted him a pension (which he never did receive). So, in spite of his intense dislike for Paris, Descartes was in an expansive mood.

As the group exchanged the usual civilities, Descartes commented "the Paris air inclines me to dreaming rather than to philosophy."

Roberval, always the tactless blunderbuss, proceeded to demonstrate Blaise's adding machine. Descartes asked a few polite questions then pointed the conversation to the primary reason for the interview — a discussion of the vacuum. Descartes and the others were especially interested in Blaise's experiments in Rouen. Such experiments could not have been carried out in Paris for want of technical instruments but Rouen, with its glass works, had provided an exceptional opportunity for experimentation.

After describing his efforts at Rouen, Blaise then asked Descartes, "What do *you* believe forces water to be expelled from a syringe?"

Descartes haughtily declared that it was a subtle form of matter.

Blaise, pain racking his body and making every word agony, mumbled a weak response. Whereupon the well-meaning Roberval leapt to the defense and interjected his own view that it was a vacuum.

Descartes imperiously spit out the words, "I wish to talk with Monsieur Pascal as long as possible for he speaks rationally. But you, you are prejudiced." Then noting by his watch that it was noon, he declared that he must leave for a luncheon date in the Faubourg St. Germain. As he bid farewell to Blaise, he added that he would return the next morning at eight. Then the gathering broke up. Descartes and Roberval rode in the same carriage toward the Faubourg St. Germain, arguing as they rode along.

That evening Roberval returned to Rue Brisemiche to find D'Alibray there before him. D'Alibray had heard of the appointment for the next morning and had come to ask Pascal's permission to be present. Blaise had graciously acquiesced and asked him to invite Le Pailleur to join the discussion. The remainder of the evening twenty-four-year-old Blaise and the feisty Roberval discussed Physics and Theology.

After a day of such excitement, Jacqueline feared her brother would be exhausted. Yet his headaches seemed to have vanished. The only after-effects seemed to have been heavy sweat and a fitful sleep Monday night.

The next morning, Tuesday, September 23rd, the drawing room was crowded. The great Descartes dominated the room. His jutting chin and prominent nose gave the impression of strength. His tight, thin lips were those of a man often lost in thought. His arched eyebrows bespoke the superiority of the man who discovers what ordinary mortals miss. At first Blaise was strangely silent. Every nerve in his body seemed to throb with pain. Descartes, who considered himself something of a medical authority, urged the young Pascal to take long rests, to stay in bed each day as late as possible and to drink strong broths. Then for three hours the conversation ranged over geometry, philosophy and theology. Blaise seemed to draw strength from the stimulating discussion. At one point, Descartes suggested an experiment which would convincingly demonstrate whether Blaise or Descartes was correct. He suggested that the height of the mercury in a tube at sea level be compared with the height in the tube at the top of a mountain. If it varied, then Blaise's conviction of the existence of a vacuum would be vindicated. If the levels were the same, Descartes' view would be victorious. Blaise nodded in agreement. For months he had planned just such an experiment. But his health had prevented him. Now he nodded politely without bothering to explain that he already had conceived such an experiment.

Finally, after three hours of pain-filled discussion, it was evident that Blaise was at the limit of his exertion. So Descartes, after expressing his best wishes for Blaise's recovery, withdrew. Shortly afterwards the house on Rue Brisemiche was silent except for the sounds of splashing as Blaise took a warm bath to relax himself.

About that time, Mersenne's Academy and the new Academy of Abbé Bourdelot, which met at the Hôtel de Condé, were eagerly discussing not only Blaise's experiments but also similar experiments being carried on in Poland by the Capuchin Valeriano Magni. Toward the end of September, Roberval, jealous for Pascal and eager that Magni not steal any of Pascal's thunder, published in Latin a summary of Pascal's experiments. On October the 8th, 1647, Blaise himself published his "New Experiments Concerning The Vacuum." He had labored through several long weeks to prepare this document. As he had sat at his writing table day by day, he took the theoretical assumption that nature abhors a vacuum and carefully showed that his experiments at Rouen demonstrated that in fact, an "apparent" vacuum does exist in the upper end of the tube. Then, his experiments went on to show that this "apparent" vacuum was in *fact* empty of all matter perceptible to the senses and therefore was a real vacuum. So he declared with a proud flourish that nature's abhorrence of a vacuum was limited. Relying strictly on experimentation, he had undercut an age old assumption and was proud of his accomplishment. Roberval and others of Mersenne's Academy were quick to congratulate him on his brilliant feat.

Meanwhile his treatise was being read by the rector of the College of Clermont in Paris, a one-time teacher of Descartes at La Fleche, Father Noel. The Jesuits who administered the College of Clermont had no particular love for the Pascals since Etienne in 1630 had protested to the royal court against the founding of a Jesuit College in Clermont. Nevertheless, Noel in the reply which he addressed to Blaise was courteous though sharp in his criticism. He insisted that the top of the tube is full of "purified air" which has entered through "pores" in the glass. On the 29th of October Blaise sent Noel an equally courteous though somewhat ironic answer. Pascal not only refuted the venerable Noel's points one by one but also condescendingly reminded the older scholar of the universal rule, which even students in the schools must recognize, that,

> "One should never make a judgment concerning the negative or the affirmative of a proposition, unless that which one affirms or denies has one of the following two conditions: namely, either that it should appear so clearly and so distinctly of itself to the senses or to the reason according as it is subject to the one or to the other, that the mind should have no means of doubting its certainty, or that it may be deduced as infallible and a necessary consequence of these principles or axioms."

Pascal discerned a strange transposition being made by the

Jesuit. He saw Noel using the authority of Aristotle and Descartes in science while at the same time the Jesuits were using experimentation and reason in their casuistry and theology. He had learned from his encounter with Saint-Ange the dangers of abandoning Biblical authority in theology. Now he was beholding the improper application of authority in science while experimentation and reason, which belong in science, were holding sway in theology. So he pointedly reminded Noel not to confuse mere "thought" for "demonstration." He appealed for priority in science to be given to the brute facts of experimentation while reserving submission to authority for the realm of theology.

> "We reserve for the mysteries of faith, which the Holy Spirit has itself revealed, that submission of mind which extends our belief to those mysteries which are hidden from sense and from reason."

A few days after Blaise sent his letter to Noel, he received a second letter from the learned Jesuit. It was delivered to Pascal by a Father Talon while several of Pascal's friends were gathered with him in his home. Father Talon, after meeting Pascal's friends, delivered the letter and said "Father Noel sympathizes with your indisposition and hopes that the exertion of writing your letter to him has not damaged your health. He begs you not to jeopardize your health by a second letter since the remaining difficulties can be cleared up by word of mouth. So he suggests that you not reply to this one. He begs you not to show his letter to anyone since he had written it just for your eyes and besides letters are such individual matters they can suffer violence when they are not kept secret." To this Pascal agreed. A few days later he would regret his acquiescence.

Friends visiting the Pascal home brought word that it was being whispered abroad, especially by some of the Jesuit fathers, that Noel's letter had so devastated Pascal's arguments that Blaise did not dare to reveal the letter. Blaise was angry. He almost shouted. "The only reason I agreed to silence was that the request had come from a reverend Father. If anyone else had asked for silence, I would have been suspicious." "Now," Blaise threw up his hands, "I cannot conceal the letter without disadvantage to the truth, nor can I reveal it without being unfaithful to my word. But I must keep my word."

Though Blaise kept his word to Father Noel, he continued to expound his views. Day after day he toiled at his desk to complete a treatise which he entitled, "Fragment of a Preface to the Treatise on the Vacuum." As the snows of November draped a white covering over Paris, his latest writing was being discussed at Mersenne's Academy. Blaise had made the distinction between knowledge which ought to be based on authority (history, geography, theology), and knowledge which ought to be based on experimentation and reason, (mathematics, music, medicine, the sciences).

This was an effective answer to Noel. Etienne and Father Mersenne could see that seeds of their planting had taken root in Blaise's mind so that now the dim outline of a hierarchy in the orders of reality was discernible in his words:

"To lend full certainty to those matters which are incomprehensible to reason, it suffices to point to where they are found in the Sacred Books . . . *because its principles are superior to nature and to reason,* and, the mind of man being too feeble to attain them by its own efforts, it cannot reach up to those lofty thoughts, unless it is sustained by a strength which is all-powerful and supernatural."

Etienne in Rouen could remember teaching this distinction to Blaise years before. Mersenne at the Academy often had suggested a similar hierarchy of knowledge. While Noel and his Jesuit friends winced on reading this treatise, Etienne and Mersenne must have smiled appreciatively when they read it.

Blaise followed this treatise by an important letter. On November 15, 1647, he took pen in hand and wrote to his brother-in-law, Florin Perier, in Clermont. He scribbled, "I am resolved to seek full enlightenment . . . by a decisive experiment. . . . This is to perform the ordinary experiment of the vacuum several times on the same day, in the same tube, with the same quicksilver, now at the foot and now at the summit of a mountain . . . to determine whether the height of quicksilver suspended in the tube will be found the same or different in these two locations. . . . Our city of Clermont is at the foot of the high mountain Puy de Dôme and I hope that out of kindness you will do me the favor of undertaking this experiment yourself. On this assurance I have led all our curious people of Paris to hope for this. Among others there is also the Reverend Father Mersenne, who has already promised in letters which he has written to Italy, to Poland, to Sweden, to Holland, etc., to notify his friends whom he has won by his merits." So an urgent appeal for execution of this experiment was sent.

Folk all over Europe were eagerly awaiting word of Pascal's latest experiments. Gassendi and Pecquet were quoting Blaise. Across the channel, the Englishman Boyle had said that his pneumatic machine was due to "the most ingenious Pascal". But fame is a dangerous gift. Jacqueline and some of her friends were concerned lest acclaim hinder Blaise's spiritual growth in grace.

The Pascals were parishioners at the Church Saint-Merri The eloquent new curate, M. Duhamel, was a Jansenist and encouraged Blaise and Jacqueline to hear the preaching of Monsieur Singlin at the Church of Port-Royal in Paris. The convent of Port-Royal had moved to Paris nearly twenty years earlier and had relocated in the Faubourg Saint-Jacques, near the Benedictine and Carmelite Convents on Rue Saint-Jacques. The Queen, Anne of Austria, often passed through the neighborhood on her way to visit the Benedictines for whom she had purchased their convent.

The Abbey of Port-Royal in Paris was unpretentious. Indeed Mother Angélique reported that when the building was being built a young woman passing by had said to her companion,

"I wonder who the unfortunates might be for whom that prison is a-building." The Church was next door to the convent. The Church was filled by throngs eager to hear the preaching of M. Singlin.

Antoine Singlin was only three years Blaise's senior. He had been an apprentice to a linen draper until he was twenty years old. Then he had come under the influence of St. Vincent de Paul. Through St. Vincent's influence he had become a priest. Later he came under the spell of Saint-Cyran who had him appointed as the confessor at Port-Royal. The humble 27-year-old Singlin was making a profound spiritual impact on Paris. So under the prodding of Duhamel and with encouragement from M. Guillebert, who frequently journeyed from Rouen to Paris, Blaise and Jacqueline had been sitting under the preaching of Singlin.

Jacqueline became so inspired that she began to talk of joining Port-Royal. She insisted that one could "be a nun reasonably in such a place as that." At one point Blaise became so concerned that he arranged an interview for Jacqueline with M. Guillebert on one of his visits to Paris. Guillebert suggested that Jacqueline talk with Mother Angélique which she did. Jacqueline long remembered that interview. Mother Angélique, 60 years old, tall and grave, sat on a stiff, cane chair listening to the eager Jacqueline. The Reverend Mother was much impressed by Jacqueline's sincerity. That was only the first of many visits Jacqueline would make to the convent. Later Singlin told Blaise that he had never seen in anyone such a clear sense of calling as he saw in Jacqueline.

Then it was Blaise's turn. Early in 1648, permission to visit De Rebours, Singlin's assistant, was solicited and secured. Fifty-year-old De Rebours was known to the Pascal family since he also hailed from Clermont. At his first visit, after the usual courtesies, Pascal began by saying, "We have read both your writings as well as those of your opponents."

De Rebours appeared delighted so Pascal imperiously went on, "It seems to me that by following the principles of common sense one should be able to demonstrate many things which the opponents of religion say are contrary to reason. After all, reason can lead men to the gateway of belief. Though I admit men ought to believe without reason."

At this, a frown appeared on De Rebour's face. He was familiar with Jansen's warnings about "libido sciendi." As he gazed at the young mathematician opposite him, De Rebours suspected that Blaise had too high and too vain an estimate of reason.

Pascal, sensing that he was suspected of pride, attempted to justify himself by saying, "I am only concerned with turning men toward the truth. Christian concern for those who do not yet believe prompts me to suggest that many could be reached for the faith if they but saw that faith is reasonable." Pascal was embarrassed. It was obvious that De Rebours felt that he was being arrogant and that he was exhibiting intellectual pride.

De Rebours, with excessive humility, began to point out the advantage of simplicity and modesty. Each word seemed to stab Blaise who stiffened defensively. De Rebours' exhortation to humility only served to distress and to confuse Blaise, whose head now was throbbing with pain. Shortly thereafter he departed for the peace of home. In each succeeding interview De Rebours kept taking aim at Pascal's pride of reason while Blaise continued to insist that he recognized the limitations of reason and the supremacy of God's grace. These conferences finally came to an end. The two men had to call it a draw. But Pascal was chagrined and felt that those at Port-Royal did not understand his desire to be their champion and apologist. To make the situation worse, Jacqueline, in contrast, seemed to find such joy in her relation with Port-Royal. When the interviews with De Rebours were terminated, Blaise scribbled a letter to Gilberte recounting his experience. The date was January 20, 1648. He closed his letter with an admission of his helplessness and his deep feeling of impotence. This was a bitter experience for a Pascal — to feel humbled and weak.

Burdened with the pain of misunderstanding, Blaise turned

back to his scientific endeavors, a realm where there is a less delicate line of distinction between the proper and improper uses of reason.

Meanwhile Blaise had placed in his hands the latest publication by Father Noel. It was entitled "The Fullness of the Vacuum," and was dedicated to the Prince de Condé. Blaise could scarcely believe what he read. In this latest writing Noel ridiculed the view that there could be "gaps" (vacuums) in nature. Blaise could not believe it. Noel's last letter had been so conciliatory. In indignation, Blaise sat down at his desk to write Le Pailleur saying that Noel in his second letter had even given up some of his earlier views though he still could not adjust completely to Blaise's view. Though De Rebours had brushed reason aside as useless in theology, Noel seemed to be absolutizing deductive reason in science. Now Pascal wished the Jesuit father would rely on inductive reason which starts with the facts instead of deductive reason which starts with presuppositions and assumptions. Blaise was indignant at Father Noel's apparent reversal.

What he did not know was that the aged Jesuit was innocent of this apparent betrayal. Noel had fallen ill and had to be kept in bed. While he was recovering, his friends found a manuscript he had written before his exchange with Pascal, took it to the printer and had it published. Poor Noel was chagrined when he discovered what had happened.

Etienne, in far off Rouen, was, however, more than chagrined at the seeming betrayal of his son by Noel. Etienne took up his pen and wrote a stinging rebuke to Noel.

Meanwhile, Noel hastened to write an account of his latest views. They *had* been modified in the exchange with Pascal.

The huge Roannez mansion nearby was aglow with lights and laughter most of that winter. The Duke was thoroughly caught up in the social world of Paris. From time to time he ran in to see Blaise. In February 1648 he breathlessly told his serious, young neighbor of the ballet in which he was dancing with other young princes of the court at the Palace of the Cardinal. The subject of the ballet was the disharmony and conflict of the passions of interest, love and glory. The Duke described his role in the second part dealing with love. He laughingly described his portrayal of both Olympus and Relee. He mimicked Roger de Lorraine, Gilles de Hautefort and other noblemen who were in the ballet. Blaise was amused and delighted by these glimpses into life at the royal court.

As the year 1648 wore on, in March Blaise completed his treatise on conic sections. Meanwhile the family was still separated. Gilberte was visiting her father at Rouen and Jacqueline was with her brother in Paris. Yet a closeness bound the family together. In a letter to Gilberte, dated April 1, 1648, Blaise expressed his happiness that they were one not only in the natural, family sense but also one in the grace of God. Yet that oneness would soon be put to the test.

In that same letter, Blaise, as he sat at his desk, painfully wrote, "So we see that Jesus Christ does not limit the command of perfection, and that He proposes a model of infinite perfection when He says: 'Be ye therefore perfect, even as your Father which is in heaven is perfect.' Moreover, a harmful and common error among Christians and even among those who profess piety lies in persuading themselves that there is a certain degree of perfection in which one is secure, and that it is unnecessary to go beyond this, since there is no wrong in stopping there, and since one may risk falling by ascending higher. . . ." Blaise was a perfectionist in science and was no less a perfectionist in religion. He demanded perfection of himself, and he hoped for perfection in others. No wonder he was sad and disillusioned both at his own frailty and limitations as well as at the weakness of others.[1]

But then in the spring of 1648, Etienne left Rouen to return to Paris. For some time he had planned to leave public life. The notoriety stirred up by the St. Ange affair still clung uncomfortably to the Pascal name. Moreover, Etienne at 60 years of age was weary after years of diligent toil in Rouen. So after public acclaim for a job well done, he returned to Paris bearing the honorary title "counsellor of state".

It was not long before Etienne discovered Jacqueline's growing desire to enter Port-Royal. Blaise came to him, at Jacqueline's request, to tell Etienne of his sister's decision to enter Port-Royal as a nun.

In a stormy scene in the drawing room, Etienne forbade Jacqueline even to visit Port-Royal. He railed at his two younger children, declaring he had lost all confidence in Jacqueline, and even in Blaise. He considered his son to have encouraged Jacqueline in her relation to Port-Royal. Etienne cornered the faithful housekeeper, Louise Default, and told her to watch them both closely and report to him any contacts they had with those of Port-Royal. His indignation, however, soon gave way to pleading. He begged Jacqueline to postpone entering Port-Royal until after his death. To this, she reluctantly agreed.

On October 1st, 1648, as his lease on the house on Rue Brisemiche drew to its close, Etienne moved his family to the quieter, more fashionable Marais section near the Place Royale where Paris society held some of its smartest gatherings. The trees overshadowing the streets brought a sense of rustic calm to this section of Paris' west bank. There Etienne ensconced his family in a gracious house on Rue de Touraine in the parish of Saint-Jean-en-Greve.

Jacqueline, seeking to be obedient to her father, yet also to her God, more and more withdrew to the solitude of her room where she practiced the spiritual discipline of a Port-Royal nun. Only once did she appeal to her father to relax his rule. As the warm weather of a Parisian summer approached, she penned a letter to her father who was in Clermont. It was June 19, 1648. In her letter, she reaffirmed her complete submission to her father but begged his permission to undertake a fortnight's retreat at Port-Royal. When Etienne found her letter on his desk, he relented to the degree that he gave her permission to make the retreat. But within the Pascal home, the spiritual warfare continued.

Meanwhile violence was brewing in the streets of Paris. The Italian Cardinal Mazarin had inherited Richelieu's mantle when the empire builder had died in 1643. Mazarin had continued Richelieu's policy of building the monarchy for Queen Anne and her young son Louis XIV against the lords of the realm. In doing so, he feathered a rich nest for himself. Rumor had it that the Queen was his mistress. His irreverence toward religion was a scandal. His charm and his tireless labors for France could not stem a growing tide of unpopularity. The peasants blamed him that they had to sell their household goods and sleep upon straw in order to pay the heavy taxes. Merchants traced the problems of commerce to the imposts he levied. The nobles resented the loss of their power which he was bringing about. The Parliament hated him because he set the throne — and himself — above the law. A storm was brewing across France.

On July 12, 1648, while Jacqueline was meditating in her room, the Parliament met at the Palace of Justice. They issued stiff demands to Mazarin, Queen Anne and the young King. Personal taxes were to be cut by one quarter. No new taxes were to be imposed without the consent of the Parliament. Royal commissioners (intendants) who ruled the provinces over local governors and officials were to be recalled. No one was to be held in prison more than twenty-four hours without being brought before the courts. These were revolutionary demands.

On August 26th, Anne and Mazarin gave answer by ordering the arrest of the aged Pierre Broussel and other leaders of Parliament. Word raced quickly through Paris that the popular Broussel was arrested. Even while a lieutenant of the Guard was removing Broussel from his house in a closed coach, his maid shouted through the window the news of his seizure to the crowds passing by. A mob soon gathered. The shops of Paris were closed hastily. Chains were stretched across streets. By nightfall the city was in an uproar. The crowds clamored for Broussel's release. Many in the crowds gathered at the Royal

Palace carried slings so they were called frondeurs, "throwers."

The next day, 160 members of the Parliament pushed their way into the Palace through the throng of frondeurs and the barricades which had been erected. The furious crowds spurred them on with shouts of "Vive le roi! A mort Mazarin!" The Queen slammed the door of her chamber in the faces of the members of Parliament. But Mazarin grudgingly chose discretion rather than valor and arranged for Broussel's release. He tentatively agreed to Parliament's terms. The Queen took flight first to Rueil, then later to St. Germain. Paris, for many months, was in a tumult.

As the Fronde was raging, in September a messenger entered the Rue de Touraine bringing a message to the Pascals that Father Mersenne had died. At first the Pascals were crushed. But their faith quickly buoyed them up.

September found Florin Perier in quiet Clermont at last ready to carry out the experiment Blaise had requested almost a year earlier. Bad weather, and the press of official duties had caused Florin to postpone the experiment so long.

Auvergne with its dark river gorges and green valleys surrounded Clermont-Ferrand. To the west of Clermont was a range of 60 extinct volcanoes. Eleven miles from the center of Clermont, seeming to tower 4000 feet above the city, was the Puy-de-Dôme, the perfect mountain for Pascal's experiment.

At eight in the morning, on September 19, 1648, Florin and interested savants of Clermont met in the garden of the Pères Minimes. Among them was the Franciscan, Father Bannier; Canon Mosnier; two magistrates, Laville and Begon and doctor LaPorte. Florin meticulously carried out Torricelli's experiment simultaneously with two tubes in the garden. In each, the height of the mercury was twenty-six inches three lines and a half. Then, leaving one inverted glass tube standing in mercury, he asked Father Chastin to remain, and to watch carefully for any change in the level of mercury in the column, while he and the others rode muleback to the summit of the mountain. Atop

78

Puy-de-Dôme, he repeated the experiment again and again, using equipment identical to that in the garden far below. Each time the experiment was repeated, the column of mercury in the glass tube was over three inches lower than the height registered in the garden in Clermont. On the descent from the summit, Florin repeated the experiment at varying altitudes and discovered that the lower the altitude, the higher the column of mercury. When at last he rode into the monks' garden, he learned that the level in the first tube had not changed during the whole of the day. The next day, Father de La Mare suggested that Florin repeat the experiment at the foot and at the top of the highest tower of Clermont's cathedral. This Florin did with the same results. Two days later a letter describing the experiments and the results was on its way to Pascal in Paris.

When news of the experiment reached Blaise in strife-torn Paris, he was jubilant. But ever the scientist, he sought to verify for himself the results of the experiment. Near their former house on Rue Brisemiche stood the Church of St. Jacques-la-Boucherie. At the base of the tower, he performed his experiment. Then Blaise laboriously climbed the high Gothic tower of St. Jacques and repeated the experiment. Again the level of mercury in the glass tube varied according to the elevation. He repeated the experiments again using a tower of Notre Dame. Still again, he performed the ritual using a tall, private dwelling. Then in the glow of victory, he sat down to write a progress report for the scientific world. With a flourish he entitled it "The Account of the Great Experiment of the Equilibrium of Liquids." "Later," he confided to his father, "I will prepare a major work on the subject." In the meantime, with great relish he recounted the results of his experiments and concluded that air is a liquid and has weight, that "liquids weigh according to their height" and that nature does not abhor a vacuum. Thus he laid the foundations of hydrostatics and delineated clearly the principle of the hydraulic press. Explicit in his paper was the glorification of experimentation and the inductive scientific method. Pascal's triumph was complete. His fame was now secure.

After Pascal sent his completed manuscript off for publication, he sat at the desk in his room trying to pen a letter to his sister Gilberte. Welling up within him was not the intense satisfaction and fulfillment one would expect from success but rather a certain dryness of soul which turned his thoughts toward God. So, on that fifth day of November, he wrote Gilberte, "We can preserve the old grace only by acquiring a new grace, otherwise we will lose that which we think we retain. . ." Referring to Gilberte's earlier exhortations about discipleship he continued:

> "You must not fear to place before our eyes the things which we have in our memory and which we must recall in our hearts. For beyond doubt your discourse may serve them better as an instrument of grace than can the idea of it which remains in our memory."

As he scribbled, a wistful longing poured out on paper for the inspiration and vitality of the faith he had known years before in Rouen. He went on: "Without the spirit which must vivify it, our memory as well as the teachings it retains is but an inanimate and Judaical body." Then lest he unmask too much and appear sentimental he concluded with advice to Florin not to overbuild the house he was planning in Clermont.

In the stillness of their home, while Jacqueline meditated in her room and Etienne brooded in his study, Blaise was lonely and restless. His new fame did not satisfy. Though he read devotional works, though he continued his experiments on the vacuum, though he worked to perfect his arithmetic machine, though he laughed with young Roannez, Blaise was lonely and spiritually dry during that long and troubled winter of 1648-1649.

Still another unrewarding triumph came to him as the weather warmed in March of 1649. The right to manufacture his arithmetic machine was given him by royal assignment on March 22, 1649. Though the twenty-six-year-old inventor had dreams of manufacturing and selling his machine, his hope was not realized. First his machines were so expensive; secondly, there were few mechanics capable of repairing such an intricate machine. His hope of financial gain from his invention died at the outset.

To add to the Pascals' unhappiness, Paris was still in the throes of becoming an armed camp. On January 8, 1649, the Parliament had outlawed Cardinal Mazarin, urging the citizenry to hunt him down as a criminal. Throughout the spring of 1649 the nobility were busily wooing Parliament in the hope of regaining their powers. The poor were fighting in the streets for crusts of bread. The Queen, safe in her refuge outside Paris, had won the support of the Great Condé whom she ordered to lead an army to blockade and to subdue a rebellious Paris.

As summer approached, distressed by the growing intrigue and dangers of Paris, Etienne packed up his family and moved them across the French countryside to the quiet and calm of Clermont. There they would spend over a year with Florin and Gilberte. There Jacqueline would be isolated from Singlin and the "fanatical" Port-Royalists. There in Clermont the family would be together for the last time.

CHAPTER SIX

THE LAST REUNION (1649-1653)

THE walled town of Clermont in Auvergne in Central France was a quiet pool of tranquility, not terribly disturbed by the rebellion raging across Paris in 1649. The citizens of Clermont looked out across their valley to volcanic hills, peering through the distant haze. It was like a jagged lunar landscape shrouded in blue mist. Eleven miles away stood the 4000 foot Puy-de Dôme, towering like a sentinel, crowned with the ruins of an ancient Roman temple at its summit. Seen from that awesome height, Clermont appeared to be nailed to the dark earth by the twin spires of its cathedral. The sturdy Romanesque basilica of Notre Dame du Port stood near the center of Clermont. Built of greyish-brown stone, it loomed large above the tiny houses which pressed in upon it as though seeking protection from the winds that swept through the valley. Near the cathedral was an expansive, sloping square where the populace gathered on festive occasions. Clermont, solid and simple, was a restful contrast to the turbulence of Paris. Montferrand was Clermont's neighboring city. Here most of the official business of the region was carried on. Here the High Court had its seat. Montferrand, where Etienne had once served as magistrate of the Court of Aids, stood sullenly beside its more lively neighbor-city, Clermont.

Ringing Clermont, as though in a loving but protective embrace, were the communities of the religious: The Priory of Beaumont, the Chamalieres Chapter, the Minims of Saint Peter, the Augustinians, the royal abbeys of Saint-Andre and Saint-

Alyre, the barefooted Carmelite Friars of Chantoin, Jacobins, Ursulines and others.

To Clermont the Pascals came! As their coach moved through the green valley of the Limagne which funneled down to Clermont, the crocuses and jonquils along the road seemed to wave a welcome. As the family jounced along, they saw in the distance the village of Gerzat where Etienne's wife, Antoinette Begon, had her ancestry. They rode within sight of Riom with its tiny Renaissance houses. They passed by the tower of Tournoel jutting upward from a rocky outcropping on the hillside like a dagger stuck in a piece of cheese.

At last their coach rattled through Montferrand and entered Clermont. The tiny basalt houses crowded in upon the muddy streets and alleys. They paused at the house that once had been their home, as Etienne peered from the coach with sad memories flooding his mind. It really had been two houses, one fronting on the Rue des Gras and the other overlooking the Rue des Chaussetiers. Here the children had been born. Here his beloved Antoinette had died, within a stone's throw of the somber cathedral. Then the coach moved on. At last it came to a halt in the lee of the cathedral, before the small house of Florin and Gilberte Perier.

What a reunion that was! Gilberte, now grown matronly and chubby, embraced her father, brother and sister excitedly. Florin was more reserved though warm in his greeting. The Perier children peered shyly from behind their mother's skirts. There was Etienne, who was seven, Margaret, who was three, and Marie, who was two. As they entered the Perier home, Florin apologized for the crowded conditions which had necessitated his putting up partitions to insure the privacy of the guests. He explained that the country house he was building at Bienassis, outside the walls of Clermont, would soon relieve the crowding. That night, Etienne Pascal's family slept once again beneath one roof.

Almost immediately, Jacqueline set herself a rigid spiritual discipline to follow. Though she was not at Port-Royal, she was of Port-Royal. She cut her hair and donned a head piece larger than that worn by most nuns. She took to wearing flat-heeled shoes and somber grey clothes. Yet her new attire could not hide the beauty of soul which shone from her pitted face. Her small, unheated room became a cell where she held spiritual retreat. She spent much of each day in her tiny room reciting her office, reading, praying and sewing. Even in summer, the air in that mountainous region was sharp and crisp. So in solitude, she sat by her window sewing woolen stockings and linen under-garments which she later took to warm the poor and the sick. Day by day, smiling and full of charm, she moved through the sometimes dusty, sometimes muddy, always dirty streets on her errands of mercy.

While engaged in this ministry of compassion, she encountered one day a Father of the Oratory (a religious order which came to France in 1631, having been founded in Italy by St. Philip Neri). This priest came to call upon her. During the conver-sation, he discovered her poetic talents and proceeded to urge her to use her poetry to glorify God. Soon afterward, Jacqueline translated the Ascension hymn "Jesu Nostra Redemptio" into rhyme. The priest was delighted.

Not so with Mother Agnes in Paris. Jacqueline had written her telling of this new adventure into poetry. Mother Agnes, ever the austere Jansenist, replied:

". . . it is better for you to hide your talents of that nature, instead of making them known. God will not require an account of them, and they must be buried, for the lot of woman is humility and silence. . . . You ought to hate your genius."

Though the gentle priest protested, Jacqueline decided to abandon her poesy never to take it up again. But not before she had completed her last poem, which like a flash of lightning across the night sky, revealed the spiritual country through which she was travelling on her pilgrimage. As she sat in her cubicle she penned the words:

"O ye dark forests in whose somber shades
    Night finds a noonday lair,
Silence, a sacred refuge! to your glades
    A stranger worn with care
And weary of life's jostle, would repair.
He asks no medicine for his fond heart's pain,
He breaks your stillness with no piercing cry;
He comes not to complain,
    He only comes to die!
To die among the busy haunts of men
    Were to betray His woe.
But these thick woods and this sequestered glen
    No trace of suffering show.
Here would He die that none His love may know.
Ye need not dread his weeping — tears are vain —
Here let Him perish and unheeded lie,
He comes not to complain,
    He only comes to die."

Though she was radiant and her sweet face seemed to glow with compassion as she moved about the city, Jacqueline had shed a flood of tears in her little room. The tug of war with her father over entering Port-Royal had left her "worn and weary." The silence of her tiny cell was a "sacred refuge" where she felt a growing identification with the man of Gethsemane. There she felt His heart's pain mingle with hers. There she accepted even as He did, death to all personal ambitions without a murmur of complaint. Then her poetry ceased forever.

But her good works continued on. She visited the poor and the sick on sunny days and in the rain. When illness invaded the Perier household, she nursed the family tenderly. When Gilberte's little daughter was sick and close to death, Jacqueline sat by her side night and day, only leaving the bedside when the tiny one slept. Even then she merely went down the hallway to recite her office in her own room. Jacqueline was dying to her own ambitions but was intensely alive to the needs of those around her. She was approaching her twenty-fourth year.

Meanwhile back in Paris the excitement was not all in the streets. Behind the soot-covered walls of the Sorbonne spiritual warfare was being waged. Nicolas Cornet, the syndic (dean) of the Faculty of Theology, was a close ally of the Jesuits. He had devoted considerable time poring over Cornelius Jansen's "Augustinus" which had been published in 1640. He had extracted seven heretical propositions which he claimed he had found in the "Augustinus." These he proposed that the Faculty of Theology condemn as heretical. The little nuns of Port-Royal were frightened.

But then Antoine Arnauld rose to the battle. Like Port-Royal's Mother Angélique, Arnauld was one of the twenty-two children of the lawyer Arnauld who had stirred the ire of the Jesuits by arguing against them in 1594. Antoine Arnauld, the younger, had also provoked the Jesuits by attacking the frequent use of communion which was enjoined by the Jesuits. He had done this in 1643 in a brilliant "Treatise on Frequent Communion." Now Arnauld left the rustic simplicity of the men's retreat at Port-Royal in the Fields to counter Cornet's attack on Jansen before the Sorbonne. He argued that the propositions did not reflect accurately the teaching of Jansen's magnum opus. The syndic reacted by reducing his extracts from the "Augustinus" to five reputedly heretical propositions. In a heated session at the Sorbonne, eighty-five bishops heard the arguments and then finally referred the whole question to the Pope at Rome. For a time it seemed that the whole matter had ended in a draw. The nuns at Port-Royal offered prayers of thanks in their simple whitewashed chapel and Arnauld withdrew to the green solitude of the Chevreuse Valley.

The good-looking young Duke de Roannez, however, was

quite unmoved by the theological furor at the Sorbonne. The turmoil and excitement of the Fronde preoccupied him and other favorites of the Court. On January 5th, 1649, the eve of Twelfth-Night, Queen Anne and two or three of her ladies shared a Twelfth-Night cake with the little King in the elegance of the royal apartment. The Queen herself found the bean hidden in the cake. Then she retired to sleep.

But in the darkness of the night, at three in the morning, she rose. She helped dress the infant King and his younger brother, led them by the hand down a secret staircase and through the gardens to a waiting coach which sped them out of the city to Cours-la-Reine. There they were joined by a coach bearing Mazarin, Gaston and Condé. Other coaches soon appeared bearing sleepy members of the Court. Soon a procession had formed which then travelled through the darkness to Saint-Germain-en Laye. The flight from Paris had been so sudden that this palace in the country had no furniture but a few camp beds. That night royalty slept uncomfortably while ordinary Parisians slept in soft, warm beds. When the people of Paris woke on January 6th, they were astonished and angered. Their quarrel was with Mazarin, not with the royal household. Paris was in an uproar over the disappearance of the royal family. Roannez had the feeling that he was a witness to history in the making. Late in 1648 the despised Cardinal Mazarin had sent secret orders to Condé to withdraw units of the Army of Flanders from the lowlands. Accordingly, Condé, with 5000-6000 men, had returned to occupy such strategic points around Paris as the Gonesse bakeries and the cattle markets at Poissy. Now, with the royal family safely out of the city, Condé began a ridiculous and ineffectual attempt to starve the city.

At the same time, though the Treaty of Westphalia (October 24, 1648) had concluded hostilities between Spain and France, sporadic warfare continued in the lowlands. Replacements for Condé's units, now in Paris, had to be sent to Flanders. Roannez was to be among them. On May 7th, 1649, he purchased four carriage horses in preparation for his service in Flanders. Then in his brilliant uniform, the twenty-two-year-old left Paris for the battlefield. But he returned to Paris frequently. Then a great honor was granted to him. On June 6th, he was promoted to Brigadier-General. July 18th and again early in August, the youthful general returned to the center of his world. On August 9th he returned to Paris to buy forty horses for his unit in Flanders. On the 13th he purchased some mules. On August 18th, when the Royal Court returned to Paris amidst the wild enthusiasm of the crowds. Roannez attended the lavish ball at the Hôtel de Ville (City Hall). But then his sense of duty called him to return to the troops at Orleux where the Count d'Harcourt was in command. There he took part in the operations at Hainaut and did not return again to Paris until November 18th. Those were days of excitement for Roannez. They were heady days of drama and bloodshed. Through it all, he remained intensely loyal to the Queen and the child-King.

Meanwhile in Clermont, Florin Perier and Gilberte noted that they saw little of her brother since Monsieur de Ribeyre had caught his fancy. In Clermont, Blaise was a big frog in a little puddle. Monsieur de Ribeyre, Florin's friend, was a Counsellor of State, first president of the Court of Aids and an important man in that region. He had taken great delight in presenting Blaise to the circle of scientists who met in his home.

At one of the gatherings at the Ribeyre's house, Domat, the "Blackstone" of the French legal profession, had met and taken a fancy to the young Pascal. Domat, like most intellectuals, was fascinated by the younger man who challenged his own brilliance. At one of the get-togethers, when the conversation had not gripped him, Domat sat sketching the youthful object of his admiration. With deft strokes, he captured the firm, almost petulant mouth, the wide-open, questioning eyes, the high bulging forehead of the young scientist. Domat was not the only admirer of the young Pascal, though. Ribeyre and most of his friends were captivated by him. But not all! Some of the younger savants, faculty members from the nearby university,[1] resented his cocky, self-assured airs.

But scientific gatherings were not the only affairs which kept Blaise busy. The best hostesses of Clermont were sure to put his name on their guest lists. It was at one of these social functions that Blaise first met a beautiful and intelligent young woman who intrigued him. For some months now, he had been touched by the warmth and affection between Florin and Gilberte. The family atmosphere had made him acutely aware of the emptiness of his own bachelor existence. He began to wonder what life would be like for him when he lost his father and when Jacqueline entered Port-Royal. So when he met a delightful charmer in Clermont, romantic yearnings stirred within him. On several occasions, he silently admired her from across the room. But he was discouraged when he learned that it was well known that she was "The Sappho (lesbian) of the land."

So Blaise was kept busy in Clermont with social functions, intellectual discussions and romantic meditations. Any spare time he had he used either to continue work on his "Treatise on the Vacuum" or to tinker on perfecting his adding machine.

One warm day in 1650, he set out for the Puy-de-Dôme with a carp's bladder half filled with air. As he rode along the road with the morning sun at his back, he intended to verify Florin's experiment of many months earlier. As he rode slowly up the road winding around the steep hillside, he paused periodically. Each time he stopped he noted that the bladder was swelling out more and more as the altitude increased and the atmospheric pressure decreased. When he reached the bleak, windswept summit, he walked about slowly. Below him, he saw a host of lesser hills covered with high green forests. In the distance, the volcanic hills blended into the sky in a sea of blue haze. On the journey downward, the carp's bladder slowly shrunk as the pressure of the air increased. As he returned to Clermont, he was jubilant. The facts once again confirmed his views on the vacuum.

The months in Clermont lengthened into a year and a half. As the frost of autumn 1650 began to spread its icy web across Auvergne, Etienne prepared to return to Paris. Sad farewells were said. Then their coach headed back to the noise and glamour of Paris.

In the chill of November, 1650, the house on Rue de Touraine was awaiting them. And so was the young Duke of Roannez. Artus Gouffier, the Duke of Roannez, was strangely attracted to Blaise. Artus always felt stimulated by his conversations with Blaise. Together they probed the mysteries of science. Occasionally their long discussions touched on religion and the Jansenist priests at St. Merri. In turn, Blaise enjoyed those occasions when he accompanied Artus to gala affairs at court. Each opened new worlds for the other during that cold winter.

As the warm summer solstice of 1651 arrived, Blaise received word that in June of 1651, it had been argued at the College of Montferrand that while Blaise's experiments on the vacuum were not original with him, he nevertheless sought credit for them. Blaise was crushed. His own self-image was largely built on his achievements in science. Now to be accused of dishonesty was shattering. His hands trembled as he read the words of the prologue to the theses that had been presented at Montferrand.

> "There are persons loving novelty, who want to say that they are the inventors of a certain experiment of which Torricelli is the author and which has been performed in Poland; notwithstanding that, these persons wanting to attribute it to themselves, after having performed it in Normandy, have come to publicize it in Auvergne."

Blaise knew that these barbed words were aimed at him. And so, since the theses had been dedicated to his friend, Monsieur Ribeyre, he took pen in hand and wrote him a heated letter. He carefully traced the development of the experiment from

91

Torricelli, to Mersenne's abortive attempt, to his own successes in Rouen. He quoted from his "New Experiments Touching the Vacuum," which he had distributed widely in 1647. (Fifteen or thirty copies had been sent to Clermont). At that time and afterwards he had always acknowledged that he was not the author of the experiment. Relentlessly, Blaise pursued the jealous Jesuits in Montferrand. He demonstrated that Valerian Magni in Poland conducted his experiment a whole year after Pascal performed his. Then he declared triumphantly, "The new knowledge that it (the experiment) has discovered for us is entirely mine." He fought fiercely to bolster his self-image. He struggled to maintain his own ego-identity. As he hugged his dearest treasures, his scientific knowledge, his reputation in things of the intellect, he didn't realize that his life was built on the hope of success in the realm of knowledge. Science was sucking the juices of his humanity from his soul. But Jacqueline, meditating in her room upstairs, had outstripped him in things of the spirit. Roannez had outstripped him in material possessions and royal recognition. Now he desperately fought to maintain prominence in the one realm left to him, the kingdom of the mind.

Meanwhile new successes came to Artus. In February and May, he danced in ballets written by Benserade and captivated the court by his performances. Then, on August 22nd, the twenty-four-year-old Duke was appointed Governor and Lieutenant General of Poitou. Poitou was strategically located in West Central France. His ancestors had long owned vast holdings in Poitou. So the Duke had eargerly purchased the governorship for 300,000 livres from the Duke de la Rochefoucauld. When the royal appointment confirmed Artus' Governorship, congratulations poured into the mansion at the head of the Cloitre St. Merri.

On September 7th, 1651, church bells rang the glad news across Paris that the majority of the young King Louis XIV had been declared. Mazarin was in exile. This became the opportunity for Artus to have his peerage confirmed. The ducal title of his grandfather, Louis Gouffier, had been given during the minority of Louis XIII and so had never been verified or registered with the Parliament. This meant that legally Artus' peerage was open to question, since without registration it was not hereditary. So Artus took steps to secure his royal status. On September 25th, he received new letters of peerage.

Meanwhile, Etienne Pascal was not well. He was feeling his years. The hot summer had wearied him. On Sunday, September 24th, Etienne died. Jacqueline and Blaise stood helplessly by his side. Then Jacqueline fled to her room to seek comfort on her knees. Blaise was bereft. Shortly afterwards a messenger was dispatched to Clermont to tell Gilberte, who was about to give birth to another child, that her father was dead. Two days later the funeral was held and Etienne was interred in the Church of St. Jean-en-Greve. That same day Artus received a royal order to leave for Poitou to resolve some troubles there.

After the funeral, Blaise returned to the house, climbed the stairs to his room and sat in hushed silence, in gloom and darkness. He was alone, terribly alone. Jacqueline belonged to God and Port-Royal. Gilberte belonged to her family. But Blaise had no one except Artus Gouffier and he really belonged to the high society of the court. The pain and loneliness was so deep that the young scientist could only sit in stunned, tearless silence.

The next day, the day after the funeral, Blaise sat at his familiar desk scratching words upon paper. This was to be a letter of comfort to the Periers. He tried to describe their father's death and funeral. But grief overwhelmed him. So he left the desk abruptly to take a short walk. At lunch he mentioned to Jacqueline that he had attempted a letter to Gilberte. Then he went to take a short nap. When he wakened he discovered that Jacqueline, thinking he had completed the letter, had posted it. Blaise lacked the spirit to start another.

As the days went by, the chill grip of death slowly began to loosen its hold upon Blaise. Reason began to take hold of his emotions. The doctrine of the Jansenists began to reassert itself.

Finally, nearly a month after Etienne's, death he sat down once more at his desk, pen in hand, to try again to write words of consolation to Gilberte. She had not been at her father's side when he died. She was pregnant, finally giving birth to a son, Louis, three days after Etienne died. Even if her health had allowed, she still would not have been able to rush off to Paris since war was raging across the French countryside making travel almost impossible. So now, having recovered his own equilibrium, Blaise sought to offer comfort to Gilberte.

He sat at his desk and scribbled rapidly. The sound of his heavy breathing cushioned the noise of the scratching pen.

". . . the end of his life was so Christian, so happy, so holy and so to be desired that beyond those whose interest arises from natural ties, there is no Christian who should not rejoice over it . . . we must seek consolation for our ills not in ourselves, not in men, and not in all created things but rather in God . . . let us view it as a decree of God's providence, conceived in all eternity to be fulfilled in the fullness of His time, in such a year, on such a day, at such an hour, in such a place, and in such a manner . . . then we shall adore in humble silence the inaccessible height of His hidden designs."

Here Blaise paused reflectively. As the scientist bows in humility before the power of God's laws in nature, he bowed to the inexorable working of the Sovereign Providence of God in human affairs. There is no comfort to be found in the wisest of men, even Seneca and Socrates. The only comfort is to be found in Holy Writ. Pascal, lost in contemplation, mused on the contradictions, the misery, the blindness of humanity. He had found no comfort, at his father's passing, from his scientific endeavours or from the worldly gambits with Roannez. So he wrote: "we must have recourse to the person of Jesus Christ, for everything in man is abominable . . . but if we consider all things in Jesus

Christ we shall find every consolation, every satisfaction, every edification . . . without Jesus Christ it (death) is horrible, it is detestable, and the horror of nature. In Jesus Christ it is entirely different; it is worthy of love, it is holy and the joy of the faithful. All is sweetness in Jesus Christ, even death."

Blaise mused thoughtfully on the death and resurrection of Jesus. He pondered Jesus' continual re-enactment of His death and resurrection in the members of His Body, the Church. He analyzed the natural horror of death which comes to men. It seemed to him that man's horror of death could be traced to man's inordinate absolutizing of the love of self.

He continued writing. "I have learned from a holy man that one of the most substantial and useful charities toward the dead is to do the things which they would want us to do if they were still in the world. . . . In so doing we somehow make them live again in us . . . let us then do everything in our power to make our father live anew in us before God." Here Blaise inwardly dedicated himself to identify more and more with his father's ideals and purposes.

"If I had lost him six years ago (before the spiritual awakening stirred by the Jansenists in Rouen), I should have been lost. . . . But we must hope that since God has decreed his death in such a time, in such a place and in such a manner, it is doubtless most expedient for His Glory and for our salvation."

Blaise then brought his lengthy letter to a close: "Saint Augustine teaches us that in every man there is a serpent, an Eve and an Adam. The senses and our nature are the serpent, Eve is lustful appetite, and Adam is reason . . . let us pray to God that His grace may so strengthen us that Adam may remain victorious. Then let Jesus Christ be the victor over Adam, and let Him reign in us forever and ever. Amen." When Gilberte received this letter she may well have wondered, "Does my dear brother who is so intoxicated by reason really realize what he is saying when he urges that Jesus Christ be the victor over Adam (reason)?"

Some time after Etienne's death, his children were reunited. Gilberte, though unable to be at her father's funeral because of her pregnancy and because the war raging across France made travel impossible, had finally reached Paris to comfort her brother and sister. Etienne's children prepared to divide up his properties. Much of his wealth consisted of credits on debtors. A series of contracts were drafted in December 1651. Jacqueline agreed to sign over her share of the estate to Blaise. In return, he promised to pay her an annual income of 1600 livres. He hoped that he could collect from his father's creditors in order to fulfill this obligation. On the other hand, if Jacqueline became a nun, Blaise would have free use of her inheritance. At the same time, a yearly income of 400 livres was provided for faithful Louise Default. Gilberte had been well cared for under her marriage contract so no provision was made for her.

As the new year approached, Jacqueline was preparing to move to Port-Royal. The date set for her departure was January 4th, 1652.

The night of January 3rd, Gilberte timidly explained to Blaise that Jacqueline was leaving the next morning to make a retreat at Port-Royal in order to learn more about a nun's way of life. Blaise sensed that this was not the whole story. He quietly and forlornly rose from his seat and went to his room without saying a word. At the time, Jacqueline was closeted in a tiny room she used for her prayers. Later Jacqueline and Gilberte retired after tearful embraces.

The next morning as daylight rolled the covering of night from Paris, Gilberte rose about 7 a.m. Hearing no sounds in the house, she tip-toed to Jacqueline's room, woke her sister, and then returned to her own room. A while later she heard the front door close and listened to the click of Jacqueline's heels as she went down the steps and down the Rue de Touraine. Jacqueline had gone. She was twenty-six years old when she entered Port-Royal. Later Gilberte was to say, "we said no farewell, for fear that we might be too moved, and I turned aside out of her way, when I saw that she was ready to go."

Afterwards, Gilberte remained in Paris just long enough to assist her brother and Louise Default in their move to smaller quarters on the Rue Beaubourg which was closer both to the Roannez mansion as well as to their former home on Rue Brisemiche. Smaller quarters would mean less expense for Blaise. It had cost Etienne 12,000 livres to maintain the household on Rue Touraine. Blaise was hard-pressed to maintain himself, a household staff of four or five servants and a carriage and horses on his much lower income of 2500 livres.[2] So the move was made and Gilberte returned to her family in Clermont.

Blaise was now alone with his books, his experiments, his work on the adding machine, and a very occasional visit with the busy Roannez. Though many came to talk with him about his science, he felt terribly alone.

Periodically he crossed the Seine and rode to the edge of the city to visit Jacqueline at Port-Royal. Those visits were always brief. Jacqueline noted that their conversations in the visitor's room seemed stiff and formal. She could see that her brother resented her leaving him. But the joy and peace of her new life overcame her sadness for Blaise. Nevertheless, after each visit her words would linger in his mind long after he had left the visitor's room at the convent.

During the first half of 1652, Blaise continued to work many long hours attempting to perfect his calculating machine. In April, he appeared in the drawing room of his old family friend, the Duchess d' Aiguillon. There amidst the silk and brocades of the nobility, he demonstrated his machine, talked about fountains and touched on the problem of the vacuum. His scientific lecture fascinated the Duchess' friends but sold no machines. It was expensive to move in high society. He needed to enlarge his income and hoped that the sale of his machine might make him rich. He resented the sham of the world, yet like a moth drawn to a flame, he was attracted to it. He described life in the world:

"We distinguish men by external appearances rather than by internal qualities! Which of us two shall have precedence? Who will give place to the other? The least clever? But I am as clever as he. We should have to fight over this. He has four lackeys, and I have only one. This can be seen; we have only to count. It falls to me to yield, and I am a fool if I contest the matter."

As he worked on his machine, he attempted to stir interest in it. In a letter that he penned to Bourdelot, the personal physician of the wealthy Queen Christine of Sweden, he described the machine in some detail. In it he paid a lively tribute to Christine who had a reputation for being a paragon of learning. Indeed, she had persuaded the great Descartes to join her household before he died. So Blaise praised the cultured Queen.

What excitement raced through Blaise when he received a letter dated March 14, 1652 in which the Queen, through Bourdelot, declared that she would be happy to receive the machine from Pascal and that he was "one of those geniuses for whom the Queen had been searching."

Excitedly, Blaise hurried the work on his machine. In June, he began to draft a letter to the Queen in which he said:

"I have devoted myself to it with as much ardor as if I had foreseen that some day it would be seen by so august a person. . . . For I have a very special veneration for those who have attained the highest rank, whether in power or in knowledge. If I am not mistaken, these latter may be considered sovereigns quite as well as the former. . . . Indeed, this second empire (of the mind) seems to me to be an even more exalted order because the mind is of a higher order than the body. . . ."

Here Blaise put down his pen and closed his eyes. Before him he could see the world of the flesh — a physical, sensual, material world, inhabited by the vast majority of men. But he also could see the much more superior realm of the mind, inhabited by a smaller elite sampling of humanity.[3] Then taking pen in hand again, he went on:

"Each of these empires is great in itself. . . . (But) no matter how powerful a monarch may be, his glory lacks something if he lacks pre-eminence of the mind."

Blaise paused, realizing that Christine combined the best of both kingdoms. Then he continued:

"In your majesty power is dispensed through the light of science, and science is elevated by the luster of author-ity. . . . Reign therefore, incomparable princess, in a man-ner that will be entirely new. . . . As for me, not having been born under the first of your empires, I desire all the world to know that I glory in living under the second. . . ."

"This, Madame, is what leads me to make this present to your majesty. . . . I desire nothing with more ardor, than to be acknowledged by Your Majesty as her very humble, very obedient and very faithful servant."

Blaise Pascal[4]

So the letter was written and posted. And Blaise continued in his attempt to perfect a machine which was marketable.

Jacqueline had been in Port-Royal for two months when Arnauld d'Andilly, Mother Agnes and Mother Angélique de-cided that her consecration was so genuine that they would count her self-imposed retreat at home as part of her novitiate and that she could be betrothed to Christ on Trinity Sunday, May 26, 1652. Jacqueline was excited! On March 7, she composed an emotional letter to her brother urging him to be present. She pleaded:

"Do not set yourself up against the divine light. Do not hinder those who do good and do good yourself; or if you do not possess the strength to follow me, at least do not hold me back. . . I look principally to you for this sign of affection, and I am inviting you to my betrothal which with God's help will take place on Trinity Sunday. . . . I am writing to my faithful (Gilberte).[5] . . . Please comfort her if she needs it. . . . But if she is coming with the idea of opposing me, I am warning her that she will be wasting her time. I must say the same to you . . . I have been patient too long.

I have only invited you to the ceremony as a matter of form because I do not believe that you would ever have dreamt of missing it. You can be assured that I shall have nothing more to do with you if you do."

When this letter, with its threats and innuendos, was delivered to Blaise by a Monsieur Hobier, he went into a rage which was followed by piercingly painful headaches. He felt misunderstood, betrayed and cut off from his younger sister.

The next day, he journeyed across the city to Port-Royal. There in the now familiar parlor set aside for visitors the two Pascals came face to face. Immediately, he began to plead with her to postpone the date. But Blaise's possessiveness melted as he stopped and gazed into her face. Suddenly he felt remorse at having caused her pain. After a few moment's conversation with Arnauld d'Andilly, he gave his approval and, eyes filled with tears, left Port-Royal.

As May 26th dawned over Paris, amidst the ringing of church bells, Gilberte and Blaise rode to Port-Royal and took their seats in the chapel. Two other girls were to be cloistered with Jacqueline that day. During the ceremony when Jacqueline went to light a candle at the offertory, Gilberte went with her, then escorted her to the altar rail to be questioned by the celebrant. Blaise sat through the long ceremony tense and sad. He watched as Jacqueline and the other girls walked to the monastery door, bowed to the abbess who cut off a lock of her hair. Then Jacqueline walked through the door and the door closed. A few seconds later the door opened to reveal Jacqueline now wearing the habit and white veil of a novice. From that moment on Jacqueline was Sister Sainte-Euphemie.

June, 1652 also saw a reunion with some of the remaining members of the Academy. With Mersenne dead, Le Pailleur had taken it upon himself to draw together the remaining members of the old Academy. What reminiscences were shared. New discoveries were exchanged. Yet a wistful longing was felt for those days before death had begun to break the circle.

As the heat of summer began to lift from Paris with the approach of autumn, Roannez was forced to quit Paris to attend to pressing problems in Poitou. With Roannez out of town and Jacqueline within the walls of Port-Royal, Blaise suddenly felt terribly alone in the vast city of Paris. In October, he cut short his research and left for Clermont where he enjoyed the family life of the Perier's until May 1653.

Then came a letter from Jacqueline which caused Gilberte and Blaise to shake their heads in indignation. Jacqueline had written that she was to take her final vows on June 5th. She asked that her share of her father's estate be given to Port-Royal. Blaise and Gilberte agreed to deny the request. A letter of refusal was drafted and sent off post-haste, and Blaise prepared to return to Paris.

When Jacqueline opened the letter, she wept. She grew ill. She talked with Mother Agnes and Mother Angélique who in their motherly way comforted her, trying to make her smile again. Jacqueline through a flood of tears blurted out, "Perhaps I should make my profession as a lay sister in the kitchen or in the garden." From Mother Agnes' rugged, round face came a kindly smile. She rejected such a notion, recommending instead that she try to placate her brother. She said, "Why not let your family keep their fortune. We will receive you without a dowry." But Jacqueline's pride was offended. Her rights were being denied. She was in agony of spirit.

A few days later the novices had a meeting with Mother Angélique. As the gathering was breaking up, Angélique took Jacqueline by the hand and said, "What, is it possible, my daughter, that you are still sad? Were you not prepared for all you see? Did you not long since learn that we should never lean on the friendship of creatures and that the world loves its own? Is it not a happy thing that God makes this truth plain to you in the persons of those from whom you had least reason to expect such a lesson and thus removes all doubt of it from your mind? Your previous resolutions are thus braved by a sort of inevitable necessity, and you may, in a certain sense, say that you are alone in the world."

The two women were now alone. So the younger burst into tears and replied, "But I already feel so detached from the world that I don't feel I need such a bitter experience."

The older woman, with her arm around Jacqueline, assured her, "God is showing you that in this thought you are mistaken. If it were so, you would look upon all that has occurred with indifference instead of grieving as you now do. You ought to feel that God is granting you a great favor and to make good use of it."

The next day as the nuns gathered for mass in the chapel, Angélique was in her usual seat in the choir. As she gazed out at her nuns, she noted the forlorn look on Jacqueline's half-hidden face. Quietly, she left the choir loft and went to kneel beside the young novice. When the service was over, she motioned to Jacqueline to follow her to her own quarters. There she let Jacqueline cry and cushioned her head on her bosom for nearly an hour.

She whispered to the young woman, "I cannot wonder enough, my daughter, that you are overcome by such a trifle. You astonished me yesterday by saying you were sad. I did not know how to answer you. I supposed that you had already forgotten the incident since your being accepted into Port-Royal is all settled whether you have a dowry or not."

The only response was more sobbing from the fledgling nun.

Then Angélique's tone became firmer. As though probing into her hidden motivations, she peered into Jacqueline's wet face and said, "Why do you weep over this thing? Or, why do you not weep as much over every sin that is committed? If you are thinking only of God's glory and the spiritual welfare of your relatives, why have you never shed as many tears over their graver faults and their more heinous guilt in the sight of God as you now do over a slight failure in the kindness due to yourself?"

Jacqueline protested that it was only the injustice to Port-Royal that troubled her.

Angélique countered, "You are mistaken, my daughter, nothing is more painful or hard to bear than wounded affection. I know that you feel deeply the injustice done to the House, but your own share in this gives you a deeper pang. Self-love mingles in everything we do. This is the mainspring of this mighty sorrow!"

Jacqueline nodded in agreement. So Angélique proceeded to probe Jacqueline's soul. "You see, my sister, it was an easy thing for you to renounce the world. God had enabled you to perceive how vain and trifling are the amusements and gaieties of life which please and fascinate other girls . . . certainly you were very much detached from earth, but there yet remained two things for you to relinquish. One was your fortune, small though it is from a worldly point of view. The other, the chief treasure of your family, was the close union and confidence which made all your interests one. On this you are unconsciously relying and resting. But God sees fit to strip you of both and to make you poor in every sense of the word, poorer even in friendship than in possessions."

The wise old woman continued by relating the experience of

others who had learned the necessity of surrendering self-love and pride to God. Then she pointed the way of Jacqueline, "I entreat you not to feel angry with your friends, not to manifest any resentment nor to allow this to alienate your affection from them. After all, for what are you contending? Only a little lucre, absolutely less than nothing! . . . Therefore, write to your friends once more, especially to her whose tenderness for you is deepest. Express your own affection without reserve. Let them see that you have, in all sincerity, given up your fortune from the sole fear of paining them. And when your brother, who is expected here shortly, comes, do not reproach him, nor even look as if anything was wrong. Appear to have forgotten all, which you really should have done long ago."

There was a long silence. Then Jacqueline, after admitting that Angélique's analysis was accurate, stated that she probably had not acted wisely in signing over her estate so quickly after her father's death.

But Angélique replied, "Don't fret over it. You acted out of concern for the will of God and the welfare of your brother who was dearer to you than the world's wealth". Then with a barb in her tongue she said, "You certainly did not give him the money in order to aggrandize him or to render his position more brilliant. Besides, with all you have done for him, he has barely enough to keep up an appearance befitting his station." Then she arose and the interview was ended.

Soon afterwards her brother arrived in Paris and appeared in the parlor at Port-Royal. As Jacqueline entered the parlor, deep emotion was evident on her pretty face. But she did not scold. She was tense but quiet. Blaise turned white and started to explode with anger. As he raged, Jacqueline became silent, eyes toward the floor, tears falling on the carpet. Suddenly Blaise realized what he was doing to Jacqueline. Embarrassed, he too became silent. Then softly he said, "I will make matters right." And he left.

Three or four visits ensued during which Blaise sought

to negotiate a reduction in the dowry. Finally on the afternoon of June 4th, Blaise, the lawyers, Jacqueline, Mother Agnes, Mother Angélique and three other religious met in the parlor.

Mother Angélique said to Blaise, "I feel bound to entreat you, sir, in God's Name, do not let any earthly consideration influence you, and if you do not feel that the spirit of charity prompts you to this deed of charity, to leave it undone. You see, Monsieur de St. Cyran taught us to accept nothing for the house of God which does not come from Him. Alms given from other motives are not the work of His Holy Spirit and therefore we have no wish to receive them."

Blaise was flustered by her indifference, but with meticulous courtesy, pledged an annual gift of 1500 livres and promised to sign over a sum of 5000 livres within six months. This was a perfectly respectable dowry. Jacqueline was saved from becoming a recipient of "charity" but rancor must have curdled in Blaise's heart.

The next day, June 5, 1653, Jacqueline took her final vows. She had reached her promised land, but her brother was more alone than ever before. Jacqueline and Port-Royal had triumphed and Blaise had gone down to defeat.

A few days later, however, the nuns at Port-Royal also tasted defeat. Word arrived from Rome that on June 3rd, Pope Innocent X had condemned the five propositions said to be found in Jansen's "Augustinus."

CHAPTER SEVEN

"SAMPLING THE WORLD"
(1653-1654)

THE ducal palace of the Roannez was a busy place in 1653. The bachelor Henri Taconnet was the young Duke's secretary in charge of Poitou. He came and went between Poitou and the Duke's Paris mansion with regularity. Nicolas Martini, an older man, was in charge of the Duke's Paris affairs. Antoine de Hallot served the Duke as his squire or riding master. Jerome Paulin was engaged in 1653 to serve as the "maitre d'hotel." The Comte d'Harcourt, the poet Saint-Amant and a host of other notables were constant visitors at the mansion on Cloitre de Saint-Merri.

Presiding over the establishment was the Duke's aged mother, the Marquise de Boisy, and her daughter, Charlotte. Charlotte, Artus' younger sister, had Isabelle Forgeau, Jacquette Bretonneau and Marie Ratier living with her as companions. Jacquette and Jerome Paulin, the maitre d', spent many hours together in a romance which finally issued in marriage. Charlotte, herself, was almost twenty and very attractive, though in delicate health.

Marie Beraudin, another grandchild of the Duke's grandfather, old Louis Gouffier, also had an apartment in the mansion. 1653 was an exciting year for twenty-four-year-old Marie. Though her engagement had been made in 1652, it was not formalized until 1653. She was engaged to Louis de Cremeaux, Seigneur de La Grange from Lyons.

Artus Gouffier, the Duke of Roannez, was still busy early in 1653 consolidating his debts and attempting to put the estates he had inherited into some sort of financial order. The worth of his holdings was estimated at millions of pounds but there also were vast debts which needed settling. Accordingly, stringent economies were imposed.

Into this household Blaise came to live for a while as a friend and counsellor to Artus. The excitement in the ducal palace helped him to recover from the defeat he had experienced at Port-Royal. The fact that Artus and Charlotte both regarded him with such reverence and that they hung on his every word made him feel wanted and important. Artus spent long hours with him discussing the latest scientific discoveries of Europe. He also sought advice from Blaise concerning a project he had been deeply interested in for over a year, Brisson's attempt to drain five sections of marsh-land on the right bank of the. Seine. Charlotte, who was fascinated by the Jansenism taught at the Church of Saint-Merri, was delighted to have Blaise near to answer her questions in theology. Together with the Roannez, Blaise made many trips to the scintillating and glamorous affairs at the royal court. He continued attending the reunions of the old Academy of Mersenne which gathered around Le Pailleur each Saturday. While part of the ducal household, he received a letter from the Periers announcing that on July 26th, 1653 a son had been born. They had named him Blaise after his famous uncle. Those were days when the world of high society was opening to him to disclose its secret treasures.

Toward the end of that summer, Artus invited Blaise to join him and some friends in journeying to Poitou. The Fronde was over. France was peaceful. It was time for the Duke to visit Poitou to make sure the pacification of his realm was complete. This meant that Blaise must get his own affairs in order before attempting such a trip. Accordingly, on the fifth of September he handed over the balance of the sum he had promised to Port-Royal. There in the visitors' parlor, through the familiar grille, he received a receipt. Then his obligation to Port-Royal seemed finished.

As autumn approached, the trip to Poitou was undertaken.[1] Early in the morning on the fifteenth of September, they gathered in the courtyard of the Duke's palace. Antoine de Hallot made a last minute check of the carriage and the horses. Artus embraced his mother and Charlotte. Then four men boarded the carriage. They were the Duke, Blaise, Antoine Gombaud the Chevalier de Méré and Damien Miton. Then with the crack of the whip the horses strained forward and the carriage began its seven-day journey toward Poitou.

As they jolted and jounced through the French countryside, their journey would bind them together for seven days of conversation and chatter. As they rode along, their conversation was at first casual. Miton reported that Marie Pastoureau, his bride of nearly seven months, was pregnant. He was excited at the prospect of becoming a father. He mentioned that when he returned his servants would have moved his family from a house on the Rue Saint-Louis au Marais to one on the Rue de la Cerisaie. It seemed appropriate for a new marriage and a new child to have a new house.

As he bounced along Blaise studied the occupants of the carriage. Miton was about thirty-five. He had a dissipated look which reflected a youth of debauchery. He was very rich and was regarded as a literary authority by his friends at Court. Since 1646, he had been Treasurer General of Extraordinary War Funds for Flanders, Artois and Picardy. Pascal felt an irritation for this man with the nervous 'tic' who could so easily leave a young bride bearing his child. Perhaps Miton, the throughly worldly sophisticate, challenged Pascal's sense of self-identity. The worldling made the scholar feel extremely uncomfortable. When he reached Poitou, Pascal scribbled some observations about Miton on scraps of paper:

109

"The self is hateful. You, Miton, hide
it; but you do not succeed in getting
rid of it. You are then always hateful?
No; for in acting to oblige everybody
we give no more occasion for hatred of
us." (141-455)

"Miton sees well that men are corrupt;
what he does not see is why they cannot
fly higher." (145-448)

"Reproach Miton for not being troubled,
since God will reproach him." (760-192)

The fourth man riding in the coach was Antoine Gombaud
the Chevalier de Méré, a member of the great Condé family.
Méré was a bon vivant, a man about town. He had traveled
widely, even reaching the shores of the New World. He was an
accomplished student of the classics with a special interest in
the Greeks. He also owned estates surrounding the Chateau de
Boussaq in Poitou. Méré was to have a profound influence on
Blaise.

As they rode through the French countryside, amidst the
changing colors of autumn and the nostalgic odor of burning
leaves, Blaise became more and more a listener. These habitués
of proper society intrigued him. From time to time he pulled
his tablet of paper from his pocket to write down insights and
thoughts stimulated by the conversation.

Méré delighted in lecturing his captive audience on the ideal
of "honnête homme," the honest man, who embodies the aristocratic stardards to be set by people of breeding and culture. The
theme was recurrent in the salons of Paris, perhaps as a reaction against the coarseness and pushiness of the Frondeurs. The
"honnête homme" is the man who has such sensitivity to the
feelings of others that he perfectly embodies consideration for

110

the rights of others. He brings out the best in others. He has good manners and is the perfect host. As Méré pointed out time and again, Montaigne's "gentil homme" helped to inspire such idealism. Montaigne, years before, had held up the standard of the "gentil homme," the gentleman who is undogmatic, kind, understanding, unassertive, intelligent and well read. Pascal, then and there, made a mental note to go back to re-read Montaigne, not this time from the perspective of theology but rather for a deeper understanding of the soul and mind of the natural man.

Finally, the journey was nearly ended. The two tall towers and the massive, grey slate roof of the Chateau d'Oiron could be seen looming above the trees in the distance. It was well known that the young Duke's ancestral home had been built nearly 30 years earlier by Louis Gouffier at a cost of over 150,000 livres. Also, that his grandfather had brought the master masons Jean Deschamps and Nicolas Caillon from Paris to oversee the stonework. The Chateau was modelled after the Chateau de Conflans.

Then the coach was entering the neatly manicured grounds of the estate. Pascal gazed out at the fountains cascading into the pool as they drove through the park surrounding the Chateau. Servants had started the pumps early that day so that the fountains would be sending water high into the air to celebrate the Duke's return. Then the carriage came to a stop under the pavilion at the main entrance.

Servants were lined up row on row on the nine steps of the staircase leading into the Chateau. The Duke greeted them warmly and then led his guests into the rich depths of the cavernous house. Pascal noted the collection of paintings and murals decorating the walls. Especially striking, he thought, were several paintings by the distinguished painter Charles Beaubrun.

So they arrived in Poitou. Méré soon left for his estates and the neighboring Chateau de Boussaq. The days that followed were enchanting to Blaise. There were rides through the fall countryside to inspect the ducal holdings. There were expeditions to survey the work of the Duke's company which was draining some of the marshes of Poitou. Pascal, being a shareholder in this company, was hopeful that the venture would increase his income. There were visits to Poitiers and Fontenay le-Comte. There were long conversations in front of the roaring fireplace when Méré's reading of long passages from Montaigne, Rabelais and Scarron would be followed by animated discussions both about their views and their pungent literary styles.

Those were days when Pascal scribbled thoughts and new insights on his pad of paper furiously. When he retired to his spacious room overlooking the park, he brooded over the conversations with his companions. He began to formulate the plan for a book which would present Christianity to sceptics like Miton and Méré in a way that would appeal not only to their minds but also to their hearts. Pascal was impressed with the role that intuition, feeling, the heart played in the lives of these seemingly rational sophisticates. He was astounded to realize that their intuitions often gave them insights which were not perceived by the most rational of men. So he scribbled on paper the insights that came to him during those stimulating days.

But their days in Poitou were numbered. As frost gripped the ground in its icy clutch, Méré, Miton and Pascal had to return to Paris. Blaise felt obligated to be in Paris when Gilberte and her ailing daughter Marguerite were scheduled to arrive, both to place the seven-year-old in Port-Royal and to consult witn the Paris doctors. So they headed homeward leaving the Duke to finish his business in Poitou.

Back in his rented rooms in the Rue Beaubourg, Blaise prepared to receive his sister and niece from Clermont. Marguerite's illness had been evident during his visit to Auvergne a year earlier. An ugly swelling had formed in the corner of the left eye, next to her nose. The swelling was growing larger and so Gilberte was bringing the seven-year-old to Paris for examination by the medical experts, Doctors Renaudot and Dalence.

With the snows of winter, Gilberte and Marguerite arrived at the Rue Beaubourg causing some small crowding in Blaise's quarters. Nevertheless, Blaise delighted in the inconvenience. The presence of those who cared for him, his own family, made him nostalgic for those days when he and Jacqueline and his father were under one roof. How he needed a family of his own.

The Paris doctors diagnosed Marguerite's ailment as a lachrymal fistula, gave her strange-smelling medication and dismissed her. Gilberte was distressed but Blaise reassured her that all would be well. A few days later Gilberte left for Clermont after placing Marguerite in Jacqueline's tender care at Port-Royal.

As 1654 dawned, Roannez was back in Paris, having returned just in time to spend Christmas with his family and friends. Blaise, after Gilberte's departure, was spending an increasing amount of time with Artus, Méré and their friends.[2]

Nevertheless, Blaise was also probing more and more deeply into the secrets of nature. He was continuing his experiments on air pressure and hydrostatics. He was writing treatises on "The Equilibrium of Liquids" and "The Pressure of the Mass of Air." Pascal was convinced of and was forcefully demonstrating the priority of experimentation in the realm of physics. The scientific method, for him, was experiment, experiment and experiment again and again. He was waging a crusade against that obscuration which based its judgments on the authority of Aristotle and so impeded the advance of new scientific knowledge.

Pascal was not locked into his intellectual pursuits, however. His society friends took him to the theater, gala balls[3] and, above all, to the gambling tables of high society. The Parisian society of the day was fascinated and captivated with the gambling fever.

One day, Méré challenged Pascal the mathematician to calculate how the gamblers should be paid off when a game is interrupted. How does one calculate the probabilities of gain or loss for each player when a game is broken off? Pascal was intrigued! During much of 1654 he attempted to determine a calculus of probabilities. He discussed this "geometry of chance" with his friends Carcavi and Roberval. He wrote the famous scholar Fermat in Toulouse. He was seeking new fields to conquer as he explored the upper reaches of mathematical knowledge. And conquer he did. He proposed a clever mathematical answer for Méré, a solution which won the approval of the renowned Fermat in Toulouse. Blaise laughingly remarked, "'I see that the truth is the same both in Toulouse and in Paris."

Now, more and more, Pascal turned to an intensive study of pure mathematics. His observation of the man of high society, the "honest man" was beginning to stir a revulsion within him. He could be gay and witty. But increasingly he struggled to be polite. Increasingly he bit his tongue, an effort which made him look angry — as though he were about to break out into a curse. The shallowness of the discussions in Madame de Sable's drawing room and at other salons was wearying him.

During his visits to the gaming tables, Pascal also probably began to develop his argument of the wager.[4] He caught the freethinker at his own game. He scribbled, "God exists or He does not. . . . In a domain beyond our reason, there is a game the meaning of which differs according as to whether God exists or not. You must take sides on the issue. You must bet." If one wagers for God and God does not exist, one has lost only that which is of finite value. But if one wagers that God does not exist and God actually does exist, one will lose "an infinity of life infinitely happy" (343-233). Pascal was yearning for his free-thinker friends to discover a higher way of life.

Pascal's own identity crisis also seemed to have been deepening. Life amongst sophisticated "gentils hommes" had only tended to help him know what he did not wish to become. It did not offer him the quality of life which could fulfill him. As he watched the "bon vivants" he saw the contradictions, the futility, the ennui in their way of life.

So it was a relief to retreat into the pure air of abstraction. He withdrew into the solitude of his study to reason, to think, to scribble. There as the weeks went by, he devised an Arithmetical Triangle which anticipated the Binomial Theorem of later mathematics. He explored the realm of Integral Calculus and the whole calculus of probabilities. When he reported his research to the Academy, it became apparent to the members that Blaise was working at a furious and intense pace. He seemed to be attempting to escape from the ennui which traps so many caught in the social whirl by throwing himself mercilessly into the abstractions of mathematics. The savants wondered, "Why is he driving himself so hard?"

They didn't realize that Blaise was experiencing a bitter crisis within. His frequent visits to the Roannez' mansion over the last year and a half had put him in close contact with sweet, sensitive Charlotte Gouffier, the Duke's younger sister. She spent long hours with Blaise, listening to him discuss the theology of Jansen and Singlin. They felt a deep spiritual bond uniting them. This closeness over the months and years had grown so deep that Blaise in his reveries dared think of Charlotte as one with whom he could share his love.[5] Yet he never dared speak of romance to Charlotte or to anyone else. Their relationship had to remain platonic. Nevertheless, he felt that she, too, was drawn to him in more than spiritual or intellectual ways. Yet a great gulf separated them. They were one spiritually and intellectually. But they were worlds apart socially. So Blaise felt the fire growing but he probably did not dare to speak of it to the one who inspired it. This frustration, coupled with the revulsion he was feeling at the terrible contradictions so evident in the souls of the worldly great, made him retreat more and more into the world of mathematical abstraction and pure philosophical thought. In the midst of his confusion, Blaise was struggling for his own identity as a person. What kind of a person was he? He was dissatisfied and unhappy with himself.

Like a moth drawn to the flame, he was constantly drawn back to his worldly acquaintances. Desiring wealth and power which would enable him to win Charlotte and impress his friends, he nevertheless knew the emptiness and folly of the worldly style of life. Man as man was an enigma to him. He was approaching a great divide when he would have to decide either to cast his lot with the worldlings and be a second class citizen amongst them or with God's help to learn contentment with his own station in life.

In the solitude of his rooms on Rue Beaubourg, he read early and late from Montaigne and Epictetus, that Greek of the first century A.D. who had described man's pride and arrogance. But Montaigne, the sceptic who had died in 1592, highlighted man's weakness, contradictions and misery. The latter spoke to Blaise's condition. Pascal was well-known. He was the talk of the Paris salons. He was the object of adulation by the rich and the great. Yet he knew within himself how wretchedly weak he really was. He was unhappy with himself. He knew there was a vacuum within. He read and reread the closing words of Montaigne's book "Apology of Raymond Sebond." He agreed that man can only rise to a higher kind of life if God reaches out a helping hand. Yet in despair he wondered if God would ever touch him. "Am I of the elect?" he cried. "Am I rejected of God? Have I sold my destiny for a mess of worldly pottage?"

One evening before retiring, Blaise took his pad and wrote:

"I had passed a long time in the study of the abstract sciences; and the limited number with whom one can treat thereof had disgusted me with them. When I began the study of man, I saw that these abstract sciences are not proper to man and that I was straying farther from my natural state in penetrating them than others did in their ignorance of them. I pardoned the others for knowing little of them, but I thought at least to find many companions in the study of man, and that this was the true study proper to him. I was mistaken; there are still fewer who study man than who study geometry. It is only from man's incompetence in studying man that he seeks the other themes, but

116

isn't this because the knowledge of man too is not the knowledge man should have, and because it is best for him to be ignorant of himself to be happy?" (756-144)

His study of science, his study of man had only led him down dead-end roads. He was still alone, unfulfilled and unhappy. The yawning vacuum within him was destroying him. He was not an authentic person, the man he once had hoped to be. He put his face in his hands in sadness and loneliness. He was alienated from himself, from others and from God. He was a terribly divided man.

Toward the end of September, Blaise journeyed across Paris to visit Jacqueline (Sister Saint-Euphemie) at Port-Royal. As Jacqueline entered the visitor's parlor, she sensed that Blaise sitting behind the grille was despondent and defeated. His shoulders slouched. His head drooped. Sadness was in his eyes. After the usual courtesies, Blaise slowly and softly recounted his research, his meetings with the famous and the great, his disappointment at the emptiness of worldly fame and amusement. It all seemed so empty. He admitted the pain his conscience had stirred within him; pain which had forced him to break away from it all.

His words came in a flood. How desperately Blaise had needed to unburden his soul.

"But," he wistfully declared, "I feel abandoned by God." He felt that he was only making an intellectual struggle to find God. His heart was not in it. His desires were still for the world, even though the world could not satisfy him.

Jacqueline dared not show it, but her heart jumped for joy within her. This was the answer to her prayers. Blaise seemed at the end of his own self-sufficiency, his own striving for success with God and man.

Then, the shadows having lengthened, they attended Vespers together. Blaise sitting in the visitor's cupola mechanically followed the prayers. Jacqueline, within the grille, prayed fervently for her brother.

That was the beginning of many such visits to Port-Royal. The brother and sister sat talking and reading for long hours that sped swiftly by. Each time, when Blaise returned home, he felt a step closer to his fulfillment. Nevertheless, he fought against placing himself under a spiritual director to whom he would have to bare his soul in complete humility and honesty. At home, he prayed. He read the Bible and dusted off other sacred writings. As the weeks went by, something began to happen within Pascal.

Drawn as by a magnet toward Jacqueline and Port-Royal, Blaise took a small house in the Faubourg Saint-Michel. From this pleasant new house, with its small domestic staff, he could walk to the convent for his conversations with his sister and for an occasional chat with the fifty-year-old, stern, inflexible Singlin, the nun's confessor.

On the evening of November 23rd, 1654 Blaise had gone to his bedroom. The door was locked. He was alone. There he sat reading from his father's Bible, a translation by the scholars of Louvain. As he turned the pages, he read:

> "Jesus said these things: then lifting his eyes to heaven, said: Father, the hour is come, glorify Thy Son so that Thy Son may glorify Thee. As Thou hast given him power over all flesh that He may bring eternal life to all those whom Thou hast given Him. And this is eternal life that they may know that Thou art true God and that He whom Thou hast sent is Jesus Christ. . . ." (John 17:1-3)

Slowly, Blaise put down the book, closed his eyes and rested his head on the back of the chair. He pictured Jesus on the eve of the Crucifixion. He thought of the Saviour about to be crucified. He suddenly realized the intense aloneness and agony of the Man of Sorrows.

Then came tears, tears for himself and tears for Jesus. His thin frame convulsed with dry sobs. Then silence!!! Blaise's eyes were closed. Jesus Christ seemed to be very near. Words he had just read pulsated in his mind. "And now I come to Thee and say these things to the world so that my joy shall be accomplished in them". For the first time in a long while, Blaise felt himself being identified with Jesus Christ and being loved by God. Joy! Joy! The joy of being fully loved and accepted by the unloved Jesus began to race through his being. Again, came tears — this time tears of joy. He was being recovered by God.

Blaise opened his eyes. Feverishly he took a scrap of paper from the table beside him. He noted it was 10:30 P.M. He scratched a tiny cross on the top of the paper and wrote, "Monday 23rd November, Feast of St. Clement, Pope and martyr, and others belonging to the martyrology. Vigil of St. Chrisogonos, martyr and others. From about half past ten in the evening until. . . ."

Pascal, ever the scientist, scribbled a record of the experience he was passing through. "Fire!" With Moses and the Apostles at Pentecost, Blaise felt aflame. It seemed to him that the whole room was aglow with heavenly fire. God was with him.

Blaise continued to write; "God of Abraham, God of Isaac, God of Jacob, not of the philosophers and scholars." There was a personal Presence with him. A living Personality had surrounded Blaise and had invaded his soul. A Person to person confrontation had occurred. He was in the presence of the Living Lord. Pascal was not in charge. He was not analyzing and controlling and manipulating thoughts. A wholly Other had come to him. Blaise closed his eyes, basking in the Presence.

"Certitude, certitude," were the next words he scribbled. The Presence of the God of the burning bush had caught up with him. God who is eternally certain of His own Being possessed Pascal with that same certainty. He knew with a sublime certainty that he was gripped by God.

119

"Feeling. Joy. Peace," were scratched on the paper. With the release of his long pent-up emotions, Blaise was feeling the joy of being accepted and loved by the One by whom he was known. His struggle for certainty being ended, he was also at peace. At last he was a whole person. His whole being was unified in God. No longer was he torn and divided between God and the world, between his desperate hunger for Eternal Truth and his desire for worldly fame and success.

He wrote, "God of Jesus Christ." The chasm was bridged between him and the eternal spaces which had so terrified him. God had come to him in Jesus Christ, the Mediator between eternity and time, between God and his soul. "Deum meum et Deum vestrum. Thy God shall be my God."

He penned the words, "Greatness of the human soul." No longer did he despise himself. Self-hatred melted in the love of God. All that he disliked about himself was lost in the overwhelming awareness that God loved him. Now he could accept himself. He who had known himself as a weak, miserable creature was realizing that he was loved by God who saw value and greatness in him. Pascal had at last discovered that God sees worth in him and in every sinful soul. Then he did not have to strive for success in things spiritual or in things temporal.

"Righteous Father the world hath not known Thee, but I have known Thee. Joy, Joy, Joy, tears of Joy." At last he had the Pearl of great price which none of his sophisticated friends at court possessed. In the fire of the love of God, he had a treasure which made all the trappings of worldly greatness fade into insignificance. He was free of worldly loves and his soul was soaring. The prodigal knew the joy of being welcomed home in God.

"I have separated myself from Him." Pride, love of the world, love of knowledge had been barriers behind which he hid from God. "My God, wilt Thou leave me?" Pascal longs to live always in the rapture of this union with God. He prayed "Let me not be separated from Him eternally." He writes, "We keep hold of Him only by the ways taught in the Gospel." What are those ways? They are summarized in the next words he wrote: "Renunciation, total and sweet." Pascal again and again was surrendering, yielding his life to Jesus Christ. So he wrote toward the end of his scribbling, "Total submission to Jesus Christ . . . and to my director."[6] Then he put down the pen, leaned his head back, closed his eyes and relaxed in the joy and peace of communion with his Lord.

For years Blaise had sought to surrender to God the ego he so disliked. But in his desperate attempt to yield himself, he had merely emphasized the self he so despised. On this mystic night, however, he had no strength left for the struggle or effort to make himself worthy, righteous, successful before God. Exhausted, with his thoughts on Jesus, he gave up the struggle. In those hours, the love of God for him, just as he was, became real in his soul. He would never again be the same.

A little over a fortnight later, Blaise still in the flush of his mystic revealing, attended church at Port-Royal in Paris. He sat with Jacqueline in the convent parlor while nones were being repeated before the sermon. When the church bells stopped ringing, Jacqueline rose to go to her place in the Church and Blaise to go to his. As he sat in the Chapel, he listened to a sermon by Singlin, the confessor to Port-Royal. It was the 8th of December, the commemoration of the Conception of the Virgin. Singlin leaned over the pulpit slowly and clearly pointed out how difficult it is for one to work out his salvation when entangled with worldly commitments. Blaise listened intently and wondered whether his allegiances to the great in society would not hinder the new life which had begun on his night of "Fire." That same day Jacqueline wrote in a letter to Gilberte, "I notice in him a humility and a submission even toward me which surprises me".

A short time later, still in the afterglow of his greatest of all experiences, Blaise felt the need to talk with Singlin, but he had returned to Port-Royal in the Fields. Fearful of undue publicity,

Blaise decided that he would quietly take his carriage to the Chevreuse valley, stop at the nearby village, leave his carriage and servants behind, and walk the short distance to see Singlin at Port-Royal. But when Singlin was apprised of the plan, he was reluctant to see Pascal under a cloak of secrecy. Shortly afterwards, he wrote a letter to Blaise appointing Jacqueline as her brother's spiritual directress. So through meetings at the parlor grille at Port-Royal, the brother was led by his sister carefully into new understandings of himself and his experience in God.

Toward the end of December, Singlin returned to Port-Royal in Paris. As Singlin and Pascal came together, Singlin seemed to feel threatened by the brilliant Pascal. The radiant young scientist confided to him his fears that he would be pulled back into the world and its allurements. Whereupon Singlin with a strange aloofness recommended that he make a retreat at Port-Royal in the Fields.

Years before Saint-Cyran had gathered a group of men who took over the deserted premises of Port-Royal in the Fields where they practiced penitence, discipline and meditation. In 1637, the brilliant Antoine le Maitre, the thirty-year-old son of Catherine Arnauld, had left his legal practice to retire to Port-Royal. There he built a small hermitage near the deserted convent. Soon his brother Isaac joined him. Later Isaac became a priest, becoming confessor to the group and changing his name into De Saci. Among the thirty or more soldiers, doctors, teachers who attached themselves to this solitary life were Arnauld d'Andilly, his son Luzanci and another le Maitre, de Sericourt.[7] Each one had some work to do. The marshes of Port-Royal were drained, gardens were made, children were taught, a printing press was built. But above all, they devoted themselves to studying the Bible and the Fathers of the Church. Singlin urged Blaise to make a retreat amongst these solitaries.

Then it was that the Duke de Roannez returned to Paris. What astonishment he felt when Blaise confided to him his experience of November 23rd. A wistful yearning for the peace,

one be sure of being in possession of truth without knowing what it is? Who can even know what being is. . . . ? And since we do not know what soul, body, space, motion, truth, good, and even being are, and since we do not know how to explain the idea which we have of them, how can we assure ourselves that this idea is the same for all men?"

"With equal thoroughness he finally scrutinizes all sciences and geometry, he points out the lack of certainty in geometric axioms and the inexactness of undefined terms such as extent, motion. He does the same with physics. . . ., with medicine. . . , with history, politics, morals, jurisprudence and the rest. He does this in such a manner as to leave us convinced that at present we merely think in some sort of dream from which we shall awaken only at death. So he takes reason devoid of faith to task so vigorously and so unsparingly that he causes reason to doubt its reasonableness."

Suddenly Blaise stopped. Gazing into the dying fire, he was lost in thought. De Saci softly repeated words from Augustine, "O God of truth! Are those who are schooled in the subtleties of reason more agreeable to Thee because of that?" Sympathetically, his soul went out to the tortured Montaigne. Then sitting up straight, De Saci said, "I am indebted to you, sir; I am sure that if I had read Montaigne for a long time I should know him as well as I do after this conversation that I have just had with you . . . I do indeed believe that he had a keen intellect, but I am not sure that with your careful linking up of his principles you are not attributing to him a somewhat better one than he had."

After citing Augustine again, De Saci said, "He brushes faith aside from everything that he says; consequently we who have faith must brush aside everything he says."

Pascal pondered the words of his confessor. Was this the type of obscurantism which he had been taught to despise?

De Saci was still speaking, "I do not condemn the author's intellect which is a great gift of God, but he might have made better use of it and offered it as a sacrifice to God rather than to the devil. Of what benefit is a good thing when one makes bad use of it? . . . You are fortunate, Sir, in having risen above these people called doctors who are engulfed in the intoxication of science, but whose hearts are devoid of truth."

Pascal slowly replied that if he knew Montaigne, De Saci knew Augustine far better. Blaise concurred with what De Saci had said, nevertheless, he could not help but say "that I take no pleasure in seeing this author's superb reason so utterly routed by its own weapons, nor do I rejoice in this bloody revolt of man against man who . . . is now cast down to the level of a beast."

"Montaigne acts like a pagan. From the premise that without faith everything is uncertain, and that so many search for the true and the good without achieving any degree of tranquility, he concludes that one ought to leave the matter to others. . . . Since the probabilities on both sides are equal, precedent and convenience overcome the balance and determine his conduct. Hence he conforms to the customs of his country because it is easy."

"I cannot conceal from you, Sir, that while reading this author and comparing him with Epictetus I found that they were assuredly the two greatest champions of the two most celebrated sects in the world and the only sects which are in accord with reason."

Then with a slight barb in his voice, Blaise said, "It is true, Sir, that you have just revealed to me admirably what little benefit Christians may derive from such studies in philosophy." But then recovering his sense of humility he went on, "With your permission I shall take the liberty of telling you what I think of them, although I am ready to renounce all the light that does not come from you."

"It seems to me that the source of errors of these two sects lies in their failure to recognize that the present state of man differs from that at the time of his creation. Now one of these sects (Epictetus) sees some traces of man's former greatness, ignores his depravity, and views nature as healthy and in no need of a Saviour; all this carries man to the pinnacle of pride."

"On the other hand, the other sect (Montaigne), conscious of man's present misery and unaware of his original dignity, regards nature as necessarily infirm and beyond repair; this causes man to despair of achieving real goodness, and so he descends to extreme baseness."

Here Pascal paused again. As he gazed into the fire, he remembered his own alternation between the arrogant pride of reason of Epictetus and the confusion amidst contradictions of Montaigne. He remembered how his own bewilderment and inner struggle with the contradictions of life had been resolved in his experience of the Gospel a few months before. Then he went on.

"It is the truth of the Gospel which reconciles these contradictions through a skill which is truly divine; by uniting everything which is true and dispelling everything false, it makes of them a veritably celestial wisdom in which the opposites, that were incompatible in human doctrines, are reconciled." So Blaise suggested that the contradictions of philosophy and of human thought could lead man to recognize his own hopelessness without faith and his need for the reconciling power of Divine Truth.

De Saci stirred and responded that although he could see that these readings might have that effect on Pascal, nevertheless he could not see that they would be helpful to the many folk whose slugglish minds would not enable them to extract pearls of truth from such rubbish.

Blaise broke in. "But I find that Epictetus has an incomparable art of disturbing the calm of those who seek it in external things, and of compelling them to recognize that they are veritable slaves and miserable blind men . . . Montaigne is incomparable in his ability to confound the pride of those who boast of real justice without faith, to disabuse those who cling to their opinions, and who believe they can find unshakable truth in the sciences. He is unparalleled in his ability to convince reason so thoroughly of its limitations and its vagaries that one is not inclined to regard mysteries as repugnant. . . ."

"But if Epictetus combats laziness, he leads to pride . . . Montaigne is absolutely pernicious to those who are inclined to impiety and to vice. . . . It seems to me that only when read together will their effect be not altogether injurious. . . Not that these readings may lead to virtue but merely that they may disturb vice."

It seemed that Pascal and De Saci were again on common ground. Pascal had arrived there through a reasoned study of these two philosophers and De Saci through simple Christian faith. But they both held that Jansenist view of man's hopelessness and impotence to attain truth without God's grace.

As De Saci and Fontaine later left Pascal and crossed the muddy courtyard, they exclaimed to each other of the wonder of Pascal's conversion.

As the days went by at winter-bound Port-Royal in the Fields, Blaise found a deepening satisfaction in his new life. Increasingly the scientist who had been a listener to the facts of nature became a listener to the whisperings of God. He read and reread the Bible in the Vulgate. He wrestled with what appeared to be Biblical contradictions. He became convinced that distortions of the Christian faith sprang out of man's opting for one truth to the neglect of its opposite. One day, after pondering seeming contradictions of the Bible, he scribbled on a scrap of paper "To understand Scripture, we must have a meaning in which all the contrary passages are reconciled."

His meditations on Scripture led him to perceive that there must be two meanings in Scripture — a literal and a spiritual meaning. Again he scribbled on a scrap of paper, "When the Word of God which is really true, is false literally, it is true spiritually." Then he added that piece of paper to a growing pile of such scraps on which he had scrawled thoughts about Christianity.

130

Each month at Port-Royal, the brothers focused their meditations on a different subject. While Blaise was among them, the mystery of Jesus' death was chosen as a subject. It was the first prayer in the mystery of the rosary. Day and night, Blaise read the Biblical accounts of Jesus' death and, lost in meditation, relived his sufferings. As he read his Bible, Blaise was transported across the centuries, back into the scenes described by Holy Writ. Time dissolved for him and he was there. Then one day, writing in the light of the small window of his cell, he began to scribble a record of his meditations. Pad of paper and pen before him, he read the Bible, closed his eyes in contemplation and prayed.

"In His passion Jesus suffers the torments imposed on Him by men; but in the agony He suffers the torments of His own imposing. . . .

"Jesus seeks at least some consolation from His three dearest friends; and they sleep; He asks them to endure with Him a little and they neglect Him entirely, having so little compassion that it could not for a moment keep them from their sleep. And thus Jesus was abandoned, alone, before the wrath of God. . . ."

Blaise stopped! His head was down, chin on his chest, eyes closed. He remembered the times when he had deserted Jesus for the glitter of high society. While he had been sipping the pleasures of Roannez' and Méré's world, Jesus had been in agony. Suddenly Pascal felt the loneliness of Jesus, the aloneness of God in a world that didn't seem to care.

He writes again. . . . "He suffers the pain and the loneliness in the horror of the night."

"I think Jesus complained only this once; but then He complained as though He could not contain His excessive pain: My soul is sorrowful even unto death. . . ."

"Jesus will be in agony until the end of the world; we must not sleep during all that time. . . ."

Again Blaise paused, scratching out words, polishing phrases. Then he closed his eyes, remembering his own night of nights and his confession: "I have fled from Him, denied Him, crucified Him."

He leaned forward writing, "Jesus being in agony and in the greatest of woes, let us pray longer."

"We implore God's mercy, not that He should allow us peace in our vices, but that He should deliver us from them."

"If God were to give us masters with His own Hand, Oh how gladly we should obey them! Necessity and events are indubitably such masters."

"Console thyself; Thou would'st not be seeking Me, had'st Thou not already found Me."

"I was thinking of thee in My Agony; I have shed such drops of blood for thee. . . ."

The Presence of Jesus was real to the young scientist. His love, His agony, His reassuring Presence seemed to fill the tiny room. He seemed to hear the Presence saying:

"I am present with Thee by My Word in the Scriptures, by My Spirit in the Church and by inspiration, by My Power in the priests, by My prayer in the faithful." He knew experientially who he was — the beloved of God. He "felt" possessed by the Eternal. In the grip of the Divine, he was in the grip of a certitude which rooted in the Eternal self-certainty. This experience transcended mere rational assurances, though it was not against reason. Transcendent, holy Love was breaking through all barriers to fill and to possess the soul of a surrendered man.

Pascal's lips moved in a fervent prayer, reminiscent of his night of Fire, "Lord, I give Thee all."

The Presence whispered, "Let the glory be Mine and not thine. . . ."

Then Blaise laid aside his paper and pen and sat in silence, eyes closed, contemplating the Mystery of Jesus' death, listening for inspiration from the Presence. The scientist had become the mystic of Port-Royal. But he would need all the inspiration he could contain to gird him for the storm that was about to descend upon him.

CHAPTER EIGHT

THE APPROACH OF THE
STORM (1655-1658)

AS THE winter of 1655 waned and the snows covering Paris melted, Blaise was again in residence at the Roannez ducal palace near Saint-Merri. The Roannez mansion was undergoing drastic alterations. A year earlier, the Duke had become concerned about repairs that needed to be done. So he had engaged Antoine LePaultre to do the work. LePaultre was well known, having worked on the chapel at Port-Royal in Paris, the Beauvais mansion, the Chateau de Villemareuil and many other well-known buildings.

Now in 1655, the mansion was undergoing full scale reconstruction. The courtyard had been repaved. Dominating the courtyard was a great archway at the top of a broad staircase. As one entered the mansion through the great archway, the vestibule of the mansion was newly paved with black and white stones brought from Caen. Looming large behind the vestibule was an elegant staircase, five sweeping steps bordered with a stone balustrade. At the top of the staircase, a massive door opened into a reception hall whose glittering tiles were polished squares of baked clay. Exquisite, massive tapestries covered the walls. Chairs covered with colorful tapestry lined the walls. Chandeliers, whose wooden arms were gilded and glistening, lighted the vast expanse. Beyond the reception hall was the Duke's private chamber. This was an enormous room dominated by the Duke's master bed on a raised platform recessed into an alcove, at the far end of the room. The wall of the alcove was paneled and ornamented with strings of gold, as were all the wood pieces in the room. On the next floor, there were four other large chambers. An infirmary for the sick was in the attic. The remodeling was to have been completed for Christmas 1654, but when Pascal came to visit the Duke in 1655 workmen were still hammering and hurrying to complete the renovations.

The Duke and the scientist spent many long hours locked in the Duke's chambers poring over Scripture, discussing passages from Saint-Cyran, Augustine and the Fathers of the Church. The Duke detected a profound new humility and tranquility in Blaise. Under the passionate tutelage of Pascal and after frequent visits to Port Royal in Paris, Roannez opened his soul to the inflow of Divine grace and began to experience the love, peace and joy which had transformed Blaise. The day came when Roannez' sensitive face glowed with the joy of one who has found the treasure above all treasures. His long, slender fingers held the Bible as he read rapturously of the Divine love. The glory of God seemed to fill his soul and to overflow into the household. Charlotte, who often joined their discussions, wept with joy as she watched her brother's conversion.

Later Roannez, in his devotion to God, would resign his governship of Poitou and influenced by Blaise's disparagement of marriage would abandon plans to marry the richest heiress in France, Mademoiselle de Mesme. Outraged at the change coming over his grand-nephew, the Count d'Harcourt blamed Blaise and arranged with the wife of the concierge in the Roannez mansion to assassinate Pascal. On the morning set for the murder, she entered Pascal's room stealthily, a knife concealed in her dress. But the bed was empty. That morning, Blaise had risen earlier than usual to go to Church.

Meanwhile other storm clouds were gathering. While Pascal had been at Port-Royal in the Fields, controversy was brewing in Paris. Ever since Pope Innocent X had condemned the five propositions of Jansen's "Augustinus", the Jansenist Arnauld and the Jesuits had kept an uneasy truce. Arnauld continued to insist that the five condemned doctrines were not contained in the "Augustinus".

Then on January 31st, 1655, the Abbé Picoté, an assistant priest at the Church of Saint-Sulpice refused to give the Duke de Liancourt absolution. His reasons: first the Duke had sent his daughter to board with the nuns at Port-Royal and secondly, he had taken under his roof two priests who were rumored to be Jansenists. To Picoté, this constituted disloyalty to the Establishment. The Duke de Liancourt protested vigorously, but the parish priest, Father Olier sided with his assistant.

Antoine Arnauld, not heeding the temperate appeals for silence by Singlin, De Saci and Du Barcos, dashed off a pamphlet defending Jansenism and condemning Picoté. It was entitled, "Letter from a Doctor of the Sorbonne to a Person of Quality" and was published on February 24th, 1655. To this the confessor of Louis XIV, Father Annat made a cutting response. In July, Arnauld took up the cudgel again in his "Second Letter from Mr. Arnauld, Doctor of the Sorbonne, to a Duke and a Peer". This book-sized letter defended the Jansenist stance. The weight of the Sorbonne now entered the battle.

As the frigid winds of January 1656 swept across Paris, the faculty of the Sorbonne gathered in its chambers. Six ushers wearing charms of gold stood at the doors. Two uniformed archers were in attendance to insure order. Chancellor Séguier, himself, began presiding over the meetings from December 20th on. Each day he would march through the streets to the Sorbonne with an escort of bowmen at his side to take his place in the hall where the meetings were held. Seated together were some forty ignorant, mendicant monks, brought in to create an atmosphere unfavorable to Arnauld. Arnauld, himself, was allowed only to state his case, but was forbidden to debate. In this biased atmosphere, the Sorbonne took up the question whether, as a matter of fact, the propositions condemned by the Pope were actually in Jansen's "Augustinus". Arnauld claimed they were not. But the Sorbonne, by a vote of 130 to 71, said they were. Arnauld was condemned! Discussion of the assertion that grace could fail the just, that Saint Peter in his denial of Christ lacked grace, was scheduled for mid-January. If Arnauld was condemned on this second point, Jansenism would be in grave danger. A chastened Arnauld sought once more to marshall arguments for his defense. In December 1655 he wrote another tedious, dull, logical letter, intended to appeal to the general public and then went into hiding in Paris.

Meanwhile, early in January 1656, Blaise journeyed to the Granges. One evening as the solitaries gathered to hear spiritual readings, the great Arnauld who, with his lieutenant, Nicole, had secretly left Paris, was in the circle to read in resounding tones his latest letter. When the reading of the letter was ended, there was an embarrassed silence. Heads hung low. Arnauld's dark, deep eyes were troubled and sad. His high forehead was knit and furrowed. His greying hair seemed to surround his square face like clouds of doom. Blaise's face was screwed up in obvious dissatisfaction.

Arnauld wearily said, "I see that you find my statement poor and I think you are right." But then his eyes flashed and he thundered, "You who are young, you should do something." He was pointing to Blaise!

Blaise, slowly and softly, responded, "I believe I see how the case could be presented. I will try to draft a letter provided that there is somebody to polish it up and to put it into a state in which it could be published."

That night the light burned late in Pascal's cell as he scribbled notes in anticipation of the battle.

January 23, 1656 the first of Pascal's letters, printed on large sheets of paper, was printed, published and sold in Paris for two sols, six derniers a copy. Howls of laughter went up from salons all over Paris as Parisians read "A little letter of eight pages dated the 23rd" and "written to a country gentleman" by a certain Louis de Montalte.

Blaise's friends at Port-Royal wondered about the significance of the name Louis de Montalte. Some suggested that Montalte was an anagram drawn from Pascal's birthplace, Clermont:

Mons Altus. Others preferred to believe the name was drawn from a rearrangement of the letters in the phrase "Talentum Deo Soli", "my talent for God alone".

The average reader of the little letter immediately identified with Montalte whom Pascal represented as an educated man with an open mind, but with little knowledge of theology. Montalte writes to inform his friend in the provinces of the latest happenings in Paris and particularly at the Sorbonne. He tells how the pompous doctors of the Sorbonne had two questions to examine. One was a question of fact. Was Arnauld correct in saying the doctrines condemned by the Pope were not really contained in Jansen's "Augustinus?" The second question to be examined was a question of right. Was the grace "without which we can do nothing, wanting to St. Peter at his fall?"

Pascal described Montalte as he turned first to a Jesuit, a follower of the 16th Century Jesuit Luis Molina, then to a Jansenist and finally to a Dominican for clarification of the debate. The Dominicans being loyal to Augustine should have gravitated towards the Augustinian-Jansenist position, but being fearful of identification with the Calvinists who also claimed Augustine, they had made an uncomfortable alliance with the Jesuits. But they really had less in common with the Jesuits than with the Jansenists. He learns that the Jesuits and Dominicans have coined a word "proximate," "which both used indiscriminately, though they understand it diversely." Thus, "By a similarity of language and an apparent conformity, they may form a large body, and get up a majority to crush him (Arnauld) with the greater certainty." The word "proximate" which means something different both to Jesuit and Dominican is used to attack the Jansenists. As Montalte goes to the Jesuit and the Dominican, he discovers hat the Jesuits are divided on the meaning they assign to word "proximate." And the Dominicans consider the Jesuits' views heretical. What division, what a variety of views are held. Yet they have all agreed to hide behind the word "proximate" as the means of attacking Arnauld and the

137

Jansenists who decline to say that the power of grace is "proximate". Pascal through the lips of Montalte declares "this is merely playing with words, to say that you are agreed as to the common terms which you employ while you differ as to the meaning of these terms . . . this is nothing better than pure chicanery". So Montalte's first letter to a provincial closes, "I shall continue to apprise you of all that happens". Pascal brilliantly showed that the doctors of the Sorbonne weren't interested in studying the "Augustinus" to see if the five condemned propositions were actually contained therein. With the cleverness of a playwright, he had shown that theology was not really the issue at all. Jesuits and Dominicans were simply joining forces to destroy the Jansenists. When Chancellor Séguier read the letter he was apoplectic. His face grew red as a beet. He had to be bled seven times.

Six days later on January 29th, 1656, the second Provincial Letter appeared! Again, the points in dispute at the Sorbonne were described to Montalte's friend in the provinces. Having touched on "proximate power" in the first letter, Pascal turns the discussion to "sufficient grace". "The Jesuits maintain that there is a grace given generally to all men, subject in such a way to free will that the will renders it efficacious or inefficacious at its pleasure without any additional aid from God". Grace then is "sufficient" because "it suffices of itself for action". On the other hand, the Jansenists hold "that a man can never act without efficacious grace." Any grace which does not of itself produce action is insufficient according to the Jansenists. The Jesuits, on the other hand, said the grace of God plus the cooperating will of man are *both* necessary to produce action. That grace which all men possess is made operative through man's free use of his will. The will of man is given priority. The Jansenists, giving an Augustinian priority to grace, clamed that the special grace of God which is given only to some men (efficacious grace) *irresistibly* influences the will of man to act rightly. That grace which all men possess is not sufficient unless a special irresistible grace (efficacious grace) is added to it. Jansenists and Jesuits were worlds apart.

The Dominicans, like the Jansenists, admit that a special (efficacious) grace must be added to the universal grace if man is to act rightly. Nevertheless this universal grace which is not sufficient is called sufficient. So a bewildered Montalte says the Dominicans "agree with the Jesuits in the use of a term" but "coincide with the Jansenists in the substance of the thing".

As Montalte quizzes Jesuit, Jansenist and Dominican in this second letter, he hears the Jansenist say: "Shall I present you with a picture of the Church amidst these conflicting sentiments? I consider her very much like a man, who, leaving his native country on a journey, is encountered by robbers who inflict many wounds on him, and leave him half dead. He sends for three physicians resident in the neighboring towns. The first (the Jansenist), on probing his wounds, pronounces them mortal and assures him that none but God can restore him to his lost powers. The second (The Jesuit), coming after the other, chooses to flatter the man — tells him that he has still sufficient strength to reach his home; and abusing the first physician who opposed his advice, determines upon his ruin. In this dilemma, the poor patient, observing the third medical gentleman (The Dominican) at a distance, stretches out his hands to him as the person who should determine the controversy. This practitioner, on examining his wounds and ascertaining the opinions of the first two doctors, embraces that of the second, and uniting with him, the two combine against the first. . . . The wounded man, however, sensible of his own weakness, begs him (The Dominican) to explain how he considered him sufficient for the journey. 'Because', replies his advisor, 'you are still in possession of your legs, and legs are organs which naturally suffice for walking'. 'But', says the patient, 'have I all the strength necessary to make use of my legs?' . . . 'Certainly you have not', replies the doctor; 'You will never walk effectively, unless God vouchsafes some extraordinary assistance to sustain and conduct you'." Essentially, the Jansenist and Dominican have similar views but for political

139

reasons the Dominicans have united with the Jesuits against Jansenism.

Again, Montalte ridicules the misuse of words by the religious establishment which was intent on destroying Jansenism. And so Paris was laughing at the foolishness and dishonesty of the theologians. Infuriated, the doctors of the Sorbonne on January 31st voted a censure against Arnauld.

Meanwhile with satiric humor, the Port-Royalists published Pascal's third letter, dated February 2, 1656. It was a short reply from the man in the provinces with the appeal "continue your letters. . . . These words, 'proximate power' and 'sufficient grace', with which we are threatened, will frighten us no longer".

But the powerful Jesuit establishment was beginning to counterattack. They were determined to stop the printing of these letters. On February 2nd at half past eleven, soldiers appeared at the shop of Savreux, the printer. They closed his shop and arrested his wife and two messenger boys. Searches were conducted at other printing shops. At Petit's shop, the printer's wife hastily gathered up the type and carried it to a friend's home where additional copies of the second letter were run off that night. From that time on, Pascal's letter had to be printed on presses hidden in private homes or hotel rooms.

Meanwhile, Blaise was on the move, spending a few days in his own house, a few days at the Roannez mansion, a few days at Port-Royal. Much of the time he was at the Sorbonne in an apartment at the hotel directly across the street from the massive buildings of the College of Clermont, a Jesuit stronghold. The hotel bore the sign of King David. Pascal, with his servant Picard, was registered as Mr. Mons.[1] From his window overlooking the dark, narrow steet, Blaise could see the Jesuit professors he was satirizing as they came and went shrouded in their caps and gowns.

Arnauld and Nicole furnished Blaise with the ammunition he needed, quotes and citations from the writings of the theologians.[2] Then Pascal undertook the writing and rewriting. When he had finished the draft of a letter, he would read it to Nicole, Arnauld,

Dubois, Saint-Gilles and others. If any one of his review board was sceptical, he kept on revising until there was unanimous acclaim. With some of his subsequent letters, three weeks passed before they were released. Some were rewritten seven or eight times.

On February 9th, the third letter was released. Copies were bought up quickly. Montalte had been waiting eagerly for publication of the Sorbonne's reasons for condemning Arnauld. Basically they came down to a condemnation of certain statements made by Arnauld which, in reality, were direct quotes from Chrysostom and Augustine. Montalte reports that M. LeMoine one of the examiners had said, "This proposition would be orthodox in the mouth of any other — it is only as coming from M. Arnauld that the Sorbonne has condemned it! . . . What is Catholic in the fathers becomes heretical in M. Arnauld . . . and new inventions, daily fabricated before our eyes (by the Jesuits), pass for the ancient faith of the Church." So Montalte concludes, "It is not the sentiments of M. Arnauld that are heretical; it is only his person." Blaise signed this letter with the initials E.A.A.B.P.A.F.D.E.P. With an ironic smile, he explained to his friends that they stood for "Et ancient Ami Blaise Pascal Auvergnat Fils D'Etienne Pascal". The long shadow of Etienne was still cast over his son.

February 25, in his fourth letter, he moved from a defense of Arnauld to challenge the ethics and practices of the Society of Jesus. Since people had no idea who the author of these much-talked-about letters was, Pascal felt quite secure. So he pressed the attack upon the Jesuits. Now he wrote, not for Arnauld's sake but for the sake of Jacqueline's Port-Royal and for the sake of Jesus Christ Himself.

As Pascal did his research on the Jesuits, reading the books on moral theology used by Jesuit confessors, he was angered. His hooked nose twitched and his expansive forehead wrinkled as he fumed. It seemed to him that the moral laxity of the Jesuits as they toadied to an indulgent society threatened the whole of Christian morality.

141

In his fourth letter, he had Montalte and a Jansenist friend quizzing a Jesuit on the meaning of "actual grace". In the course of the conversation the Jesuit declared "that an action cannot be imputed as a sin, unless God bestow on us, before commiting it, the knowledge of the evil that is in the action, and an inspiration inciting us to avoid it". This means that the hard-hearted and insensitive cannot be accused of sin. Montalte declared, "I see more people . . . justified by this ignorance and forgetfulness of God, than by grace and the sacraments." To Pascal, this strategem of the Jesuits to lessen men's feeling of guilt was contrary to Scripture and utterly repugnant to God.

On March 20th, his terrible fifth letter appeared.[3] In it he exposed the Jesuitical casuistry which attempted to apply general principles to specific cases. In certain extreme cases this tended to lower moral standards, bringing morality down to man rather than man up to the moral standards. The devious opinions of men on such applications were considered to have "probable" authority. The opinion of one serious doctor can render a teaching "probable". There is no human action which cannot be justified if one can find a single serious authority who says it is probable. So the doctrine of probability was brought before the public. The Jesuits used the probable opinions of men as authoritative instead of the certain teachings of the *Scripture*. But Montalte declares, "Probable won't do for me. I must have certainty." Here Pascal was attacking Jesuit innovations in morality while defending the verities of Scripture and the tradition of the Church.

This letter stirred the consciences of men and women all over France. No longer were people laughing. Pascal had exposed a moral sickness, the lowering of moral standards, and was accusing the Jesuits of infecting society with the disease.

A few days later, after the publication of the sharp fifth letter, the people of Paris were shaken by the news that a miracle had taken place at Port-Royal. To many it seemed as though God had intervened on the side of Port-Royal.

142

The condemnation of Arnauld had resulted in the closing of Port-Royal in the Fields. The solitaries had left their home in the Chevreuse Valley. The Abbess of Port-Royal in Paris spent the day in prayer and lamentation when it happened.

About that time an eccentric priest, M. de la Potherie, a collector of relics. offered to lend Port-Royal a thorn from the crown of Christ. This treasure he kept in his private chapel in the Faubourg Saint-Jacques. The Abbess decided to accept the offer and to venerate the relic on the Friday commemorating the death of Jesus.[4]

So, encased in a gilded reliquary, the sacred thorn was carried to Port-Royal on March 24th. In the chapel the nuns sang the Antiphon and then one by one went to kiss the case containing the relic.

Then a file of children, students at the convent, came forward to kiss the relic. One by one, they came. Then it was Marguerite Perier's turn. The young daughter of Florin and Gilberte Perier approached. For two years she had been afflicted with a lacrymal fistula. Between her eye and nose an abscess had developed, from which foul-smelling puss drained into her mouth and throat. The odor was so nauseous that the little one had to live apart from the other girls. As little Marguerite stepped forward and kissed the case, Sister Flavie, on impulse whispered "Pray to God for your eye, child," and then touched the reliquary to her eye. Marguerite moved on.

That night Marguerite confided to a friend, "My eye is cured, it doesn't hurt me anymore." After one of the nun's examined her and found that the child was indeed healed, word was carried to Mother Agnes. The next morning Jacqueline, the child's aunt, was informed.

The end of the week, on March 31st, the child was examined by the surgeon d'Alancay who had been treating her for nearly two years. When d'Alancay arrived, he said impatiently to a nun, "What do you expect me to do? Haven't I told you that it's incurable?" Then he proceeded to examine the child. He applied pressure to her eye. He put a spatula up her nose. Startled,

143

he laughed nervously and said, "There is nothing wrong with her." When Sister Flavie explained what had happened, he exclaimed, "It is a miracle. However, let us wait to see if the fistula returns."[5]

However, word had already begun to spread. On Wednesday, April 5th, Florin Perier arrived by coach from Clermont. On Good Friday some of the most famous doctors of France gathered at Port-Royal. The first surgeon to the King, Felix, was an official representative of the Crown. The Duke of Orleans' doctor, Guy Patin, was there. Altogether, an eight man committee examined little Marguerite. Their conclusion: the cure "surpasses the ordinary forces of nature, and that it did not take place without a miracle, which we assure to be veritable." The great and the small of Paris had been awaiting confirmation that God had worked a miracle at Port-Royal. Crowds swarmed about the monastery. It appeared to many that, by Divine intervention, the cause of the Jansenists had been vindicated. The solitaries were allowed to return to Port-Royal in the Fields. Even the diocesan authorities, early in June, set in motion the machinery for confirming the miracle.

But the enemies of Port-Royal were unwilling to give up. Father Annat, provincial of the Jesuits and confessor of the King, wrote that the miracle had occurred as a sign to convert the Jansenists from their errors. The Jesuits were still determined to crush Port-Royal in spite of this seeming miracle.

On his part, Blaise spurred on by God's apparent approval of his cause,[6] began to press the attack against the Jesuits even more fiercely. On April 10th, the sixth Provincial Letter was published, and on April 25th, the seventh. In them, Blaise attacked the whole ethical system of the Jesuits. In these letters he exposed the ways probabilism and casuistry were being used to destroy Christian morality and to lead the multitudes astray. Masses of people were being taught that their sins were not sins. The Jesuits were lowering Christian standards so as not to upset anyone and in order to make everyone feel comfortable in the Church regardless of his style of life. Montalte hears a Jesuit saying, "Men have arrived at such a pitch of corruption nowadays, that unable to make them come to us, we must even go to them. . . . The grand project of our Society . . . is never to repulse anyone, let him be what he may, and so avoid driving people to despair." Thus the Jesuits were accomodating the Gospel to the sins of men. In matters of morality, they chose to follow the modern casuists as "probably" of more relevance than the ancient fathers of the Church. The Jesuits practiced "directing the intention" whereby a man might violate any commandment if his intention was honorable. So one man might kill another if his intention (i.e. defending his honor) was worthy. Pascal exposed the dangers of the Jesuit's ethical system to the people of France. Everywhere people were shaking their heads in amazement as they read how the Jesuits even justified killing and murder. The dangerous premises of a lax moral theology were laid bare as Blaise led his readers to see what dangerous conclusions could be drawn from such soft accommodations of the Gospel to the sins of men.

But the Jesuits were beginning to suspect that Blaise Pascal was behind the letters which had made them the laughing stock of France. One day early in May, the Jesuits sent Father de Fretat to the inn which bore the sign of King David to consult Florin Perier who had come to stay with Blaise for awhile. Father de Fretat, accompanied by a lay brother, had come to urge Perier to apply pressure to make Blaise desist. As the two religious sat in Perier's room, spread out on the bed were some twenty copies of the latest Provincial Letter. They were fresh off the press and were drying. Florin was tense. The lay brother was sitting close to the bed. Would he notice what was there? Pascal, in the next room, scarcely dared to breathe.

Florin's response to Father de Fretat's warning that Blaise ought "not to continue, because if he did he might get into trouble" was the rejoinder that "Monsieur Pascal cannot prevent you from suspecting him. If he were to say that it is not he, you would not believe him. There is therefore nothing to be done." With that the Jesuits left.

Florin rushed into the next room. There he and Blaise exploded with laughter and relief that they had survived such a close call. Then they continued the task or preparing additional copies of the seventh and eighth letters for release.

When the ninth letter was published on July 3rd, the Jesuits suffered even further ridicule in the drawing rooms and salons of Paris. Father Barry's "Paradise Opened by a Hundred Devotions Easily Practised" and Father Le Moine's "Devotion Made Easy" disclosed the attempt of the Jesuits to win a following by "easy" religion which demands no sacrifice or discipline. The doctrine of "mental reservations" was unveiled which allowed that: "After saying aloud, 'I swear that I have not done that', to add, in a low voice, 'today'." Going even further, the Jesuit says, "no more is required of them to avoid lying, than simply to say that they have not done what they have done, provided they have, in general, the intention of giving to their language the sense (meaning) which an able man would give to it." And again, the Jesuit tells Montalte, "listen, then, to the general rule laid down by Escobar: 'Promises are not binding, when the person in making them had no intention to bind himself'." Finally, the Jesuit, citing Escobar again, even points out a way one may hear mass very quickly. If four masses are going on at once, one may hear the commencement of one, the gospel of the second, the consecration of the third and communion of the fourth. This "easy" style of religion espoused by the Jesuits startled Montalte and shocked Pascal.

No wonder Blaise closed his tenth letter with words of holy indignation. "The license they have assumed to tamper with the most holy rules of Christian conduct amounts to a total subversion of the laws of God. . . . Thus are rendered worthy of enjoying God in eternity those who never loved God in all their life. Behold the mystery of iniquity fulfilled."

By this time, a wave of popular protest was sweeping France. On May 12th, the syndic of the priests of Paris proposed an examination of the questions raised by the Provincial Letters. On May 20th, Du Four of Rouen preached a powerful sermon in the presence of the Archbishop and eight hundred clerics against a lowering of moral standards. Du Four became the leader of a protest movement demanding the condemnation of such teachings as were professed by the Jesuits. On August 7th, the priests of Paris joined the swelling tide demanding condemnation of the Jesuits.

But on August 3rd, 1656, all Arnauld's writings published since his censure by the Sorbonne were condemned by a decree of the Index in Rome. Though the influence of the Jesuits had declined among the people of France, the order had suffered no lessening of power in Rome. But the jubilant Port-Royalists took the condemnation calmly. Did they not have the Jesuits on the run in France?

On August 18th, the eleventh letter was published. Herein Pascal justified his use of ridicule. Montalte's satirical method was used by the Fathers of the Church, by Scripture and by God Himself. Pascal hammered away at the Jesuitic impiety shown to the truths of God while they defended the impiety of the falsehoods of men. In his twelfth letter dated September 9th, he bitterly rejected the names cast his way by the Jesuits and proceeded to examine the Impostures of the Jesuits.

Meanwhile, in August of 1656, Charlotte Roannez, seeking a cure from an ophthalmic illness, made a nine day retreat at Port-Royal in Paris. On the 4th of August, Charlotte attended a mass celebrating the miracle of the Holy Thorn in the Chapel. During the service she burst into tears. The grace of God was touching her heart. When she returned home, she told her brother that she wanted to become a nun. Knowing that the family would oppose her decision, Artus took his sister with him to Poitou to give her time to consider her decision carefully. Their mother accompanied them.

From Poitou, Charlotte and her brother Artus were in constant touch with Blaise by letters that were carried back and forth by messenger.[7] These new converts were experiencing many pressures from friends and relatives who were distressed to see these "darlings" of the court withdrawing from the affairs of the social world. In a confidential letter to Blaise, the Roannez shared their problems with their friend and spiritual counsellor.

In response, he penned a letter to them in September, in which this man so immersed in the Scriptures said: "A little while ago I was reading the thirteenth chapter of Saint Mark. . . . Since everything that happens to the Church also happens to every Christian as an individual, it is certain that this chapter also foretells the state of each and every person who by his conversion destroys the old man within him. . . . This prediction of the ruin of the rejected temple indicates that no passion of the old man shall be permitted to remain."

"But here is an astounding word: When ye see abomination where it should not be, then let everyone flee without re-entering his house to take anything at all. It seems to me that this word foretells perfectly the present time when corruption of morals is to be found in houses of holiness and in the books of theologians and monks where it should not be. . . ."

"This Chapter of the Gospel, which I should like to read with you in its entirety, concludes with an exhortation to watch and to pray that we may avoid all these misfortunes; moreover it is meet that prayer be unceasing for the peril is increasing."

Then Blaise promised to pray for them, shared the news that a nun of Pontoise had been cured of a dreadful headache by consecration to the Holy Thorn and thanked them for the gift of a relic they had sent him. When the Roannez received his letter, they were profoundly encouraged to continue on in their devotion.

A little later, on September 24th, he sat at his writing desk and wrote again to encourage Charlotte and Artus. He was warmly concerned for them as persons. Justifying his attacks on the Jesuits, he said, "that since the coming of John the Baptist, that is to say, since his (Jesus) coming into the world, and consequently since his coming into each faithful person, the Kingdom of God suffers violence and the violent ravish it." He scribbled, "We must resolve to suffer this warfare all our life, for there is no peace here below. . . . One must admit with the Scriptures that the wisdom of this world is but folly before God. . . ."

Shortly afterwards, on September 30th, he released one of the most terrible of the Provincial Letters, the thirteenth. He attacked the "doctrine of mental reservations and ambiguous statements," which allowed one to read a passage aloud while saying inwardly that the writer meant something else. This allowed the justification of murder, slander and a host of other ills. Pascal accused the Jesuits of dreaming of worldly domination in which the end justified ungodly means. This charge was certain to increase the tempo of retaliation from the furious Jesuits.

Meanwhile, he continued to minister to his friends in Poitou. In October, he wrote again to the Roannez, "Thanks to God, I no longer have any fears for you . . . I try as much as possible to let nothing trouble me and to make the best of everything that happens . . . it seems obvious to me that when He discloses His will to us through events, it would be a sin not to adjust oneself to them."

Realizing that the climax of his battle with the Jesuits was approaching, Blaise went on. "It is a thing which makes those who are truly committed to God tremble when they see the impending persecution not only of persons (that would be little) but of the truth. . . ."

"I sympathize deeply with our friend who was persecuted. . . ." The pressures upon Jansenists and their sympathizers was building. The Jesuits, though their influence had declined among the crowds in the street, still had the ear of the King and dominated the power structure. Their hatred of Port-Royal which had been fanned by the Provincial Letters, was increased as Pascal's fourteenth letter appeared.

On October 23rd, letter fourteen was published. In it Pascal sought to horrify the world by the Jesuit's views on homicide. The permission to kill, granted by the Jesuits on so many occa-

149

sions, illustrates how far the Society of Jesus has wandered from the law of God. They commit the worst sacrilege of all by usurping the prerogatives of God.

At the end of October, the inquiry into the miraculous healing of Marguerite Perier was concluded by the ecclesiastical authorities. The miracle was officially recognized and announced by the vicar-general, A. de Hodencq. On October 27th, a service of celebration was held at Port-Royal. Blaise was among the throngs who attended.

Early on that rainy morning, a crowd gathered in the Church at Port-Royal. The little altar in the choir was decorated in white. The reliquary containing the Holy Thorn, surrounded by a forest of candles, crowned the altar. The Vicar-General who was celebrant of the mass, surrounded by sixteen deacons, ceremoniously carried the Holy Thorn from the little altar to the main altar where he placed it in an elaborately decorated tabernacle. The nuns, veils lowered, knelt and sang the hymn, "Exite filiae Sion" and the antiphon, "O Corona." Kneeling on two large flagstones so she could be seen by the whole congregation was Marguerite Perier, clothed in grey. Then the small altar was removed and Mass was celebrated. At last the Holy Thorn was venerated, kissed by the ministers at the altar and carried by a priest to be kissed by the people.

Blaise, surrounded by the throng, felt a deep joy in the vindication of Port-Royal. As his turn came to kiss the relic, tears flooded his eyes.

Later that same day, Blaise wrote to Charlotte and Artus. "It seems to me that you are sufficiently interested in the miracle for me to send a special word to you that its verification was completed by the Church." But then having pondered why God did not intervene again and again he said, "If God revealed Himself continually to me, there would be no merit at all in believing in Him. . . . Ordinarily He conceals Himself and He reveals Himself but rarely to those whom He wishes to engage in His service. This strange secrecy, into which God had withdrawn and which is impenetrable to the eyes of man, is a great lesson to lead us into solitude far from the eyes of man. He has remained hidden under the veil of nature which hid Him from us until the Incarnation . . . I believe that Isaiah saw it in this state when he said in the spirit of prophecy, 'Verily Thou art a hidden God'. . . . Let us return infinite thanks, that inasmuch as He had hidden Himself from others in all things, He has revealed Himself to us in all things and in so many ways."

Blaise thus shared with his friends a profound insight from out of his own experience. For years he had been blind to the revealing of God and disheartened by His impenetrable concealment. Then after his own night of "Fire," his eyes had been opened both to God's revealing and to the reason for God's concealment. So, he opened his soul to explain to his beloved friends something of God's hiddenness as well as His revelation. He wanted them to have faith even in those dark hours when God seemed absent.

In November, he wrote again to encourage the Roannez. He was amazed at their zeal "for it is far more rare to see people continue in their piety than to see them enter into piety." He quoted Saint Paul, "Lord, achieve Thou the work which Thou hast begun."

In the meantime, Blaise received a letter from his friends in Poitou. In it, they expressed their fear of schism if Port-Royal rebelled against Rome. They desired to remain loyal Catholics.

Pascal responded almost immediately. "I am writing the details about this condemnation which had frightened you . . . with all my heart I praise the slight fervor that I have observed in your letter for union with the Pope . . . I do not know whether there are persons in the Church more attached to this unity of the body than are those whom you call ours."

"I shall never separate myself from communion with him, at least I pray God to grant me that grace, without which I should be lost forever. . . . For sixteen hundred years the Church has been grieving for you. It is time to grieve for her and for us. . . ."

As the chill winds of late November bristled about Paris, Pascal's biting fifteenth letter exposing the Jesuits' use of calumny was published on November 25th. Following close behind was his sixteenth letter dated December 4th. He zealously defended Port-Royal. "I know, father, the work of the pious recluses who have retired to that monastery and how much the Church is indebted to their truly solid and edifying labors. I know the excellence of their piety and their learning."

With the ringing in of the new year, 1657, Blaise shifted his attack to the head of the Jesuit order, the powerful Father Annat. In his seventeenth and eighteenth letters, Pascal engaged in a duel of wits with Annat, confessor to the King. He addressed these letters to Annat. In the seventeenth he said: "Your former behavior had induced me to believe that you were anxious for a truce in our hostilities. . . . Of late, however, you have poured forth such a volley of pamphlets, in such rapid succession, as to make it apparent that peace rests on a very precarious footing when it depends on the silence of the Jesuits. . . ."

"It is full time, indeed, that I should, once for all, put a stop to the liberty you have taken to treat me as a heretic. . . . You are well aware, sir, that heresy is a charge of so grave a character that it is an act of high presumption to advance without being prepared to substantiate it. I now demand your proof."

Blaise declared he was not a member of the Port-Royal community. "I have no sort of connection with any community except the Catholic, Apostolic and Roman Church, in the bosom of which I desire to live and die, in communion with the Pope, the head of the Church, and beyond the pale of which I am persuaded there is no salvation. . . ."

He went on to assume full responsibility for his letters. "Nobody is responsible for my letters but myself. . . ." Then followed a lengthy discussion of the distinction between a question of doctrine and a question of fact. Pascal insisted that as a matter of fact, the doctrines condemned by Rome were not in Jansen.

In February, 1657, bad news came to Blaise, news that caused him to shudder. On February 9th his letters had been publicly burned by the public executioner at Aix. The Parliament of Provence condemned his letters on February 21st. Then on March 11th, 1657, a messenger from Rome handed the King a copy of Alexander VII's Bull dated October 16, 1656. Three days later the papal nuncio, Piccolomini, presented the President of the Assembly of the Clergy with a copy. Pope Alexander in this Bull, confirmed the stand of his predecessor Innocent X and condemned the five propositions. The Bull condemned and prohibited the "Augustinus". . . . "With all other books, manuscript as well as printed, and all those which might perhaps be printed in the future, in which the doctrine of the said Cornelius Jansen herewith condemned is or might be established or sustained." Now, with the official delivery of the Bull, action had to be taken. The Assembly of the Clergy proceeded to draft a "formula" condemning the propositions of Jansen. The formula would have to be signed by all clergy. All that kept it from being enforced was the French Parliament. Enforcement of a Papal Bull required the consent of the King, the clergy and the Parliament. King and clergy having accepted the Bull, it was now up to the Parliament.

As Blaise was drafting a nineteenth Provincial letter, he suddenly broke off the attack. He shifted fronts. Once the papal Bull was officially received and registered by the Parliament of France, the Formulary would be published requiring the signatures of and endorsement of all religious. This registration of the Bull had to be stopped.

Accordingly, early in June a new letter was making the rounds in Paris. Its title — "Letter of a Lawyer at Parliament to one of his friends concerning the Inquisition that they wish to establish in France, upon the occasion of a new Bull of the Pope Alexander VII." The author of the arguments in the letter was Pascal, though the writer of the letter was Le Maistre.

The lawyer sensed a conspiracy. He wrote: "We were about to see the establishment of an inquisition in France. . . . The agents of the Court of Rome and some bishops who dominated the Assembly cooperated toward its establishment and for its basis they chose the Bull of Pope Alexander VII on the five propositions. . . . It was decreed in the Assembly that it should be subscribed to by all the clergy of the realm without any exception, and that all those who would refuse to sign it should be proceeded against with all the penalties directed against heretics."

". . . God knows, once it has taken root, how much the inquisition will grow in a very short time. We shall see how in no time at all that no one will be safe in his own home. For you will merely need powerful enemies to denounce you and accuse you of being a Jansenist, simply because you have Jansenist books in your study or because you have spoken somewhat freely about these new Bulls, as you know that we lawyers often do."

Le Maistre went even further disavowing the Pope's infallibility. . . . "The Church has never recognized this infallibility of the Pope but only in the universal council to which unjust decisions of the Pope have always been appealed. . . ."[8]

". . . We maintain that only the councils can require belief."

". . . Is it not obvious that if this Bull is accepted, there is none that we shall not be forced to accept . . . whenever it pleases Rome, those in the opposition will be treated as heretics." Pascal and LeMaistre appealed for Parliament to examine the Pope's judgment — to see whether the five condemned propositions actually were taken from Jansen and to reject the Bull. The letter closed, "If Parliament takes up this matter, I have good enough data to show how great a difference there is between the primacy which God has truly given to the Pope for the edification of the Church and the infallibility which his flatterers would like to give him for the destruction of the Church and of our liberties."

The members of the French Parliament read the letter and enjoyed it. But the papal nuncio and Father Annat were indignant. Pressures were brought to bear. On June 25th, the Council issued a decree suppressing the letter. But the damage was done. The members of Parliament were in no mood to register the Bull.

For awhile it appeared that Blaise could lay down his cudgels. But the appeal of the Jesuit Father Morel, Prior of Saint Foy, that when a reconciliation was achieved Montalte should point his pen toward the thousands of libertines and sceptics in Paris, revived Pascal's dream of writing a "Vindication of Christianity." So he began to gather together the scraps of paper on which for several years he had been scribbling his thoughts.

Suddenly he also intensified his study of mathematics! Throughout most of his tug-of-war with the Jesuits he had managed to keep up some correspondence with the mathematician Sluse, Canon of Liege. Now he renewed his study of curvilinear curves.

Then a thunderbolt struck! On September 6th, amidst great pomp the Cardinals of the Holy Roman Church filed into the Church of St. Mary Major in Rome. Seated beneath the lofty ceiling of the vast Church were the Inquisitors General from many lands. Finally Pope Alexander VII entered amidst wave after wave of applause. Then there was silence.

A voice loudly intoned the words: "Our Holy Father, Pope Alexander VII, by this present decree forbids and condemns the books hereinafter mentioned, and has resolved that they be considered condemned and forbidden under the penalties and the censures contained in the decree of the Holy Council of Trent, and in the index of forbidden books, with whatever other penalties it shall please his Holiness to exact."

"Eighteen letters written in the French language and having the following titles:

1. Letter written to a provincial by one of his friends on the subject of the present disputes at the Sorbonne. . . ." (then followed a listing of the 18 letters).
   Letter of a lawyer in Parliament to one of his friends regarding the inquisition.
   The following works of Antoine Arnauld. . . ."

When news of the condemnation reached Paris, Blaise was distraught and in tears. For an instant it seemed to him as though his world had collapsed and that his cause had failed. Perhaps he agonized "Why had God not intervened? Have I been wrong?" But if these thoughts flashed through his tormented mind, they did not linger. He could never deny the reality of the Presence that had possessed him. When the Church and the Pope seemed to falter, the Presence was real. Of this he was certain. And so his identity as God's man kept him resolute even when his writings were condemned at Rome. He retired to his room and fell on his knees with the prayer, "When my letters are condemned in Rome, Lord Jesus, to Thy tribunal I appeal."

The months that followed were months of silence during which Blaise continued his correspondence with Sluse and continued to gather material for his "Vindication of Christianity" to the sceptics.[9]

Joy revived in Blaise's soul when he received word that Charlotte had entered Port-Royal. Against the opposition of her mother, she had entered the peace of the convent. A few years later, she would seek release from her vows, would re-enter the world and enter an unhappy marriage with the Duke de la Feuillade. But for awhile, Charlotte enjoyed the peace of the sanctuary and Pascal was glad. If he could not have her, he was happy to surrender her to God.

Yet the argument with the Jesuits could not be forgotten. In order to clarify his own views on grace, he scribbled what he called his "Writings on Grace," which he then left one piled on another in a drawer of his desk. They consisted of analyses of Protestant, Jesuit and Augustinian views on grace. Pascal's understanding of grace was clearly that of Jansen and Port-Royal.

As Christmas festivities were sweeping Parisian society in 1657, a new book stirred up controversy within the religious community, Father Pirot, a Jesuit, against the counsel of many colleagues, anonymously published a book bearing the title

"Defence of the Casuists against the Slanders of Jansenism." In a series of questions and answers he attempted to answer Pascal's charges in the "Provincial Letters." And more, he made a sharp counterattack against Pascal and Port-Royal. He stooped to the charge that the Port-Royalist, like Luther and Calvin, wished to abolish the celibacy of the clergy. He accused Arnauld of financial skullduggery. He claimed that the secretary of Port-Royal (Pascal) was guilty of unchastity. The list of charges went on and on. "The Defense of the Casuists" was the opening volley in a new wave of hostility. The people of Paris were not pleased.

The parish priests of Paris, now openly sympathetic to Port-Royal, referred the book to the ecclesiastical authorities and to Parliament for condemnation. They asked Pascal to write their defense in a "Case for the Priests of Paris." Singlin and Mother Angélique tried to restrain him, counselling prayer and silence, but Pascal would not be restrained.

As the new year 1658 entered, Pascal was busy writing and rewriting the first in a series of "Cases". On January 25th his first tract appeared. During the first half of 1658, others would appear. Several were written by Blaise. One was from the pen of Arnauld and another was by Nicole. In his "Cases", Pascal brilliantly summarized the arguments against the Jesuits, concentrating on their undermining of Christian morality.

In the battle which raged between the parish priests and the Jesuits Pascal hurled the charge, "we find them obstinately approving vengeance, avarice, sensuality, pride, a false conception of honor and all the passions of fallen human nature, the profanation of the sacraments, the corruption of all the offices of the Church and a contempt for the Fathers. . .; and though we see that the Church is on the point of being submerged beneath this sea of corruption, for fear of disturbing the peace we dare not cry out to those who are leading it: save us for we perish."

One after another Pascal's "Cases" appeared. At the same time, Arnauld and Nicole published their "Statements by the Parish Priests of Paris". Across France, parish priests began to demand a condemnation both of Pirot's book and the teachings of the casuists.

The chastened Jesuits proceeded to disown Pirot. Then on August 21st, the Inquisition in Rome placed Pirot's book on the Index. For a while, Port-Royal and Pascal seemed to have triumphed.

CHAPTER NINE

THE FINAL CONTEST (1658-1661)

AS THEY assembled in the library of the Granges at Port-Royal des Champs, the "gentlemen" of Port-Royal chatted almost gaily. Some, like Pascal and Roannez, had just arrived from Paris. Through the partly open windows came the sounds of children playing in the sunshine of the Chevreuse valley. In 1658 the cause of Port-Royal seemed to be prospering.

Seated together with Pascal in the familiar long room, they listened eagerly for two hours as Blaise outlined the plan for his magnum opus, a "Vindication of Christianity" aimed at sceptics. Blaise had done his homework well. He had read many of the historic Defenses of Christianity. He had given special attention to Montaigne's translation of Raymond Sebond's "Theologia Naturalis", Charron's "The Three Verities", Hugo Grotius' "Treatise on the Truth of the Christian Religion" and the four-hundred-year-old "Pugio Fidei Christianae" of Raymond Martini. Pascal had even gone to the effort of learning Hebrew so that he could follow Martini's argument better. But he made it clear to his listeners that he would not use the traditional metaphysical arguments. Instead he would use the moral and historical approach since this would speak to a man of the world where he lives.

Blaise, obviously excited by this new project, sketched the first part of his book. He intended to paint a portrait of man without God. He would attempt to shatter the sceptic's complacency by confronting him with the enigma of man's condition. The feebleness, fragility and folly of man's existence would be contrasted to man's greatness and nobility. Man, thus, would be described as the riddle and paradox of the universe. Hopefully the reader, after seeing man as a paradox, would be ready to seek answers to explain the contradictions in man. Pascal would outline the dead-end answers offered by the philosophies and the non-Christian religions. Then he would call attention to a unique race, the Jews. From their history and prophecies, he would point to the miracles of the Bible and finally to Christ and the Church. All of this he suggested would be woven into dialogue form which he had used so successfully in the "Provincial Letters".

When Blaise stopped speaking, the others broke into a babble of voices, each trying to express his congratulations at the ingenuity of such an approach. Thus encouraged by his friends at Port-Royal, Blaise continued scribbling thoughts for his book on scraps of paper which he planned to group into chapters. The "thoughts" which would be worked into separate chapters were strung together on strings.

As summer 1658 poured its heat upon the sprawling city of Paris, Blaise found his diversion in wrestling with an ingenious mathematical problem, the cycloid, more popularly called the "roulette". Scientists in many places were discussing the problem of determining the area and properties of a cycloid. (the cycloid or roulette, it was said, was formed by tracing a point on the edge of a wheel moving on a plane surface in a straight line. It forms an arch or half of an ellipse.)

One warm evening Blaise was suffering with a painful toothache which made his head throb with pain. As his thin body lay on the bed in his room, he was unable to sleep. The pain mingled with the heat prevented him from drifting into slumber. To take his mind off his pain, he turned his thoughts to the problem of the cycloid. One thought led to another. Insight seemed to flood his mind. Suddenly it seemed that he saw a breakthrough, a solution to the perplexing problem of the cycloid.

In the days which followed, he confided the solution to his friends. Roannez was thrilled and insisted that Blaise publish it. Artus reasoned that the prestige of such a discovery would enhance Blaise's outreach to the sceptics of Paris. The Duke even suggested that a challenge to other scientists should be made through a competitive contest which would offer a nominal prize of forty pistoles for the best solution.

Blaise was reluctant to seek new glories yet acceded to Roannez' pressure. Accordingly, in June a circular letter was published anonymously, outlining six problems to be solved. Four of the problems had already been solved by Pascal's friend Roberval though Blaise didn't know it at the time. Solutions were to be sent to the president of the judges, Carcavi, by October 1st.

When the deadline arrived, only two other official entries had been received, though Huyghens, De Sluse, De Ricci, Wrenne and others had evidenced interest. One of the official entries was from an English mathematician, the Savilian professor at Oxford, Wallis. The other was from the Jesuit Father Lalouere of Toulouse. As Blaise and the judges perused the entries, they saw that Wallis' proposal contained several serious mistakes. Lalouere, on the other hand, having discovered errors in his own calculations sent word that he withdrew from the contest. On November 24th, the judges met and awarded the prize to Blaise.

During December, Blaise released further results of his own research in a letter to Carcavi. He signed the letter with a pseudonym, Amos Dettonville. Soon afterwards in letters to De Sluse and Huyghens, Blaise enunciated principles which would open the way into the mysteries of integral calculus.

But Wallis and Lalouere did not take Pascal's mathematical victory kindly. Wallis criticized the form of the competition. The shortness of time discriminated against scholars outside of France. He accused Pascal of using insights from other entries to arrive at his own solutions. Lalouere while claiming to possess solutions to the problems refused to enter them in the competition. Pascal was ruthless in his counter-criticism of the two competitors. He was, once again, the victor.

Perhaps in order to keep his pride under subjection, Blaise undertook a self-imposed discipline. He began to wear under his clothing an iron belt studded with nails. When an impulse to pride stirred in his mind, he would press the hidden belt. But even iron spikes cannot destroy arrogance and pride.

When 1659 was ushered in, Pascal's health was deteriorating. As March winds swept through Paris, Blaise was exhausted! But he kept scribbling away at his "Vindication". Between periods of intense weakness which confined him to bed, he stirred himself to write and rewrite notes for his book.

In June, his doctors prescribed special broths and strong soups to stir him and to energize him. But these medications seemed to offer only temporary invigoration.

With this state of weariness upon him, Blaise seemed to withdraw more and more into stern, disciplined isolation. Frivolity and friendship were swallowed up in stern, austere, self-discipline. He began to reprove Gilberte and her children for any display of affection. As if afraid of emotional entanglement on the human level, he espoused love for God as the only proper duty.

Jacqueline Perier, now a 15-year-old student at Port-Royal, was coming into the bloom of young womanhood. Her parents, Gilberte and Florin, were contemplating her marriage to a very wealthy young man but the powers that were at Port-Royal advised against it. Jacqueline had not been consulted. Her "calling" had not been considered. Blaise delivered the decision of Port-Royal to his sister and brother-in-law. He said to them that marriage was "the most dangerous and the lowest of the conditions of life permitted to a Christian." His illness and loneliness seemed to some to be warping his perspective on the human scene.

Yet that worldly pride which sometimes had prodded him to seek the adulation of others was being dealt with. He tried to explain to a bewildered Gilberte that, "it is wrong that men should bind themselves to me, even if they do so with pleasure and of their own free will . . . I am not the last end of anyone and have not the means to satisfy them". Blaise more and more wanted men to love God, not himself. So he backed away from the common, intimate relationships of life.

As his pains and weakness increased, Blaise sank more and more into isolation and loneliness. On one of his better days, he sat in a chair in his room and wrote on a pad a "Prayer asking God to use illnesses to a Good End".

He painfully and laboriously poured out his soul on paper. "Lord, . . . not only all prosperity but even all afflictions that come to Thine elect are the results of Thy compassion. . . ." Man can bear almost anything if he discerns some meaning and purpose in his pain. Blaise clung tenaciously to the faith that God in His loving Providence had a reason for the pains that daily plagued him.

Blaise, troubled by a deep sense of guilt, interpreted his sickness as chastening sent by God. "Thou hadst given me health that I might serve Thee, and I have profaned it; now Thou dost send me illness to correct my ways. . . . If my heart was filled with love for the world while it had some vigor, annihilate this vigor for my salvation, and render me incapable of enjoying the world. . . ."

The Jansenists with their stern ethic and almost ascetic ideals had often frowned upon Pascal's forays into the world of high society with Roannez. Now Blaise identified himself more closely with the perspective of Jacqueline and the Port-Royalists. He condemns his worldliness and interprets his illness as chastening sent from God to shake him loose from his love of the world.

He continues his prayer: "But I recognize, my God, that my heart is so hardened and so filled with the thoughts, cares, anxieties and ties of the world, that neither illness anymore than health, neither discourses, books, Thy holy Scriptures, Thy Gospel, Thy most holy Mysteries, alms, fasting, mortification,

163

miracles, partaking of the Sacraments, the sacrifice of Thy Body, neither all my efforts nor those of the whole world together can be of any avail in beginning my conversion, if Thou dost not accompany all these things with the quite extraordinary aid of Thy grace. . . . Since the conversion of my heart which I ask of Thee, is a work that surpasses all the efforts of nature, I can but turn to the Author and omnipotent Master of nature and of my heart." Pascal pleads for a new conversion, a new work of grace. "Open my heart, enter into the rebellious place which vices have occupied and which they hold in subjection . . . Lord, take my affections which the world had stolen . . . yet the world is still the object of my delights."

The gambits into high society, the pride engendered by his literary abilities and his scientific accomplishments, the worldly striving for success and fame had built up a sense of guilt which now formed a formidable barrier to sweet fellowship with the Servant Lord.

As he surveyed his life, he remembered, "persistent repugnance to Thine inspirations; ill use of Thy most august Sacraments; contempt for Thy Word; idleness and uselessness of all my acts and of my thoughts; complete loss of the time Thou hadst given me only to adore Thee." And so, he penitently confessed, "All that I am is odious to Thee. . . ."

Pascal had experienced a conversion of sorts in Rouen years before. He had tasted a climactic conversion in 1654. But, his soul had again and again been gripped by the worldly desire to be superman, to outstrip all theologians and mathematicians. The "libido excellendi" held him in its grasp and he yearned for the spiritual joys he once had known. "Lord, what shall I do to constrain Thee to shed Thy spirit on this miserable earth? All that I am is odious to Thee. . ." His old self again and again had asserted itself reviving a crisis of identity. Was he to be God's man or the darling of French society? Each time that question had recurred, each time he became uncertain of his identity, he experienced doubts of himself, doubt of God and fear for his existence.

But all his strivings had not availed to bring some new re-vealing of God's Spirit and grace. So, exhausted he writes, "I ask of Thee neither health nor sickness, nor life, nor death, but that Thou wouldst dispose of my health and my sickness, of my life and my death for Thy glory, for my salvation, and for the welfare of the Church and of Thy Saints to whom (I hope through Thy grace) I belong. Thou alone knowest what is meet for me; Thou art the sovereign Master; do as Thou wilt." Echoing his Master's plea in Gethsemane, he rests his destiny in God's sovereign will.

"Unite me with Thee; fill me with Thee and Thy Holy Spirit. Enter into my heart and into my soul, there to bear my suf-ferings . . . so that it shall no longer be I who live and who suffer but that it shall be Thou who dost live and suffer in me, O my Saviour. . . ." Blaise was dying to his own ambitions and goals that the image of Christ might be formed in his life. For him this meant continued isolation and loneliness.

More and more during that painful 1659,[1] he became a familiar sight hobbling into church to share in the Little Hours of prayer which centered around the One-hundred-nineteenth Psalm. There he would alternately sit and kneel, drinking in words of refreshment and inspiration.

Early in 1660, his life was shaken by the unforseen. He and some friends had boarded his carriage and were being drawn by four stalwart horses on a holiday ride to the Bridge of Neuilly, near the Bois de Boulogne on the western edge of Paris.[2] The sunshine, the puffy white clouds scudding across the blue sky, the freshness of the air, the beauty of the en-chanted forest put the occupants of the carriage in an expansive and free-as-a-bird mood. As they approached the Bridge, the horses were galloping spiritedly.

Suddenly, the horses got the bit in their teeth and swerved toward the edge of the bridge. Since there was no railing on the bridge at that point, over the horses went into the waters of the Seine. The carriage was dragged toward the edge and hung

165

suspended for one perilous moment. Then the reins snapped and the carriage held on the bridge. Quickly the occupants alighted breathlessly.

Blaise was strangely silent almost in a state of collapse. In those brief moments of peril, death had loomed large before him and he was not ready. As the party rode slowly back home, he remarked, "Henceforth, I'll abandon my drives abroad and devote myself completely to God."

This he did! Shortly afterwards he sold his horses and carriage. He auctioned off his beautiful tapestries, his silver and most of his library. He began a life of severe austerity, keeping only those possessions which were necessities. He even forsook his scientific research. He began to devote his time to prayer, the Bible and works of charity.

Through Charles Maignart de Bernieres, a Port-Royalist who had become chief assistant to St. Vincent de Paul in his battle against the miseries of the Fronde, Blaise learned of the needs of the poor. Blaise had known the Bernieres family in Rouen. Now he set his face to securing subsidies for Bernieres' work. When his own pain abated sufficiently, he took to visiting the poor in their crowded, cold tenements.

When Spring 1660 burst into full bloom, Blaise left for his last visit to Clermont. Those were twenty-two days of agony. Part of the time Pascal rode in a carriage drawn by horses deliberately slowed to a slower, softer speed. By carriage, he traveled only three or four miles at a time. Then he would rest. More often, he travelled on the smooth waters of the canals. Most of his journey he floated on the placid inland waterways, resting on mattresses placed for him by friendly barge captains. So he alternately sailed and rode through the green countryside, sprinkled with jonquils and narcissus. Finally, after nearly a month of travel this very sick man felt the tender greeting of warm-hearted Gilberte.

The Periers were staying at their home in the country. Bienassis was their small chateau on the vine-covered slopes outside

Clermont. Its graceful arches dated from the Middle Ages though it had been rebuilt by Florin Perier just a few years earlier.

There he rested. He drank in the warm, Auvergne sunshine. He prayed, read the Bible, and made a few feeble efforts to work on the "Vindication". Those were days of refreshing, but the terrible pains continued. He was unable to walk without a cane. Yet he never complained. He bore his pain with serenity and joy. This was a source of constant inspiration and amazement to the Periers.

One day in August, he received a letter from his long-time correspondent, the renowned mathematician Fermat. As he read Fermat's labored hand-writing, he learned that he, too, was ill. Fermat was in Toulouse. Fermat, in a letter dated July 25th, 1660, suggested that since Pascal, in coming from Paris to Clermont, was already over half-way to Toulouse, perhaps he might go a little further to meet Fermat at a point midway between Clermont and Toulouse. Since neither one was strong enough for the whole trip, perhaps they could meet half way thus reducing the round trip journey to about 238 miles for each.

With great effort, on August 10th Blaise penned a letter of reply to his friend:

"Sir, — you are the most delightful person in the world and I am one of those who can appreciate your qualities and admire them unboundedly when I find them allied to talents such as yours. All this compels me to acknowledge with my own hand the offer you make, in spite of the difficulty I have in writing or reading. I tell you, Sir, that if my health allowed it I should fly to Toulouse, and I would not have allowed a man like you to take one step for a man like me. This must be added, although I consider you the leading geometer of Europe it is not for that reason that I should come, but because I should enjoy the fun and honnêteté of your conversation. Speaking frankly, I find geometry the noblest exercise of the mind, yet I know it to be so useless that I see no difference between a geometer and a clever artisan. I call it the loveliest occupation in the world, but only an occupation. I have often said that it is good as a hobby but not as a vocation. I would not take two paces for geometry and I feel perfectly sure that is your own view. But also, I am now engaged upon studies so remote from these that I should find it difficult to remember what they were all about. A singular chance about a year or two ago did set me at mathematics, but having settled that matter I am not likely ever to touch the subject again, apart from the fact that I am not yet well enough."

"I am too weak to walk without a stick and cannot stay on a horse or drive more than two or three leagues in a carriage. It took twenty-two days for me to come here from Paris. The doctors order me to take waters at Bourbon in September, and I am pledged since two months ago to spend Christmas at Saumur with the Duke de Roannez, who has much too high an opinion of me. But my route to Saumur by river would take me through Orleans and if my health forbids further travel I should return to Paris from there."

"There you have my present condition. I had to tell you only to make clear the impossibility of my enjoying the honor you offer, and to say how greatly I wish to meet you, either in your person or in your sons to whom I am devoted, having a particular veneration for those who bear the name of the world's greatest man.

I am, etc.,
Pascal"

So the summer passed. But it was filled with pain. As the cool of autumn drew near and the cool winds began to sweep down from the jagged hills, Blaise determined to return directly to Paris. A journey to visit Roannez at Saumur seemed increasingly impossible. So, before the chill of winter could freeze the canals,

168

Blaise departed for Paris. The winds of November were sweeping the streets, when he arrived back in the big city.

The city was still throbbing with the excitement of the events of the summer. On Tuesday, August 26th, the new King Louis XIV and his new young Queen Marie-Therese had entered the city. The city was flooded with sunshine and brilliantly decorated. Triumphal arches had been erected. Crowds, many from the provinces, jammed the city streets to see their King and the Spanish Infanta. The clergy, the doctors of the University of Paris, the guilds marched in procession, paying their homage to the King as he received them all morning long at the edge of the city. Then at two o'clock in the afternoon the Court moved into the city in a four-hour-long procession. The households of Mazarin, the King, the Queen moved first. Further along came Chancellor Séguier wearing golden robes and a black velvet hat. He was mounted on a white horse and surrounded by pages and equerries clothed in satin and velvet.

The golden-haired young Queen rode in an open carriage. She was escorted by princes of the Houses of Lorraine, Guise, Elbeuf along with the Spanish ambassador. The handsome, manly, young King was resplendent. The city went wild in welcoming him and his queen.

Into a city worn out from its gaiety, and yet happily expectant that a marriage between Spain and France would insure peace, Pascal came. His friends eagerly described to him what had transpired in Paris while he was gone.

Pascal, in his house on the Rue des Francs-Bourgeois-Saint-Michel, just a stone's throw from the Bridge Saint-Michel, now had his oldest nephew Etienne Perier living with him. Etienne was studying philosophy at the College d'Harcourt. Nine-year-old Louis Perier and his brother Blaise also filled the house with boyish enthusiasm. Louis and young Blaise were in Paris awaiting openings in the school at Port-Royal. Amidst the youthful clamor in the house, the second week in November Blaise received a note from Jacqueline. She said, "I only write to felicitate you on being the father of a whole family, in the sense that God is the Father of all of us; and to ask your pardon for the trouble it gives you. It is my doing entirely; it will not last long, and I believe you will enjoy it."

Concerned for the proper upbringing of his own nephews, he penned three "Discourses on the Condition of the Great". They were written for the Duke of Chevreuse, the son of the once-powerful Royal Falconer, the Duke of Luynes, but they evolved out of Pascal's concern for his nephews growing up in a royal society. Pascal stressed that noblemen must develop personal qualities which will win respect. They should not expect respect by virtue of their inherited status. The true nobleman, if he is to be an "honnête homme", should act like a king who wins the people's love so that they follow him out of desire, not out of fear. The truly noble man should aspire towards the practice of charity. Pascal underscored a proper respect for social conventions as long as they are recognized as mere conventions. He was not ready to tear down the structures of society but he did long to see them purified.

Blaise was busy, not only caring for his own but also for outsiders. Word had reached Paris of the famine which gripped the poor of Blois. Amidst the colorful countryside of the Loire valley so lavishly dotted with fairy-tale castles, the peasants were starving. The fertile mind of Pascal sought a way to secure help for the hungry.[2]

For some while, he also had been thinking of a way to assist the poor of Paris who lacked adequate means of transportation. Only the affluent could ride in carriages. Why not provide public vehicles which would transport folk at little cost? The dream of public bus service was born. Pascal discussed his dream with Roannez. Here was a way both to help the poor of Paris and to raise funds for the starving in Blois. But it was only a dream at this point.

At the same time Pascal continued some contact with the world of high society. The Marquise de Sablé, one of the "precieuses", presided over a notable salon near Port-Royal in Paris. Madame de Sablé had warm ties with Mother Agnes and a deep affection for Blaise. Upon his return to Paris, he visited her several times and she helped him by putting him in touch with the Protestant medical doctor, Menjot. Madame de Sablé considered her friendship with the much younger Pascal an instance of that platonic love, "la belle galanterie", which had been the fashion among the precieuses during the days before Molière and others had begun to stir up laughter against them.

Then the storm clouds began to gather once again. During Blaise's sojourn in Clermont, the ecclesiastical authorities in Paris had condemned the "Provincial Letters" as defamatory and heretical. The Church in Paris thus confirmed the condemnation of the Pope, the French Church and the Faculty of Paris. Their edict dated September 23, 1660, provoked a burning of the letters by the public executioner at high noon on October 14th in the Carrefour de la Croix-du-tiroir.

Behind the scenes, the agents of young Louis XIV also were at work. Louis XIV, influenced by Cardinal Mazarin his prime minister, had decided to destroy Jansenism once and for all. He was weary of the tug of war between the Jesuits and Port-Royal. It divided his Kingdom. King Louis said of Port-Royal, "Well intentioned they were no doubt, but they were also ignorant and willfully ignorant of the dangerous consequences which their errors must entail." So in December 1660, the Assembly of Clergy, under pressure from the throne, acted to revive the Formula. The Bull "Ad Sanctam" was to be obeyed and the Formula signed. Now bishop after bishop began to insist that the Formula, condemning the five propositions purported to be in the "Augustinus," be signed.

As 1661 dawned, the Port-Royalists were divided as to their course of action. Some led by Arnauld and Nicole favored a forthright confrontation, a straight-forward defense of Jansen's views as thoroughly orthodox and consistent with the teachings of Aquinas and Augustine. Pascal's sympathies were completely with Arnauld and Nicole.

171

On the other hand, De Saci, Barcos, Guillebert of Rouville and others insisted that no defense of Jansen should be attempted. They advocated acceptance of Jansen's condemnation while maintaining for themselves the Augustinian position as Augustinian, not Jansenist. Jansen's interpretation of Augustine would be ignored or overlooked and treated as though it never had been written.

On February 1st 1661, the Assembly of the Clergy, under continuing pressure from the throne, declared that every ecclesiastic and teacher must sign the Formula condemning the five propositions. The storm was about to break in full fury over Port-Royal.

Then on March 9th, 1661, Cardinal Mazarin died in the Castle of Vincennes. For several days Louis XIV and Anne of Austria had occupied rooms in the Castle. On the morning of the ninth, the handsome young King rose to discover that crafty Mazarin was finally dead. Louis dressed, summoned his ministers and announced that they should conduct no business at all without consulting him. Thus, the manly young king took firm control of the kingdom. High on his list of priorities was the extermination of Port-Royal. Accordingly, on April 13th, the Council of State ratified the action of the Assembly of the Clergy in calling for affirmation of the Formula. In addition, stern punishments were decreed for any who refused to sign.

Shortly thereafter the order was issued commanding the convent of Port-Royal to send all its scholars and novices back to their families. On April 23rd, Mother Angélique, sick with dropsy, left Port-Royal in the Fields for Paris. As she prepared to board the carriage, she stopped, turned and said to her brother, Father d'Andilly, "Goodbye my brother, be of good courage whatever happens."

He replied, "My sister, fear nothing. I am full of courage."

Her eyes twinkled and she answered, "My brother, my brother, let us be humble. Humility without strength is cowardice; but courage without humility is presumption."

Then she boarded the carriage for the jolting ride back to Paris. When she arrived at the convent in the city, she looked around her into the sad, tearful faces of her nuns and exclaimed, "What! I believe there is weeping here. Come, my children, how is this? Have you no faith?"

Like a mother hen, she drew her brood around her and prayed, "My God, have pity on Thy children. My God, Thy holy will be done." A few days later the novices and scholars had all been sent home. An ominous silence hung over both Port-Royal in the Fields and Port-Royal in Paris. The laughter of the little children had vanished.

The friends of Port-Royal continued their maneuvering. The question of "fact" still remained. As a matter of fact were the five condemned propositions actually *in* Jansen's writings? They were willing to admit the heresy contained in the five statements. These they could condemn. But as a "matter of fact" they did not find that the five propositions were in Jansen's teaching. So, they pressured the Grand Vicars of Cardinal Retz to publish on June 8, 1661 a "Charge" which defined what was involved in signing the Formulary. It stated that to sign meant submission on the question of right doctrine but indicated silence on the question of fact. This, most Port-Royalists could sign.

But not all! On June 22nd and 23rd, Jacqueline, as she penned a letter to a friend, declared, "We may perhaps be cast out from the Church! True, and yet who does not know that no one can be really detached from the Church except by His own will? Forgive me, my dear sister, I beg. I speak in the agony of a grief which I am certain will kill me unless I have the consolation of seeing that some are willing to come forward as martyrs for the faith, to protest either by refusal or by flight against the acts of others, and to become themselves champions of the truth" . . . "Since the bishops have the courage of maids, the maids should have the courage of bishops. It is not our task to defend the truth, it is ours to die for the truth and sooner to suffer everything than to abandon it." She sent a copy of her letter to Arnauld!

173

Mother Angélique, meanwhile, was dying. In the storm over the Formula, she whispered from her sickbed thanksgiving to Heaven that her illness spared her from being involved in this "mystery of iniquity".

In early July, under the persuasion of Arnauld, all the members of the Port-Royal community signed the Formula except Jacqueline and the Prioress. These two were convinced that remaining silent on the "question of fact" was a miscarriage of the truth. It was betrayal by silence. Both these courageous women became ill after this act of compromise. Eventually, however, Jacqueline too would affix her signature. But her heart was broken. Being weak and tubercular, she never recovered from the shock of this betrayal.

On August 6th, Mother Angélique died. She was only one month from her seventieth birthday. Among her last words were, "Oh Jesus! Thou art my God. Thou art my righteousness. Thou art my strength. Thou art my all".

Later in August, a new superior of Port-Royal was appointed. He was Monsieur Le Bail. He immediately undertook a visitation of Port-Royal. He questioned the nuns, one by one. On August 22nd it was the sub-Prioress Jacqueline's turn. She sat stiffly on a cane chair before him.

Monsieur Le Bail asked her name and said, "Have you perceived any change in the doctrine taught in the convent since you have been here?"

Jacqueline nervously replied, "I have not been here long but nothing has been taught me that I was not taught since childhood".

"As a child, did you learn that Jesus Christ died for all men?"

"I don't recollect that it was so stated in my catechism."

"Since you have lived here, have you been taught anything on this subject?"

"No."

"What is your opinion on it?"

"I am not accustomed to delve into matters unconnected with

duty but it seems to me that we ought to believe that Christ died for all men, for I remember some line in a volume of devotion which I owned before I took the veil, and have kept ever since, where addressing our Saviour it says: 'For the salvation of all men, Thou didst humble Thyself to be born of a Virgin'."

The examiner smiled slightly and asked, "Very good, but how comes it then that so many are lost eternally?"

She leaned forward and answered, "I confess to you, sir, that this thought often troubles me, and when I am praying, especially if kneeling before a crucifix, and it recurs to me, I cannot help saying internally to our Lord, 'Oh my God! How can it be, after all Thou hast done for us, that so many souls should miserably perish?' But when these thoughts come, I repress them not daring to pry into the secrets of God and I find satisfaction in praying for sinners."

Her superior continued, "That is quite right, my daughter. What books do you read?"

"At present, St. Basil on Morality but more often my rule, the rule of St. Bénedict."

"How do you occupy yourself?" he queried.

"Before the novices and candidates for the veil were removed," she responded, "I took charge of those who were here. But now the number is limited to a few nuns, a novice and some lay sisters."

Le Bail shifted position and went on.

"It was a hard trial for you when the novices were removed was it not?"

Jacqueline, tears in her eyes, explained that grief had overwhelmed the whole community. She wept for the spiritual dangers the novices had to face out in the world.

Her examiner was moved. He said, "Do you teach your novices that Christ died for all men, and the reason why some men are holy and others are wicked?"

Head now erect, Jacqueline answered, "Since I avoid puzzling myself with these topics, it is not likely that I should seek to

175

puzzle them. On the contrary, I try to have them as simple minded as possible."

He pursued the point, saying, "Do you teach them that they alone are to blame when they do wrong? Or do you not believe this yourself?"

"Yes sir, and I know it by my own experience. I assure you that when I commit a fault, I blame no one but myself, and for this reason I endeavor to repent and atone for it."

"You are right", he nodded, "God be praised for it. I believe you are speaking to me in all sincerity. My daughter, always maintain this belief, whatever you may hear and teach it to the novices. I thank God with my whole heart for having kept you from error for it is really horrible that any man should be found to teach that God draws some from the corrupt mass and leaves others to perish as it pleases Him. It is horrible. God be praised that you have not fallen into this great error. Have you any complaints to make?"

"No sir; by God's grace I am quite contented."

"That is wonderful. I sometimes meet with nuns who keep me two hours listening to their complainings, but I find nothing of this sort here."

"Truly sir, by the grace of God we live in great peace and harmony. I think it is because each one does her own duty, not meddling with that of others."

He exclaimed, "That is indeed a blessing. God be praised for it, my daughter. Send me the sister next in order to yourself."

So Jacqueline left. Her inquisitor was pleased and felt assured that once these Port-Royalists signed the Formula all would be well.

Meanwhile on July 7th, the King's Council seeing through the loopholes in the signing of the Formula, had nullified it and replaced it with another of crystal clear and brutal clarity. There could be no escaping a condemnation of Jansen this time. After incredible pressure was applied, even Jacqueline signed.

176

But poor Jacqueline was spared the grief of seeing the men of Port-Royal squirm even more. Thirteen weeks after signing, on October 4th, she died. The morning she died, the Introit being sung in the chapel by her friends bore the words, "God forbid that I should glory save in the cross of our Lord Jesus Christ." When the news of her death reached Blaise, he breathed deeply. He knew that Jacqueline had at last outstripped him, not only in loyalty to God's truth but in attaining the eternal goal. But now he no longer yearned to surpass her. His experiences with God had purged his soul of such rivalry. He was too secure in his own relationship with God to deal in comparisons with others. Now, in humility, he only longed to emulate her.[3] So he simply whispered, "God give us grace to die as well as that."

On October 31st the Grand Vicars signed the new Formula. On November 20th, it was read in the churches. Now the Port-Royalists had two weeks to decide whether to sign this new condemnation of Jansen or to accept the bitter consequences.

Late in November, a sickly and lonely Pascal composed a "Writing on the signature of the Formulary." In the spirit of his beloved Jacqueline, he condemned any middle course. Nicole at Port-Royal countered with his "Examination of the 'Writing on the Signature. . . .'" He now opposed Pascal's conclusions.

A meeting was called at Pascal's home. Head throbbing with pain, Blaise tried to explain his position. At his side were Domat, Roannez and young Etienne Perier. Arnauld insisted that for the nuns to sign the Formula was a concession to maintain the unity of the faith. He admitted that it only ambiguously safeguarded the doctrine. Arnauld was advocating expediency and compromise. Nicole and Arnauld then went off into the theological hair splitting which seemed to win over most of the other Port-Royalists sitting about the room.

Suddenly, for Blaise the room began to spin. His eyes grew dim and he fell over in a faint. Alarmed, everyone jumped forward. Soon the house was almost empty and silence prevailed. His friends had carried him to his room.

When he regained consciousness, Gilberte standing by his bed, whispered, "What happened?"

Turning his head away and closing his eyes again he said with great sighs, "When I saw all those persons waver and succumb, who should have been the defenders of the truth, and to whom I believed God had made the truth known, I confess that I was so overcome with grief that I could not endure it, and so I collapsed."

What a crisis this was for Pascal! Progressively through the years all his idols had been taken from him. Reason had been dethroned when Pascal came to see its contradictions and limitations. That had precipitated an identity crisis in Pascal. Then the glamour of the world had been found to be shallow, humiliating and unsatisfying. With that realization Blaise had tasted again of despair as he evaluated the futility of his life in the world. Even after that mystic night when his identity as God's man was made explicit, God seemed to continue toppling al! authorities which tended to be idols. The Pope, the church and now even his beloved Port-Royal were seen as frail vessels, full of sin and compromise. Such a revelation had stripped Pascal of all external support. Now he was alone. But he was certain of the Presence of Jesus Christ. That would be sufficient for this man who knew his identity as the beloved of the Lord.

CHAPTER TEN

"THE LAST CONVERSION" (1662)

BLAISE was terribly torn within. He felt he was being pulled apart by his loyalty to the Church and his loyalty to the truth. He felt unbearably alone in his witness to the truth, against the Pope, the ecclesiastical establishment and even his friends. This was bitter agony.

But then he gave up the struggle! In weariness, he withdrew. He lacked the strength to continue the warfare.[1]

It was like a new conversion. With what strength he had, he turned to consider his own salvation and the practical needs of others in 1662.

He spent long hours in his room which was now stripped of carpets, ornaments and niceties. He swept his own room, made his own bed, carried his own plates to the kitchen. His room became a monastic cell in which he reread the Bible and especially lived in Psalm 119.

He secured a copy of the "Spiritual Almanac" that was published annually by Father Martial du Mans. It listed the special ceremonies, services, processions and displays of relics that were occurring in Paris day by day. His frail form became a familiar sight at the religious happenings in Paris. He attended vesper services, offered prayers, followed religious processions with fervor. His outward submission to the rites of holy Mother Church signified a profound inner penitence and surrender to the Church.

Not that he would ever abandon his convictions about grace.

179

Not that he forsook his stand on Jesuistical casuistry. But he had come to the place where he rested his case at the tribunal of Jesus Christ. God the Lord was Sovereign. He would judge. He would accomplish His Sovereign will. So Pascal left the theological issue in God's hand and turned to a day by day seeking and doing God's will in the maelstrom of life.

He visited the poor in the hospital. He handed out alms to the poor, shivering in the cold winter of 1662. One day as he returned home from Mass at the church of Saint-Sulpice, he bumped into a poor young girl, fifteen years old. She was standing bedraggled and begging on the street corner. Fearful for her safety, Blaise spoke to her. He learned that her father was dead and her mother was in the hospital. Blaise persuaded her to return with him to Saint-Sulpice where he gave a priest money for her support. The priest, ignorant of Pascal's identity, took the money and made provision for the girl's future. Then Pascal went on his way.

In his home, he entertained visitors. Occasionally he saw Arnauld and other Port-Royalists. But sceptics were specially welcome. He sought to be gentle and patient with them. He struggled not to overwhelm them with his brilliance and eloquence.

He took to live in his home a poor family named Bardout. The mother, father and little children not only received lodging but also food and firewood. They blessed him for his goodness an even named him godfather of one of their children.

Concern for the poor prompted him to engage in a new venture. Often distressed to see the poor trudging wearily through the streets of Paris, he had conceived of a carriage-bus company which would provide the poor with transportation for a fare of five sols.

On November 6th, 1661, Pascal, the Duke de Roannez, the Marquis de Sourches, Arnauld de Pomponne and the Marquis de Crenan had organized as shareholders in the venture. A company was formed. A license from the King was issued on

February 7th, 1662. On March 18th the first route was established with seven carriages which ran from the Saint-Antoine Arch near the Bastille, across the river Seine to the Luxembourg. On the first day of operation, long lines formed at each stop as weary Parisians sought to ride in the carriage-buses.

On April 11th a second route was initiated, running from Rue Saint-Antoine to Rue Saint-Honore. In May, still another route was opened from Rue Montmartre to the Luxembourg, Coachmen, wearing blue cloaks with the arms of the King and the City of Paris embroidered upon them, collected fares. Unfortunately, soldiers, pages, lackeys, manual laborers were not allowed to ride the carriages under the royal license. But those who could board the crowded carriages breathed sighs of thankfulness.

As the venture prospered, Blaise sought to borrow against the profits. He wanted desperately to send relief money to the hunger ridden peasants of Blois.

When the summer heat descended on Paris, Blaise was drained of energy and exhausted. He was unable to sleep nights. His weight dropped. He began to have terrible abdominal pains.

Then one of the Bardout children in his house contracted small-pox. Rather than move the family out of his house, Pascal went to stay with the Periers in their little house near the banks of the Seine between the Bridge Saint-Marcel and the Bridge Saint-Victor. There Gilberte tenderly nursed him.

July 3rd, the Queen's physician Guenaut was brought in. He agreed with the other doctors that there was no danger. Blaise was simply to be douched, purged and bled.

But Pascal knew better. He sent for the priest of Saint-Etienne-du-Mont, Gilberte's parish. Father Beurrier responded to his call.

As the two men sat together in Gilberte's little house, Blaise stated that he wished to put his soul and conscience in Beurrier's hands. He described his illness. He told the priest that two year's earlier he had sold his possessions and had broken with his earlier life. He shared his concern for unbelievers. He unburdened his distress at the moral laxity of the casuists. He opened his heart to reveal his heartache over the divisions among Christians. He discussed his unhappiness about the confusion over the complicated questions of grace and predestination. He declared that because he feared he might have said too much or too little, he wished to make a complete submission to the Pope, the Vicar of Christ.

As their long conversation drew to a close, Blaise asked Beurrier to remember him in prayer, that he might live and die a Christian. "The one thing I desire," he declared, "is in all things to accomplish His will". With Beurrier's assurance given, the two men parted.

Throughout July, Pascal grew weaker and weaker. After one of his visits to Blaise, Father Beurrier remarked, "He is like a child; he's as humble and submissive as a child."

On August 3rd, Blaise felt somewhat stronger so he called his lawyers, Gueneau and Quarré, to the Perier home. There he dictated to them his last will. As the lawyers wrote, Pascal dictated. He affirmed his faith "as a good Catholic, Apostolic and Roman Christian". He "recommended and recommends his soul to God, begging that by the merits of the precious blood of our Saviour and Redeemer Jesus Christ, it will please Him to forgive him his faults and receive his soul when it departs this world, imploring to this end the intercession of the glorious Virgin Mary and all the saints in Paradise. . . ." He asked that he be buried at Saint-Etienne-du-Mont and that Florin Perier both arrange the funeral and serve as executor.

Then followed a list of bequests: 1200 livres to Louise Default's sister, Francoise; 1000 livres to Anne Polycarpe; an income of 100 livres to Esdune his cook; gifts to Etienne Perier, Etienne's nurse, and to hospitals in Paris and Clermont. Then wearied by his exertion, Blaise excused the lawyers.

A few days later Blaise was confined to bed. The physician Homes and Cardinal Mazarin's doctors Brayer, Renodot and Valot held a consultation over him. Again, the doctors agreed that his condition was not serious and after prescribing various remedies departed.

Blaise, however, knowing that something was desperately wrong, pleaded for Gilberte to send for the Last Sacrament. But Gilberte and Florin, believing the doctors and not wanting to trouble the parish priest at night, declined.

The doctors, however, had prescribed the taking of much water. For several days, this seemed to purge and relieve the patient. But on the sixth day, severe dizziness and a stabbing headache returned. When the doctors were consulted, they insisted that this was merely the result of water vapors.

Again, Blaise begged to receive Holy Communion. But he was admonished to wait until he was well again and could go to the Church to commune.

Blaise pleaded, "They do not feel my illness; they are mistaken; there is something extraordinary about my headache". But seeing he was unable to persuade his family, he said no more of it.

Instead, he made a new request, "As this grace has been refused me, I should like to make up for it by some good action, and since I cannot have Communion in the Head I should like to do so in the members, and for that I thought that I might have here some poor sick person to whom the same services can be rendered as to me. For I am distressed and confused at finding myself with such assistance while a vast number of poor people, who are sicker than I, are deprived of the barest necessities. Let a nurse be engaged for the purpose and let there be no difference between him and me. . . ."

Unfortunately when Gilberte asked if Beurrier knew such a person, he did not. Blaise then wanted to be taken to the Hospital for Incurables. Again his family objected.

In mid-August the pains were increasing. But the doctors kept on insisting there was no danger. "It was only the effect of his migraine and the vapors from the waters."

On August 17th as night fell, Pascal was so weak he pathetically begged Gilberte to send for a priest. This time she too became alarmed. But Father Beurrier was away. So she sent to Port-Royal for Pascal's old friend Claude de Sainte-Marthe. There in Pascal's room De Sainte-Marthe heard Pascal's whispered confession.

As the night wore on, Blaise's body shook with convulsions and he plunged into a coma. Through the dark streets a messenger ran to summon Father Beurrier who had returned home during the evening. When Beurrier entered Pascal's dimly lit room, suddenly and miraculously the sufferer returned to consciousness. As he opened his eyes, he heard Beurrier, gleaming silver chalice in hand, saying, "Look I am bringing you Him whom you have so greatly desired."

Blaise struggled to raise himself to receive the sacrament. When Beurrier asked the usual questions of faith, he responded weakly, "Yes, Monsieur, I believe them with my whole heart".[2] Then he received the Holy Viaticum and Extreme Unction as tears flooded his eyes. When Beurrier had concluded, Pascal softly thanked him and whispered, "May God never abandon me!"

Shortly afterwards convulsions tore his thin body again. For the next twenty-four hours they shook his body periodically. At one o'clock in the morning on Saturday, August 19th, Blaise Pascal died.

On Monday, August 21st at 10 o'clock in the morning, the funeral was held at Saint-Etienne-du-Mont with about fifty friends present. His body was buried in the Church behind the High Altar amidst the remains of generations of men and women who had gone before him.[3]

Later Gilberte and a servant undertook the sad task of sorting her brother's belongings. As they folded up his clothing to dispose of it the servant felt a bulge in the lining of Blaise's coat. Opening the lining, they discovered a folded sheet of parchment bearing words Blaise had scribbled years earlier. It was his Memorial, the record of his mystic night of revealing in 1654.

184

For eight years he had carried this record with him. It closed with the words:

"Let me never be separated from Him.
He is preserved only in the ways taught in the Gospel.
Renunciation, total and sweet."

Blaise would not need this paper ever again. His renunciation now was total and sweet. He would never again be separated from the Lord to whom he had gone. His two hours of a foretaste of heaven which had been the basis of all his hopes had at last given way to ultimate fulfilment and to final certitude in eternity.

CHAPTER ELEVEN

"THE VINDICATION OF CHRISTIANITY"

AND YET Pascal lives on! After his death bundles containing nearly one thousand scraps of paper were found in his rooms. Most were clustered together into over twenty groups. Each bundle was tied by thread. Other scraps of paper were loose. Gilberte, Etienne Perier and friends from Port-Royal made two complete copies of these papers just as they were found. One of the copies has kept the order in which they were found. So a manuscript emerged which was a rough draft of Pascal's dream for a "Vindication of Christianity". They would be called "The Pensées". The papers were grouped into twenty-seven piles which became chapters. There were thirty-three or thirty-four other portions which were unclassified.

The "Pensées" have gone through many editions and have had many editors since the first Port-Royal edition, prepared by an informal committee composed of the Perier family, Jean Domat, the Duke of Roannez, Filleau de la Chaise and some friends from Port-Royal.

The public was eager for more of Pascal's writings. But partly because Port-Royal was undergoing fierce attack from the throne and partly because of the difficulty of deciphering and arranging the host of fragments, the book was not published until 1670. Finally, when it appeared that his book would not aggravate Port-Royal's perilous position, a Port-Royal edition of his "Thoughts" was published. Etienne Perier provided the introduction which summarized Pascal's Port-Royal lecture in which he had delineated the plan he intended to follow. Then followed those of Pascal's thoughts which would not antagonize or agitate the powers of the age which had brought about an uneasy truce between Port-Royal and the Jesuits. This editing undoubtedly muted the force of the edition.

Through the years which have intervened, many other editions have been published. The most widely used is a version edited in 1905 by the French scholar Léon Brunschvicg. Brunschvicg disregarded the evidences of Pascal's intended order and regrouped the fragments into what he thought were coherent groups. More recently, Dr. H. F. Stewart, Louis Lafuma and others have regrouped the thoughts into the order suggested by Pascal's lecture at Port-Royal.[1] Thus they have recaptured something of the power of his argument.

Nevertheless, the "Pensées" is only a shadow of what Blaise intended to be his "Apology". It is a skeleton without flesh and bones. It is not the series of letters vindicating the Christian faith, which he probably intended to write. It is not what he hoped would persuade a sceptical world of the truth of Christianity.

In spite of its incompleteness, the "Pensées" has caught the attention of thoughtful millions and has become an inspiration to a host of readers ever since 1670.

Pascal seems to have planned to start with man. He intended to describe the respectable, intelligent man who tries to live without God. He wanted the "honnête homme", the sophisticated sceptic, the cultured broad-minded man to see himself as he really is without God.

In the foreword and introduction, Pascal sought to prod man to seek answers to the human dilemma. He readily admits that man is both mind and conditioned automaton. He recognizes that custom conditions our subconscious which drags the unthinking mind behind it. Our first duty is to seek answers to the issues which affect our destiny. (7-252) He points out that since "men live in darkness far removed from God, that God has hidden himself from them . . . that he will only be seen by those who seek him with all their heart. . . ." (11-194)

Blaise had watched sceptics like Miton and Méré who seemed content to run from one social event to another, who sat at the gaming tables hour after hour without facing up to their own identities and their own peril. He hopes to convince the worldly sophisticate, who professes to be rational, of the unreasonableness of his position. So he prods the sceptic to search for an understanding of his own nature and destiny. He wants the sceptic to see the conclusions to which his position carries him. He asks, "How can a reasonable man argue thus: I don't know who put me in the world, or what the world is, or what I am . . . I see these frightful spaces of the universe that enclose me, and I find myself planted in a corner of this vast extent without knowing why I am put in this place rather than in another, or why the brief time given me to live has been assigned to me at this moment rather than another. . . . All that I know is that I must soon die, but what I know least is that death I cannot dodge." (11-194)

"It is monstrous to see in one heart, at the same time, this sensibility about the slightest matters and this strange insensibility about the greatest". . . . "There are two kinds of people who can be called reasonable: those who serve God with all their hearts because they know Him, and those who seek Him with all their hearts because they do not know Him. . . . But as for those who live without knowing Him and without seeking Him, they adjudge themselves so little worthy of their own concern that they are unworthy of the concern of others." (11-194)

In his first chapter, Blaise intended to deal with "Order". "I must begin by showing that religion is not contrary to reason." (35-187) He wants to stimulate men to wish it was true and then to show that in fact it *is* true. He continued, "I might well have organized this talk on order as follows: to show the vanity of all sorts of states of life, show the vanity of ordinary life, then the vanity of philosophic, pyrrhonian (sceptical), stoic lives. But the order would not have been kept. . . . " (47-61)

So the second chapter on "Vanity" follows. Pascal warms to

the task of describing man's misery. He intends to show that the Biblical diagnosis of man is an accurate representation of man. He points out tha treason is constantly being prostituted by deceptive appearances and imagination. "The greatest philosopher in the world may walk a plank amply wide; if there is an abyss beneath his imagination will prevail, though reason convince him of his safety" (81-82) Pascal knew from experience how his own imagination had deceived him and distorted reason. At times, during the writing of the "Provincial Letters", Blaise may have been in despair in his room at the King David's Inn frightened by thoughts of the power of the Jesuits and the Crown. If he imagined what the consequences of the struggle could be, he may have had to wrestle with his thoughts, to realign them with reality. He knew that reason could be terribly distorted by appearances and by the fantasies of imagination.

He knew also that one's physical condition affected one's view of reality. "We have another principle of error: illness. This distorts our judgment and our senses" (81-82) Sickness of the emotions or of the body distorts man's perspective. Pascal had experienced this distortion and knew how painful it could be.

Above all our self-love, our inflated self-esteem not only warps our view of reality but also even leads us to hate the truth. Pascal confessed that he too had been victimized by self love. "A soldier, a soldier's servant, a cook, a porter boasts and wants his admirers, and even philosophers want them . . . and I, writing this, have perhaps this desire" (94-150) Pascal could recollect his letter to M. de Ribeyres, his epistles to Father Noel and many other times when he had been jealous for his own glory. He could hearken back to his younger years when he vied with Jacqueline for glory and praise.

As he analyzed this "amour-propre," he asked, "But what can a man do? . . . He wants to be great, he sees himself small; he wants to be happy, he sees himself wretched; he wants to be perfect, he sees himself full of imperfections; he wants to be the object of men's love and esteem, and he sees that his faults deserve only their aversion and their scorn. . . .He conceives a mortal hatred for this truth that reproves him and convinces him of his faults." (99-100) Man's oft-vaunted objectivity and reasonableness thus is a myth to the man who subconsciously is prejudiced against the truth because it condemns him by its analysis of his imperfections. Man's vanity distorts the truth and encourages falsehood, deceit and hypocrisy.

Blaise's third chapter on man's "wretchedness" describes man's hopelessness. Man's vain reason has corrupted everything. Justice and truth become lost in a world of vain imaginings. Only custom remains. The hateful self makes itself the center of everything and expects others to subject themselves to it. Pascal had watched Miton and other social butterflies in their arrogance, demanding that others adore them, tyrannizing over others. Now he deplores the wretchedness and misery of men who talk of goodness, justice and happiness without being able to live them.

The fourth chapter speaks of the "Distress of mind — the ennui of man." Blaise had wrestled with the question, "Who am I?" He is acutely aware of the agony of soul each man undergoes as he seeks his own identity. He pictures the man without God like a ship without rudder or sails. "Where then is this me. . . .?" (167-323) Man struggles to flee that calm repose which will force him to face his nothingness. So in an agitated state, man tries to develop those qualities which will win him an illusory love and happiness, but he still is empty, unfulfilled and restless.

In Chapter five he planned to discuss "Causes and Effects." He undercut man's presumption by pointing out that society is built on an illusion of justice. Justice is inaccessible. The social order is built on the madness of common, street-corner notions of justice which are illusions. Force, custom and appearances sustain and legitimatize the commonly accepted ideas of justice. "Justice without power is impotent; power without justice is tyrannical (192-198) Our highest efforts for social good thus end in a recognition of our own frailty and inability even to discover or to define ultimate justice.

Yet the fact that we recognize our wretchedness is evidence of greatness. "Man's greatness lies in his knowing himself to be wretched" (218-397) Chapter six points to man's capacity to transcend himself, to think, to aspire to truth, justice and happiness. "By space the universe comprehends me, swallows me like a speck; by thought I comprehend it" (217-348). But in his analysis of man's reasoning power, Pascal points out that man's thinking process builds on the foundation of certain "cognitions of the heart". Man's awareness of essential first principles, space, time, motion, numbers comes to him through the heart. "The heart has its reasons that reason does not know". (224-227) Greater than all first principles is the knowledge of God which also comes through the heart. "It is the heart that feels God, not reason." (225-278)

Throughout his "Pensées", Pascal continued to speak of the heart as an instrument of knowledge. Its superiority is derived from the superior knowledge which it apprehends. Knowledge begins and is born in the heart. He speaks of an intuitive apprehension of reality by a man's whole personality. Such knowledge precipitates itself into thought but it is first apprehended in the heart. The heart was seen as the center of personality which transcends and enfolds thought, feeling and willing. The heart perceives principles, order and the highest and deepest truths of life. It is in the heart that God is felt and known.

Pascal had sought God with his intellect. During the years following his first conversion in Rouen, he had read and searched for more of God. But his quest was primarily rational. Then came his discovery of "honnêteté" which sees things in their totality and which discerns deeper values in life. The world of the heart began to open to Blaise. At last came the mystic night of November 23rd, 1654 when his heart was stirred and filled with a glorious awareness and certitude of God. Out of his own painful pilgrimage came his words humbling reason by pointing out the superiority of the heart.

In preparing chapter seven, Blaise sketched the contradictions of man. "What a chimera then is man! What a novelty, what a monster, what a chaos, what a subject of contradictions, what a prodigy! Judge of all things, witless worm! Casket of truth, sewer of incertitude and error, glory and refuse of the universe". (246-434) Blaise saw man's contradictions clearly focused in the clash between the sceptics and the dogmatic stoics, those who believed too little about man's abilities and those who believed too much. The sceptics taught that man was corrupt and incapable of any truth. The stoics taught that man was superlatively capable of both knowing and doing truth. Both dealt in half-truths. Pascal judges that "we are incapable of being absolutely ignorant and of knowing certainly." He affirms a paradox — that there are two truths to be affirmed. "One is that man in the state of creation or in that of grace is raised above all nature, made like unto God, participating in his divinity. The other is that in the state of corruption and sin he has fallen from that state and has been rendered like unto beasts." (246-434) This, then, accounts for the fact that man dreams of knowing and doing truth (his destiny) but actually is corrupted and incapable of knowing and doing truth (his nature). Reason cannot explain man's true identity but Scripture can.

In such a state, man tries to avoid facing his alienated condition. Chapter Eight deals with "Diversions". "I have often said that all men's distress comes from one thing only, not knowing how to sit quiet in a room." (269-139) "We seek the commotion that distracts us from thinking of our state and diverts us." "Put it to the test; leave a king alone, with no satisfaction for the senses, no concerns in his mind, no company, no diversions, to think of himself at his leisure; you will see that a king without diversions is a wretched man." (270-142)

Blaise had watched Roannez, Méré, Miton as they had sought to avoid facing themselves. He watched them gambling at cards. "Give him every morning the money he can win that day, on

condition that he doesn't play and you'll make him unhappy.
. . . Then make him play for nothing; he won't get excited, he
will be bored." (269-139) Men love the exhilaration of the
chase but the capture of the quarry disappoints them. So men
chase the bluebird of truth but would let it go if they ever captured it. Men must be doing. Men love the excitement of diversion. They avoid quiet reflection upon their sick selves. At
times, Pascal himself had sought diversion in science and in
the world in an effort to escape his own soul sickness, in an
effort to flee his own identity crisis and in a frantic effort to
flee from God.

In Chapter Nine, Blaise discusses the philosophers. Some
say you will find happiness within yourself (Stoics). Others
say seek happiness outside yourself in diversion and pleasure
(Epicureans). All the philosophers deal in partial truths without realizing that that which is opposite to their views also
contains some truth. All man's truth and goodness is mingled with falsehood and evil because fallen man is a mixture of
noble aspiration and selfish, sin-tainted desires.

With Chapter Ten, Blaise shifts his emphasis. The first nine
chapters were designed to show man his own identity crisis
and emptiness and to create a hunger for higher truth and goodness. "It is a good thing to be wearied and worn by the vain
search for the true good, so that one may hold out one's arms
to the liberator." (306-422) But where will man find that
sovereign good? "This emptiness he strives futilely to fill with
everything about him. . . . And these are all incompetent, because the infinite gulf can be filled only by an infinite, immutable
object, that is, by God Himself." (300-425)

As he proceeds into Chapter Eleven, Blaise insists that the
true religion which can fill a man's soul with God must explain
man's identity and account for both the greatness and the
wretchedness in man. In the wisdom of the God of the Bible
lies the answer. It says, "I created man holy, innocent, perfect;

194

I filled him with light and intelligence; I communicated to him My glory and My marvels . . . He wanted to become his own center, independent of my aid. He departed from My rule. When in his desire to find his felicity in himself, he tried to become My equal, I abandoned him to his own courses . . . so that today man has become like unto beasts. . . . That is the state of men today. Some feeble instinct remains of the bliss of their first nature, and they are plunged in the miseries of their blindness, their concupiscence, which has become their second nature." (309-430) So Pascal points the sceptics toward the Christian faith which offers man an understanding of who and what he is. Divine Wisdom resolves man's identity crisis.

Chapter twelve, entitled "The Beginning" commences his case for Christianity. The Christian life begins with a leap of faith, a gamble, a wager. Each individual stands solitary and alone before the great decision. "We must act as if we were all alone" (327-211) "Either God is or He is not. Which side shall we lean to? Reason can't determine anything about it. . . . A game is going on in the farthest reaches of this infinite distance, where heads or tails will turn up. What will you bet? According to reason you can't choose either; by reason you can't defend either choice." (343-233)

"Yes, but you must bet! It's not up to you; you're in the game!" . . .

"If you win, you win everything, and if you lose you lose nothing. Bet then that He exists, without hesitating." . . .

"Here there is an infinity of infinitely happy life to win, a chance of winning against a finite number of chances of loss; and what you are staking is finite. . . .

"And thus our proposition has infinite force, when the finite is to be waged in a game wherein there are equal chances of gain and loss, and the infinite is to be won". . . .

"I tell you that you will win in this life, and that at every step you take along this road you will see so much certainty of profit, so much void in the things you stake, that you will finally learn that you have bet on a certainty, infinite, for which you have given nothing." (343-233)

But the thinking man will ask, "Is it necessary to abandon reason?" In Chapter thirteen, Blaise discoursed on the use of reason. "There is nothing so conformant to reason as this disavowal of reason" (367-272). "Reason's last step is to recognize that there are an infinity of things that surpass it" (373-267) Blaise seeks to put reason in its proper perspective, to humble it. He is careful to point out that man's reason is motivated by man's desires and choices. A man believes intellectually what he wills to believe. "The will is one of the principal organs of belief. . . . The will, which prefers one to another, dissuades the mind from considering those aspects it doesn't like to see" (375-399). Then look carefully, Oh man, your beliefs are conditioned by what you will to believe in the deep subconscious chambers of the mind.

As if to humble man further, Blaise went on in chapters fourteen and fifteen to make a transition from the knowledge of man to the knowledge of God through Jesus Christ. He focuses on the infinite universe in the tiny atom beneath man. He points to the starry universe above man. Man is poised perilously between two infinities, the infinitely great and the infinitely small. Everything is bound to him. To know himself, man must know the infinity which encompasses him. This is to know God.

"Man is only a reed, the weakest in nature, but he is a thinking reed. . . . Even if the universe should crush him, man would still be nobler than that which kills him, because he knows he dies; and he knows the advantage the universe has over him. . . . All our dignity, then, consists in thought". (391-347) Man, dignified by thought seeks to understand the infinite. But such knowledge is only given by God.

In Chapter sixteen, Pascal turned to consider the "Falsity of Other Religions." Herein he highlighted the characteristics of true religion." The true religion must then teach us to adore him only, to love him only . . . the religion that informs us of our duties must inform us also of our impotence and teach us the remedies for it." (399-489) He then throws the spotlight on the falsehoods in other religions. "The other religions, like the pagan ones, suit the masses better, for they are external; but they are not for the elite. A purely intellectual religion would suit the elite better, but it would be of no use to the mass. Only the Christian religion is suited to both, being a mixture of external and internal." (413-351) In other words, true religion will be universal and will meet the needs of all men in all conditions. The religions of falsehood will meet the needs of a limited number.

Moreover, true religion will confront the root of all sin, self-deification. "Whoever does not inwardly hate his own self-esteem and that instinct that impels him to make himself God is much blinded . . . no religion has noticed that that is a sin, or that we were born to it, or that we were obliged to resist it; and none has thought of giving us the cures for it." (418-492) But, he laments, "man has the power not to think of what he doesn't want to think of . . . thus the false religions are preserved." (420-259)

As Pascal focused on the arguments for the Christian religion, he writes in chapter seventeen about sincerity as the hallmark of the true seeker. "In matters of religion we must be sincere." (425-590) "How then can one have anything but a good opinion of a religion which understands the failings of human nature so well, and what can we do but wish that a religion, which promises such desirable remedies should be true?" (427-450)

He might have planned to ask the question, "If Christianity is true, are you willing to follow it? Or are there sacrifices involved which you are unwilling to make?" It is in that spirit that he tests the sincerity of his reader to see if he, at least, would be willing to accept Christian faith if it could be proved to be true.

As he proceeds into chapter eighteen, the "Foundations of

Religion and Reply to Objections", Blaise highlighted the fact that God is both hidden and revealed. He declared that the Christian religion has obscurity mingled with clarity and that any religion which does not explain the hiddenness of God is not true. He sees the Biblical emphasis on man's will. "God prefers to mould the will rather than the mind. Perfect clarity would be a help to the mind and harmful to the will." (441-581) "There is sufficient light to enlighten the elect and sufficient darkness to humiliate them. There is sufficient darkness to blind the damned and sufficient light to condemn them and make them unpardonable" (443-578) The essence of religion forbids a revelation with such clarity that men would be bludgeoned into belief. The fact is that the Christian religion is an admingling of clarity and obscurity so that the will is free to choose. Another foundation stone of religion must be its breadth in dealing with antinomies, paradox and seemingly contradictory truths. "With each truth we come upon, we must remind ourselves of the truth which is opposed to it" (460-567) "The origin of all heresy is the exclusion of one or other of these truths." (462-862)

In chapter nineteen, Blaise discussed symbolism as a key to the understanding of the Bible. He said "two kinds of error: 1. To interpret everything literally; 2. to interpret everything in a spiritual sense." (486-648) "Thus, in order to understand Scripture there must be an interpretation which reconciles all the conflicting passages. . . . In Jesus Christ all the contradictions are reconciled." (491-684) He points out that the Hebrew mentality saw not only historical reality in the happenings and rituals of the Old Testament but also deeper symbolic meaning. Jesus Christ becomes the key to penetrating the deeper meanings underlying the physical occurrences of the Old Testament. So, there is a deeper spiritual meaning underlying the material, historical events of the Bible. The key to understanding that deeper significance is Jesus Christ. This "hiddenness" of the deeper significance traces to God's plan that man should not be forced into accepting His truth. There are enough passages where the deeper meaning breaks forth clearly to stimulate men to search while there are also enough other passages where the real significance is hidden to give man freedom to reject. So a figurative or symbolic interpretation is espoused for Biblical passages which seem obscure or contradictory. Prophecies and miracles seen in this deeper symbolic way point toward Jesus Christ and find their significance in Him. Thus Old and New Testaments together form one whole witness to Him.

Using the principle of figurative interpretation Pascal presents to his readers the truth of Christianity. In Chapter twenty he traces the ancient doctrine of original sin from the Talmud to Christianity. In chapter twenty-one he introduces the argument of the perpetuity of the doctrines of the Fall and Redemption. They have always existed. The Old and New Testaments are one in dealing with these two themes. Pascal found it extraordinary that "The only religion which is against nature, against common sense, and hostile to our pleasures, is the only one that has always existed." (543-605) Biblical religion which cuts cross grain to man's natural drives, has persisted through all ages. "Let us remember that from the beginning of the world the expectation or worship of the Messiah has never ceased to exist" (550-617)

This is in sharp contrast to those religions which derive from momentary flashes of light in the darkness, instants of insight in the maelstrom of time. The history of the Jews and of the Church astound Pascal when he considers that they teach a morality which opposes the natural passions of humanity.

In chapter twenty-two, Blaise deals with Moses. Assuming Mosaic authorship of the Pentateuch, he explains Moses' ascribing length of years to the men of antiquity. Their longevity reduces the time span separating them from Moses and thus raises the credibility of the Mosaic account.

Pascal reaches a climax in chapter twenty-three on the "Proofs of Jesus Christ". The roster of "proofs" includes miracles, prophecies, the testimony of the Jews, the testimony of the apostles and even the testimony of pagans and heretics. His highest proof, however, derives from the magnificent holiness of Jesus' life and teaching.

Basic to these "proofs" or evidences is Blaise's understanding of the heart. "The heart has its own order; the intellect has its own order which operates by means of principle and demonstration; the heart has a different one . . . Jesus Christ and St. Paul possess the order of charity, not of intellect; because they wished to warm the hearts of people, not to instruct them." (575-283) In the heart, warmed by God's grace, the evidences of Christ converge convincingly to become proofs. Each proof, by itself, would not be sufficient to convince the sceptic. But when all these "proofs" converge in the open, surrendered heart of man, the grace of God molds them into conviction and certainty.

Pascal further sees reality composed of three orders. Each is separated from the other by an infinite gulf. The first is the physical, material realm wherein men strive for power and wealth. The second is the realm of the mind wherein men struggle for intellectual honors and supremacy. The third and highest is the realm of charity and love where material and intellectual greatness are forgotten but where the holiness and glory of God are all in all. The lower orders cannot rise up to the higher. There is great discontinuity. But the higher orders can break into the lower with meaning, purpose and direction.[2] Jesus Christ represents the highest order. "It would have been pointless for Our Lord Jesus Christ to come as a king, in order that his reign of holiness should dazzle;   but he certainly came with the splendor which belongs to his order." (585-793)

In his vision of reality, Pascal and a twentieth-century Frenchman, Teilhard de Chardin, have some things in common. Both came from the Massif Central (Chardin was born near Clermont Ferrand.) Both saw in Jesus Christ the highest order of reality, the Alpha and Omega of the universe, the Love which moves all things. Both saw Jesus Christ as the goal, the Point Omega who influences and draws all creation toward Himself. Each saw and understood the order of the mind, called by Chardin noosphere, as being profoundly directed and influenced by the higher order of Love. Each saw the structures of creation, the material order, receiving meaning from the higher orders. In all this, they discerned the reconciliation of science and religion in the wholeness of the universe. One cannot but wonder how much Pascal's thought may have influenced his fellow-countryman.

Blaise had explored the realm of material greatness. His expeditions with Roannez to the royal court had enabled him to know at first hand the kingdoms of the world. His genius had allowed him to penetrate more deeply than most into the realms of the mind. Years had been spent probing the secrets of science, mathematics and abstruse theology. But his highest joy and fulfillment had come when Jesus Christ introduced him to the supernatural order of holy, Divine, sacrificial love. Now, from the apex of reality, Blaise could look back and see how infinitely separate and inferior the lower orders are from the highest. But it is in and through the heart that man experiences this highest realm. And it is in the heart warmed by grace that the evidences of Christ's grandeur (which evidences by themselves are mere probabilities) will converge and coalesce into the certainty of "proofs" for any man.

In chapter twenty-four, Pascal returns to the recurring theme of the "Prophecies." "The most convincing of the proofs of Jesus Christ are the prophecies." (626-706) Divine truth, like a vast underground stratum of rock, has erupted into the light of day in many outcroppings. The prophets stand at these junctures in history declaring what God's actions mean to men. The ruin of the Jews, the birth of the Church, the outpouring of holiness through the Church were foretold and came to pass. The persisting miracle of the prophetic stream of voices all proclaiming the same basic message is convincing evidence to

Pascal of the truth of the great ground swell of Biblical revelation throughout history.

Chapter twenty-five discusses the Old Testament events which prefigure the life of the Church, and which indicate that the eruptions of God's truth in the Old Testament are of the same stuff as those in the New Testament.

Finally, Blaise brings his work addressed to sceptics right down to the warp and woof of life. In chapter twenty-six he focuses on "Christian Morality". "Christianity is strange. It bids man recognize that he is base, even abominable; it also bids him desire to be like God." (667-537) Christianity begin with man where he is — in his wretchedness. But it points him toward the sky. This new life is not isolated individualism. It is fellowship with other believers. Pascal had tried to "go it alone". But he had discovered that his faith was strong and vital only in fellowship with others who believe. His spiritual relationship with his family, Roannez and the people of God at Port-Royal had sustained and strengthened him through many tests. So he declares "When God had created heaven and earth . . . he wanted to create beings who would be, and who would form, a body of thinking members." (676-482) In that Mystical Body of Christ, our estimate of ourselves is purified and corrected and our faith is nurtured and grows.

Pascal has said much about hating oneself. But he makes it clear why we hate ourselves "(for we are hateful on account of our concupiscence)." (699-485) "Everything to be found in the world is concupiscence of the flesh, or concupiscence of the eyes or pride of life. . . ." (696-458) But when man is given a new identity by being lifted into the realm of Christ's love and is knit into the Body of Christ he learns through that Body to love himself as Christ loves him. "In order to regulate the love that we should have for ourselves, we must imagine a body consisting of thinking members because we are members of everything, and see how each member ought to love itself." (684-474) Blaise had known the agonies of despising himself in his wretched condition as a worldling. But when the love of Christ gave him a new identity, he came to accept and to love himself as a part of Christ's beloved Body in the world. So he writes, "By loving the body it loves itself because it has no being except through and for the sake of the body . . . we love ourselves because we are members of Jesus Christ." (688-483) Here then is the wellspring of Christian morality. "To have life, being and movement only through the spirit of the body and for the sake of the body." (688-483) So the Christian life is one of joy, for evil desire will be extinguished within him as he dwells more and more in the realm of God's holy love.

Finally, Pascal draws to his conclusion. Proofs and accumulated evidences are not sufficient. The realm of the intellect is inadequate. "What a vast distance there is between knowing God and loving Him!" (727-280) God must give the gift of faith. "The prophecies, even the miracles and the proofs of our religion, are not of such a nature that we can assert that they are absolutely convincing. . . . But the evidence for is such that it surpasses, or at any rate it equals, the evidence against religion. . . ." (736-564). But in the final analysis, "God inclines the hearts of those whom he loves" (732-287). "We shall never believe with a vigorous and unquestioning faith unless God touches our hearts; and we shall believe as soon as he does so" (730-284) So we must humble ourselves before God to receive His gift of grace.

Thus Pascal has brought the sceptic to see his wretched, alienated identity. He has brought him to see the reasonableness of the redemption and new identity offered man by the Christian faith. He closes with the words, "Thus there is sufficient evidence to condemn and not sufficient to convince, so that it may be apparent that those who accept it do so by grace and not reason; and that those who turn their backs on it, do so through concupiscence and not reason." (736-564) Those who reject do so because they desire something else more than they desire God. Those who accept do so because of the miracle of God's grace and discover their true identity in God.

CHAPTER TWELVE

PASCAL AND THE ANATOMY OF DOUBT

PASCAL was essentially an evangelist. He was deeply concerned about the sceptic, the doubter. He, himself, had known times of intense doubt. He had watched his sceptical friends at the royal court as they staggered through life without faith in God. He had chatted with scores of sceptics in his own home. He wanted to help the doubter to an experience of faith. He had developed a strategy of "pre-evangelism." He elaborated this strategy in "The Pensées."

"Pre-evangelism" to Pascal consisted of helping the sceptic to see his true identity and perilous position, to understand the implications of his unbelief, to see the conclusions which must logically follow the presuppositions of unbelief. Pascal had devoted many chapters of his "Pensées" to a description of man without God. Blaise hoped to lead a reasonable man to search for God because he had had his eyes opened to his own identity crisis of misery and lostness.

At the same time, he was acutely aware of some of the deeper reasons men doubt the Christian faith. Those reasons basically have not changed with the passing of the years. Men still doubt. Essentially the reasons for scepticism have not changed because essentially man is the same.

Religious doubt has at least three causes. The least common cause of doubt is emotional sickness which may render a sick soul incapable of faith. Psychiatry is familiar with the man who deeply doubts his own identity and projects his inner doubt of self into the universe around him. A variety of emotional disorders may cause an inability to choose, to decide, to believe. These folk may need patient counselling and therapy to be freed of the emotional disorders which cause a man to doubt.

A second source of religious doubt is the more purely intellectual or rational to which Tennyson referred in the phrase, "The faith that lives in honest doubt." It usually is based on an inadequate understanding of the Subject/Object of faith.

Some sincere searchers doubt the Christian faith because they misunderstand it or because they have only a partial understanding of it. Often these doubt an ugly caricature of Christianity which, more often than not, is a distorted carry-over from childhood days. An intelligent businesswoman recently admitted that she harbored doubts about the existence of God. Questioning revealed that the God she doubted was a doddering, white-haired projection of her grandfather. Such images of God are repudiated by all intelligent, Biblically-oriented Christians. The fact that many reject the Christian God because of such misunderstandings highlights the need for clear, Biblical exposition in the language and thought patterns of contemporary men and women.

The third, and perhaps most common, source of doubt is not in the mind but in the heart of man. It has been traced to a prior commitment of the heart and will to that which is not God. Many men doubt the Christian God because their hearts are already commited to other "gods." This type of doubt was the object of Pascal's scrutiny.

Even when the Christian Gospel has been lucidly set forth, some will continue to doubt and by their doubt reject the truth. Why? Clues to the answer were found scribbled on scraps of paper which were gathered together to form "The Pensées," that timeless analysis of man's plight and God's deliverance. Their author, Blaise Pascal, a pre-modern modern, was a devout believer and also a brilliant scientist in whom the forces of faith and doubt grappled painfully. After his death, many scraps of paper were found to contain thoughts which Pascal had planned to weave together in an apologetic masterpiece designed for the doubter, the sceptic. Many of these thoughts provide incisive insight into Pascal's personal battle with scepticism. They serve as a scalpel to open and to probe the doubts of all men.

Pascal saw man as a whole, integrated being in which the mind, the will and the heart are not isolated parts of the personality, independent of each other. Man cannot be bifurcated into parts. Man's heart, will and mind are functions which, like fields of force, influence and interpenetrate each other. He pointed out the strategic importance of the heart which influences both the will *and the mind.* (575-283) To Pascal, "the heart" was the center of human personality, underlying, transcending and enfolding thought, feeling and will. Pascal pointed out that what a man loves in his heart, man chooses with his will and exalts in his mind.

To Pascal, man is riding a piece of fluff in the vastness of the infinite spaces. Lost between the infinity above him and the infinity beneath him, man grasps at things he can see and control. These "things" he loves. These "loves" provide man with just enough relief from anguish in the face of the infinities and contradictions of life to keep him from seeking complete satisfaction in the love of God. When man's love of created things fills his heart, his heart attracts the will to choose and serve these false gods and then captures the mind which rationalizes and justifies this idolatry by creating doubts and false beliefs. Man's thoughts thus are drawn as by a magnet to that which he loves in his heart. Some men love the flesh, others love knowledge, still others *love power.* (696-458) Most men lust after that which is not God because that which is not God usually does not challenge man's greatest love, his substitute for God, his own ego. Thus man's illicit loves control his heart, energize his will and permeate his thoughts.

All the while man thinks that he is master of his thoughts. He is often blind to the subconscious influences of the loves which have drugged and captivated his ego, which is his real god. Man is unaware of his real identity. As Pascal peels away the layers and dimensions of man's existence, he recognizes at the core of man a destructive self-love which causes us to hug the tidbits of life in our hearts. He declared, "He who hates not in himself his self-love, and that instinct which leads him to make himself God, is indeed blinded" (418-492). This self-love satisfies itself by drawing into the heart of man loves which, like magnets, exert a pull on the will and the mind, so that they point toward those things *man loves*. (375-399) So, many men obsessively doubt and even deny God in their minds because in their hearts they love themselves and the things which flatter and tickle their egos. A modern case in point was another Frenchman, Albert Camus. He refused to acknowledge God in Christ. Perhaps a clue to his unbelief lies in these words of his from *The Fall*.

"How intoxicating to feel like God the Father and to hand out definitive testimonials of bad character and habits. I sit enthroned among my bad angels at the summit of the Dutch Heaven and I watch ascending toward me, as they issue from the fogs and water, the multitude of the Last Judgment. And as for me, I pity without absolving, I understand without forgiving and above all I feel at last that I am being adored."[1]

Because he is his own god, he wants no other. John Baillie, the sage Scot, once said that wrong belief is always mixed with wrong desire.

Thus many men hide from Jesus Christ behind a barricade of doubts. They shiver in the Presence of One who judges their "loves" and idolatries. The truth of Christ pierces to the core of man's being, exposing his sin and his true identity as an *idolator*. (99-100) If the demonstrations of mathematics were related to the totality of man's life so that they judged man's love and actions, we can be sure that the axioms of mathematics also would become the object of widespread doubt and controversy. However, it is the Christian faith which penetrates to the personal, ethical levels of life; so men often hide from the Invader from eternity behind an intellectual wall of doubts because their hearts are cluttered with the thorns and stones of ugly loves. Men don't want these loves disturbed. They don't want to see who and what they really are. Even those who believe find that their hearts need constant cultivation by the Word and Holy Spirit so that the areas of forbidden loves may be fertilized and made fruitful. Men still cry, "Lord, I believe, help Thou mine unbelief."

How then can a man find faith? Pascal found the answer in an invasion of man's heart and will by *God's grace.* (730-284) The winds of God's grace point a man's soul toward God who can enable man to see himself as he really is, to see his true identity. When the grace of the God of the Cross has brought a man to the place of humility and surrender, the mysterious miracle takes place in his *heart and will.* (441-581) Man, however, must reach the point of exhaustion. Humbled and broken from his strivings after things, he *turns to God.* (306-422)

After years of struggling, questioning and doubting, on the night of November 23rd, 1654, Pascal surrendered totally. Wave after wave of the fire of God's grace invaded his heart. Ever the scientist, he feverishly scribbled notes of this two-hour experience. He wrote, "Renunciation, total and sweet. Total submission to Jesus Christ and to my director."

The God of Abraham, Isaac and Jacob — a Person — flooded his soul with grace that cleansed his heart like fire. The old loves melted. Henceforth, his great love and passion was Jesus Christ. When his love of lesser things vanished in the advent of the love of God, doubts evaporated. A sublime certitude, even the certitude with which God is certain of Himself, gripped him. He wrote, "Certitude. Certitude. Feeling. Joy. Peace." He was possessed by the Living Truth. Henceforth, his mind would reflect the reality of the love and certitude of God who filled his heart. His thoughts had become reflections of the Divine Truth which had captured his soul.

What advice does this convinced Pascal offer to those who

doubt? First, he urges all men to search after the truth of God since man's eternal destiny is at stake. By carefully delineating the dilemmas into which man has been led by unbelief, Pascal hoped that he would have prepared man to search for relief from his misery and lostness. It is sheer stupidity and monstrous sin for a man to ignore the possibility that the Christian faith, with its promise of blessedness in time and eternity and its warning of a doom that is eternal *may be true.* (11-194) Pascal warns that if a man's heart is so weighted down with worldly lusts and loves that he will not inquire after the truth or falsity of the claims of Christ, he deserves separation from God. Yet he pleads with men to search, to study, to inquire.

Secondly, he admonishes men who seek the truth to humble themselves, to acknowledge the limitations of human reason in the face of infinity that stretches *before them.* (362-272) This involves man's facing up to his identity between two infinities.

Thirdly, he counsels men to recognize that the basic issues of life are decided in the arena of the heart and will, not *in the mind.* (375-399) Man's thoughts, though of immense value, are usually but shadowy reflections of what is in the heart of man. A college student may be convinced intellectually by hearing a brilliant discourse on the evidences of God's existence. He may be persuaded by logical arguments. An hour later, however, these arguments seem to disappear as new doubts arise, born of the shadowy inclinations and lusts of his heart. Pascal urges us to see that the source of our doubts is usually in the heart and will of man. He teaches us to doubt our doubts by searching our hearts for the desires which give birth to doubt. What is it you desire most, God or the world? God or ego? God or popularity? God or pleasure? God or power? To possess God or to be possessed by God? Expose your desires and you expose your doubts. Conversely, "Ye shall seek me and find me when ye shall search for me with all your heart" (Jer. 29:13).

Fourthly, Pascal advises earnest men to experiment, to gamble, to "act-as-if" they believed, though honestly admitting to any and all that they are simply seeking. Seekers should seek to live the life Christ has taught. Action is more efficient than syllogisms of the intellect in inducing faith. Wasn't this why Pascal urged sceptics to *wager on God?* (343-233) They should read the Bible and try to obey it. They should seek to pray, "God, if you are real, help me. . . ." They should seek to pray and fellowship with Christians, exposing their lives to God active in the life of His Church. Many an inquirer has "acted-as-if" the Christian faith was true and has become convinced along the way. Many, by attempting to *do* God's will, have found their lesser loves challenged in an existential experiment. Thus, the truth in Jesus' words, "If any man will *do* His will, He shall know of the doctrine, whether it be of God. . . ." (John 7:17) becomes apparent. As one steps out, acting-as-if, he becomes aware of his own need and inability; he exposes his life to the means of grace; he opens his life more and more to the advances of God's Spirit which already has been pointing his soul to inquire about the truth. This willingness to make a grand experiment, to act-as-if the Christian faith was true, separates those who humbly and sincerely seek the truth from those diletantes who, as Unamuno, the Spanish Pascal, put it, simply want to play with the blue-bird of the truth and would release it if they ever caught it since they really love the exhilaration of the chase. Men who sincerely ask, seek and knock, will receive. They will discover who and what they really are in the light of Divine Wisdom. They will find that the doorway to God is wonderfully open. They will discover that they would not be seeking God if they had not already been found by Him.

CHAPTER THIRTEEN

PASCAL AND THE ABSENCE
OF GOD

ONE of the Twentieth Century "death of God" theologians, William Hamilton, has said, "We are not talking about the absence of the experience of God, but about the experience of the absence of God."[1] "The experience of the absence of God" is not unknown in human history, though recent theothanatological interpretations are novel.

Blaise Pascal was among those in the course of human history who have experienced the absence of God. His cry, "The eternal silence of these infinite spaces terrifies me," (392-206) reflects an experience of the absence of God. His complaint, "I look everywhere and everywhere I see only darkness," reveals the same experience (13-229). Again he wrote of the terror of the absence of God: "When I consider the brief span of my life, absorbed in the eternity of time which went before and will come after it, the tiny space that I occupy and even that I see plunged in the infinite immensity of the spaces which I do not know and which do not know me, I am terrified and astonished to find myself here rather than there, for there is no reason why I should be here rather than there, why now rather than then. Who put me here? By whose order and design were this place and time allotted to me?" (116-205).

"When we behold the blindness and wretchedness of man, when we look on the whole dumb universe, on man without light, abandoned to his own devices and appearing as though lost in some corner of the universe, without knowing who has

213

placed him there, what he is supposed to be doing, what will become of him when he dies, incapable of all knowledge, I am overcome by fear. . . . (389-693). Yes, Pascal knew the horror of the absence of God, the terrible sense of meaninglessness which seems to pervade the universe when man is unsure of his own identity and when God appears to have vanished, to be dead. How did Pascal interpret this experience?

First, he turned the focus of his study upon man's identity as he experiences the absence of God. In Pascal's speech to the gentlemen of Port-Royal, he had outlined the plan for his apology for the Christian faith. He declared his intention to begin with the identity of man, a portrait of man as he is. He planned to hilghlight the small amount of light man has and the "darkness enveloping him on almost every side."[2] So, early in "The Pensées," Pascal describes man. "Man is nothing but a creature full of error . . . nothing reveals truth to him. Everything misleads him . . . the senses mislead reason by deceitful appearances . . . the passions of the soul upset the senses and give them false impressions," (82-83). Hence, "we desire truth and are dogged by uncertainty," (125-437). Man is filled with contradictions. The goodness and justice he yearns for are beyond his grasp. The senses, reason, all channels of knowledge end in contradictions and dead ends. Man is blind and bewildered as to his identity. The truth about himself and about God is beyond him. Unaided he cannot discover truth and only knows ambiguities about himself and therefore is overwhelmed by the seeming absence of God.

At the same time that Pascal saw man in his blindness and misery, he also caught glimpses of greatness in man. "Man transcends man," (246-434). Man yearns for truth, goodness and happiness though he possesses it not. "The greatness of man is apparent in his very concupiscence, because he has found a way of extracting an admirable code from it and turning it into a veritable picture of charity," (222-402). "The greatness of man is great in so far as he realizes that he is wretched," (218-397).

"The whole dignity of man lies in his power of thought," (232-365). "Thought is the hall-mark of man's greatness," (233-346). "Man knows that he is wretched; he is therefore wretched because he is so; but he is very great because he knows it," (237-416). So Pascal sees man's identity, including both blindness and potentiality. "What sort of a monster then is man? What a novelty, what a portent, what a chaos, what a mass of contradictions, what a prodigy! Judge of all things, a ridiculous earthworm who is the repository of truth, a sink of uncertainty and error; the glory and the scum of the world. Who shall unravel such a tangle?" (246-434). Being a child of his times, Pascal had focused on the individual. He had studied man as he experiences the absence of God. The cultural climate of his day was becoming befogged by a preoccupation with the self-consciousness of individual man. Indeed, Descartes was about to plunge generations of subsequent thinkers into the abyss of man's inner consciousness with the words, "Cogito ergo sum".

Unlike Descartes and his descendants, however, Pascal did not stop with a study of the self-consciousness of man. He saw man mirrored against transcendence. He went on to discover answers to the riddle of man's identity crisis in Jesus Christ and the Bible. "Let us learn about our true nature from uncreated and incarnate truth," (246-434).) He saw that an objective unchanging standard of reference is needed if man is to understand himself and be lifted above confusion.

Pascal rejected the Cartesian split in reality which isolated the experiencing creature from the world, from his fellows and from the Divine Transcendence. "Descartes useless and unreliable," (297-298). Unlike Descartes, Pascal saw man existing in vital relation to the physical universe about him. Man has something to learn from the natural world. "Let man, therefore, contemplate all nature in her full and lofty majesty; let him turn his eyes away from the lowly objects which surround him. Let him look upon the dazzling light placed like an eternal lamp to illuminate the universe. . . . What is man in face of the infinite? . . . let him seek out the tiniest of objects known to him . . . I will show him a fresh abyss in it. I will describe for him not only the visible universe, but the whole inconceivable vastness of nature enclosed in the abridgement of an atom. Let him see in it an infinity of universes. . . . Anyone who regards himself in this way will be terrified at himself, and seeing himself sustained in the body that nature has given him, between the two abysses of the infinite and the void, will tremble at the sight of these wonders. . . . For after all, what is man in nature? A void in comparison with the infinite, a whole in comparison with the void, a middle term between nothing and all. . . . Let us therefore understand our limitations; we are something and we are not everything. . . . That is our veritable condition. It is that which makes us incapable either of certain knowledge or of absolute ignorance," (390-72). Man, in the middle between the infinity of the vast universe above him and the infinity of the tiny universe beneath him, sees both his puniness and his greatness reflected in his relationship to the physical world of nature. The universe thus becomes a mirror before which man can learn of his contradictory position. The physical universe highlights his identity crisis.

Suspended between two infinities, man is blind to God, is incapable of discovering and knowing God. Why? Because alienated man is fallen man. In his "Exposition of the Problem of Grace," Pascal expounded the Augustinian view of man which was his own. He said of the Augustinians, "They believe in two estates in human nature. The first is the one in which nature was created in Adam, pure stainless, just and upright, coming from the hands of God, from whom nothing can come which is not pure, holy, perfect."

"The other is the state to which human nature was reduced by sin and the rebellion of the first man by whom that nature became sullied, abominable and detestable in the eyes of God."[3]

216

Again in "The Pensées", Pascal put these words in the mouth of Divine Wisdom: "You are no longer in the state in which I created you. I created man holy, innocent, perfect; I filled him with light and intelligence. . . . He wanted to be his own centre and to be independent of my help. He withdrew from my dominion . . . I abandoned him to his own devices . . . so that today man has become like the beasts and so far removed from me that he scarcely retains even a confused image of his author; to such an extent has his knowledge been extinguished or dimmed!

"That is the state of men today. There remains in them some faint desire for happiness, which is a legacy of their first nature, and they are plunged into the miseries of their blindness and lust, which have become a second nature to them," (309-430).

Thus, Pascal traced man's blindness and identity crisis back to Adam and the Fall. Man, in his second nature, sees only darkness and experiences the bitterness of the absence of God. Transcendent Divine Wisdom becomes the key to understanding man's crisis of self-understanding. Man, suspended between two infinities, only understands his nature and his destiny through Divine Wisdom.

Pascal, in response to the downdraft of God's grace into his life on November 23, 1654, reaffirmed the meaning of God's transcendence in an age when a nominalistic concern for singulars seemed to be chopping the world up into meaningless fragments. On the basis of both his experience, and the teaching of the Bible, he maintained that the transcendent God actually existed above and beyond man's experience of His absence. However, the transcendent God hides Himself! Herein, he found the second answer to man's experience of the absence of God. Pascal put it that Scripture "declares that God is a hidden God; and that since the corruption of nature, he has left man in a state of blindness. . . ." (49-242). Again, he says, "religion . . . maintains that men live in darkness far removed from God, that God has hidden Himself from them, that this is the very name that He gives Himself in the Scriptures, Deus Absconditus

(Isaiah 16:15)," (11-194). "All things are veils which hide God."[4]

"Since God has so hidden himself, every religion which does not declare that God is a hidden God is not true; and every religion which does not give the reason is not a teaching religion. Ours does both: 'Truly . . . Thou art a God of hidden ways!' (Isaiah 45:15)," (449-585).

The God who revealed Himself to Pascal is a hidden God. The secrets of nature hide God. "He has remained hidden under the veil of nature."[5] He is even hidden in His self-revealing in the Bible, the Church and Jesus Christ. Pascal recognized the ambiguity of hiddenness in the Bible. "When the word of God, which is true, is false in a literal sense, it is true in a spiritual sense," (506-687). "The veil which hides the meaning of the books of the Bible from the Jews does the same for bad Christians. . . ." (514-676). "That is why the prophecies have a hidden meaning, a spiritual meaning, to which the people were hostile, underlying the materialistic meaning which appealed to them," (518-571). He saw the hiddenness of God in the Church. "In the Church it (truth) is hidden," (530-673). Even in Jesus Christ, there is hiddeness. "What do the prophets say about Jesus Christ? That he will manifestly be God? No; they say that he is truly a hidden God; that he will not be recognized. . . ." (435-751). So it became apparent to Pascal that though God has revealed Himself, yet there is the ambiguity of hiddenness. God reveals enough of Himself to be recognized by those who seek Him and hides enough of Himself to be invisible to those who do not seek Him. "He has given signs of Himself which are visible to those who seek Him, and not to those who do not seek Him." (309-430).

What is the reason for God's hiding Himself? Is He like a malevolent demon, playing hide and seek with His creation? No! Pascal declares, "Instead of complaining that God has hidden Himself, you must thank Him for revealing so much of Himself. . . ." (310-288). He has revealed Himself in delicate

218

tension with His hiddenness so that those who desire Him may recognize Him and those who do not want Him will not be bludgeoned by the evidence into believing against their will. "It would not have been right, therefore, for Him to appear in a way that way plainly divine and absolutely bound to convince all mankind; but it was not right either that he should come in a manner so hidden that he could not be recognized by those who sought Him sincerely. He chose to make Himself perfectly knowable to them; and thus, wishing to appear openly to those who seek Him with all their heart, and hidden from those who flee Him with all their heart, he tempered the knowledge of Himself, with the result that He had given signs of Himself which are visible to those who seek Him, and not to those who do not seek Him," (309-430). So God respects man's freedom by giving enough light to enable man either to accept or to reject Him. The will of man determines, then, the road a man will take, either out of blindness or deeper into the abyss of darkness.

Pascal first traced the experience of the absence of God to the identity crisis, the spiritual blindness of fallen, alienated man. However, probing even deeper, he discerned, secondly, the sovereign will of God which respects man's freedom so much that it decrees that a Divine hiddenness must be balanced with the Divine revealing.

He was saved from anything even approximating a theothanatological dead end by his repudiation of the Cartesian split in reality. Pascal did not isolate man from either the natural world or transcendent reality. Therefore, he was able to discern that man's blindness to the presence of God was paralleled by man's blindness to truth scattered throughout the physical universe. Though he analyzed the consciousness of man minutely, nevertheless he saw man as intimately related to the world and the cosmos around him. Pascal did not isolate man from the cosmos around him. He saw man's blindness viz-a-viz the universe; therefore, he recognized man's blindness as a part of man's fallen nature and therefore to be a primary part of the explana-

219

tion of man's experience of the absence of God. Secondarily, Pascal took seriously the message of the Bible, and so he understood not only that sinful man was incapable of recognizing the transcendent God but also that God Himself, respecting the integrity of human selfhood, chose to hide Himself as well as to reveal Himself.

However, the question still remains, if man is blind and sinful and if God only reveals Himself to the man who desires Him, how does sinful, blinded man come to the point of desiring God? Certainly not by philosophical argumentation! "The metaphysical proofs of the existence of God are so remote from men's method of reasoning and so involved that they produce little impact; and even if they did help some people, the effect would only last for a few moments. . . ." (381-543).

Rather, man only desires the God who reveals Himself after God's grace touches man's heart, creating both a hatred of one's own selfish concupiscence and a God-inspired desire for God. Then, man's eyes open to behold the signs of God's reality. Then man believes. "He inclines their hearts to believe," (730-284).

Pascal saw man existing in an ordered universe ruled by a Transcendent Deity of Holy love. Man is drawn upwards, to transcend the material and the intellectual realms into the highest order of Divine Holy love. This occurs, however, only as the God of Holy love comes from above to touch man's heart with the outgoing love and certainty which characterize God Himself Thus God draws man toward Himself at the apex of creation. When man is quickened by God's grace he realizes his true identity as the beloved of God; then he can view all creation from the point of view at the apex of creation, and sees God in and behind all things. He increasingly comes to understand who man is and what man ought to be as he views man in the light of Divine Wisdom. Viewing things from the apex of creation resolves man's identity crisis as man sees himself from the perspective of Divine Wisdom.

God's revealing Himself is inextricably bound up with a definite historical figure. It has nothing of the existential vagueness of a Bultmann. "We only know God through Jesus Christ," (380-547). "It is not only impossible, but useless to know God without the intermediary of Jesus Christ," (382-549). "Thus I hold out my arms to my Saviour who, after being foretold for a period of four thousand years, came to suffer and die for me on earth at the time and in exactly the circumstances which had been predicted. . . ." (466-737).

So Divine Love, the highest order of reality, wholly free and all powerful produces a response of love, certainty and new vision in the human heart which it touches. The human heart, that aspect of man's mind which intuitively comprehends value and meaning, grasps and responds in love to the infinite value of the holy love of God. By an invasion of the human heart, God's grace from above turns man to love God more than himself and to trust the faithfulness of God even as God trusts himself. The abstract god of the philosophers, therefore, is replaced by the living "God of Abraham, God of Isaac, God of Jacob . . . God of Jesus Christ," (737-). A new self, unlike the old "moi haissable," is born to share in the love and self-certitude of God and to see all things as God sees them.

Moreover, Pascal sees God's descent to stir some and not others as rooted in the free choice and election of God. He stated that the Augustinians, among whom he reckons himself, "hold that God has divided this mass (of men), all of whom are equally guilty and fully worthy of condemnation; that He has willed to save part of them by an absolute act of will founded upon His mercy which is wholly pure and wholly free; that, leaving the other part in damnation where it was and where He might justly have left the whole mass. . . ."[6] So God freely wills to touch the hearts of some, creating within them a desire for God and opening their blind eyes to recognize God's Presence "There is sufficient light to enlighten the elect and sufficient darkness to humiliate them. There is sufficient darkness to blind the

221

damned, and sufficient light to condemn them and make them unpardonable," (443-578). This is Divine Freedom. Those whose hearts and souls He opens share in His eternal self-certitude.

God becomes a living reality to those whose hearts He chooses to touch and to redeem. Those who are untouched, those who do not believe, those for whom God is a dead abstraction, demonstrate two facts. First, that trapped in the unresolved identity crisis of fallen man, they are lost in their blindness. Secondly, that God has chosen to remain hidden to their eyes. They are the uncertain, the lost. However, those who, like Pascal, have been chosen to receive the touch of God's grace, hear God's whisper, "Thou would'st not be seeking Me, if thou hadst not found Me . . . I am present with thee by my word in the Scriptures, by my spirit in the Church and by inspiration, by my power in the Priests, and by my prayer in the Faithful."[7] For such men, the hidden God is vibrantly alive. They can never say, "God is dead," because Divine Wisdom has made clear to them, with a certainty which is God's own certainty about Himself, what their real identity is in God's universe.

Pascal, in affirming man's true identity, recognized man's intimate relationship with creation but disavowed a natural continuity between man and the universe or between man and God. Pascal rejected immanentism and called for a renewed emphasis on transcendence. He reaffirmed the necessity of God's revealing grace without which the riddle of man's true identity is unanswered and God is hidden in darkness.

CHAPTER FOURTEEN

PASCAL AND JOY

FOR TOO long Blaise Pascal has been identified with a gloomy, morbid style of Christianity. The fact of the matter is that his Christian faith brought the mature Pascal deep joy and happiness which he longed to share with others Probe beneath his studious, scholarly thoughtfulness and one will discover a sweet and gentle stream of happiness. Dig behind the pained expression caused by years of misery and illness and one will find a sense of joy and satisfaction which few men have known. Pascal, after the night of November 23, 1654, was a man of joy, celebrating the reality of God's grace which had come to him.

But it was not always so! For years, Pascal, like every man, had yearned for happiness but found it to be elusive and beyond his grasp. In the first part of the Pensées, he analyzed man's misery and unhappiness which really had been his own. In the second part, he described the nature and source of true joy and happiness.

Pascal traced both man's desire for happiness and his subjugation to misery back to the Fall. "That is the state of men today. There remains in them some faint desire for happiness, which is a legacy of their first nature and they are plunged into the miseries of their blindness and lust which have become a second nature to them." (309-430). Man's hunger for happiness is a carryover from man's original innocence in the unsullied image of God. "All men seek happiness; there are no excep-

223

tions" (300-425). But man's sin has made him blind. He lives with half-truths, deception and falsehood. Pascal emphasized that the taproot of natural man's unhappiness is moral, spiritual and intellectual blindness. Man is alienated from reality. He is separated from the glories of truth. "The people are silly, however sound their opinions; because not seeing truth where it is, which means finding it in places where it does not exist, their views are always very unsound and very misguided" (173-328). So, Pascal traced man's unhappiness in life to his blindness, his alienation from the truth of reality.

Man's ignorance about reality is essentially a knowledge crisis. Fallen man is blind even to his own identity and position in the universe. An identity crisis of major proportions is the crux of man's unhappiness. "What reason is there for rejoicing when we cannot look forward to anything but incurable unhappiness. . . . I do not know who placed me in the world, what the world is, what I myself am; I am in a state of terrible ignorance about everything." (11-194). Man is saturated with ignorance of himself, of life, of the universe, of death. He projects his blindness outward and so becomes lost in darkness and misery. "When we behold the blindness and wretchedness of man . . . without knowing who has placed him there, what he is supposed to be doing, what will become of him when he dies, incapable of all knowledge. . . . I am amazed that people do not fall into despair over such a wretched state." (389-693).

Add to this blindness, man's inner alienation and conflict and man becomes hopelessly tormented and unhappy. "Internecine war in man between his reason and his passions. If he only had his passions. If he only had reason without passions. . . . If he only had passions without reason. . . . But since he has both, he is bound to be in a state of interior conflict . . . he is always divided and at odds with himself." (253-412). Pascal had walked this road of inner strife. During his days with young Roannez, he had felt this warfare raging within him and had been tormented and sad.

Yet a yearning for happiness, a throwback to man's first state of innocence, persists. Men search for happiness. "The Stoics say: 'Go back unto yourselves; it is there that you will find peace.' It is not true. Others say: 'Go out of yourselves: seek happiness by amusing yourselves.' And that is not true." (286-465). Unhappiness in the present moment causes men to look to the future. ". . . the present is usually painful." (84-172). Men, like the tramps waiting for Godot, sit in the painful present waiting, waiting, waiting in the hope that there may be happiness out there in the future. "The present is never our goal; the past and present are our means; the future alone is our goal. Thus we never live, but we hope to live; and as we are always preparing ourselves to be happy it is inevitable that we never are happy." (84-172).

But the future holds only more of the same blindness and ignorance about life and about oneself. Moreover, out in the future awaits death which for the natural man is the ultimate misfortune, the final mystery. "Let us imagine a number of men in irons, and all condemned to death, some of whom are slaughtered each day in the sight of the others, so that the survivors see their own state in that of their fellows, and, looking at one another in sorrow and without hope, await their turn. It is the image of the human condition." (314-199). The natural man sees in death the final darkness, the final termination of his hopes. And so man avoids thinking of death. He seeks diversions and distractions in a frantic effort to avoid facing the ultimate unhappiness.

Thus men seek relief in activity. "Men's sole good therefore lies in the discovery of some form of distraction which will stop them from thinking about their condition; some business which takes their minds off it; some novel and agreeable pursuit which keeps them occupied, such as gambling, hunting, or an entertaining show — in a word, what is known as amusement." (269-139). But such distractions only provide temporary relief. The sadness returns. "No matter how unhappy he is, if we can persuade him to take up some pastime man will be happy as long as the game lasts; and no matter how happy he is, unless his mind is occupied by some passion or pastime which keeps away boredom, he will soon become gloomy and wretched. . . . But think what sort of a happiness it is that consists in being diverted from thinking about ourselves!" (269-139).

So, men become trapped in a mad whirl of activity, ever trying to avoid facing their essential condition. It is the pursuit of the bluebird of happiness, it is relentless activity which brings momentary relief not the actual capture of the bluebird. "We never seek things, but the pursuit of things" (276-135). Men run from one external activity to another, frantically trying to avoid having to face their essentially perilous and sad condition. Man seeks temporary happiness outside himself and so amusements, people, business, partying and even philosophizing occupy his time and keep him from thinking about death, misery and his own identity crisis.

Again, Pascal had walked this painful road. His excursion into the glittering world of high society, his tireless experiments in science, his involvement in theological disputation bore the mark of being diversions which were subconscious attempts to evade facing up to the ultimate issues of life. So Pascal had felt the unhappy frustration which comes to those who feel powerless to help themselves. "What then are avidity and impotence crying out to us if not that in other days true happiness existed for man, that all that remains of it is man's empty shell which he is trying in vain to fill up with anything that comes to hand, seeking from absent things the help that he does not obtain from present things; but they are equally incapable of helping him because the bottomless gulf can only be filled by an infinite, unchanging object, that is to say by God Himself." (300-425).

Then came Pascal's leap out of sadness into joy! On the night of November 23, 1654, his soul was filled with God. The God who forgives cleansed Pascal's soul with FIRE. Blaise furiously scribbled on parchment a record of that mystic experience. One word dominated the paper, "FIRE" That was the purifying fire which could free him from his past sins. It was the illuminating fire of God which could dissolve blindness and dispel darkness. It was the fire of the Presence in whose light reality becomes visible. So Pascal later could write. "Such are my feelings, and every day of my life I bless my Redeemer who placed them in me and who has turned a man riddled with frailties, sorrows, sensual desires, pride and ambition into a man who is free from these failings by the power of His grace to which all glory is due because wretchedness and error are my only contribution." (748-550).

Reality had broken through to Pascal. Identified with Jesus Christ, now Blaise saw the panorama of reality as God sees it. He was being accepted, loved and identified with the "God of Abraham, God of Isaac, God of Jacob, not of the philosophers and the scholars." The personal Being of God was flooding Blaise's heart, mind and will, giving him a new vision of reality, even of his own identity as the beloved of God. So there was "Certitude, Certitude, emotion, joy, peace." In the years that would follow, Pascal would reflect "that ultimate happiness lies in knowing him with certainty" (15-194). Cleansing and certitude was followed with the joy of being a whole person. Now he experienced the new humanity, "the greatness of the human soul."

The words fairly leap from the Memorial, "Joy, Joy, Joy, tears of joy." God, the Eternally joyous and whole Person for whom all other persons are named, was pouring new love and life into Pascal's being and he quivered with the joy of the wholeness of God Himself. No longer did Blaise have to run in fear from the darkness of past, present or future. He was possessed and secure and fullfilled in the love of God who is Perfection.

No wonder one day he would write, "It is a good thing to be worn out and exhausted by the unsuccessful pursuit of true good in order to hold out one's arms to the Saviour." (306-422).

"In order to make man happy religion must show him that there is a God; that we are bound to love him; that our true happiness lies in being in him, and that our only sorrow is to be separated from him." (309-430). "Happiness is neither outside nor inside us; it is in God, and outside and inside us." (286-465).

Now Pascal could see clearly the wisdom of God which says that man "wanted to be his own centre and to be independent of my help. He withdrew from my dominion; and when he made himself equal to me by his desire to find his happiness in himself, I abandoned him to his own devices." (309-430). Now Pascal could understand that man's unhappiness derived from his sin in separating himself from God in order to play god. Now Pascal could look back over his life and understand that he had to go through his bitter wretchedness to learn his need of God.

He wrote, "The first thing which God inspires in the soul which He truly deigns to touch is an understanding and a quite extraordinary insight by means of which the soul considers things and itself in an entirely new manner. This new light brings fear to the soul and an agitation which disturbs the repose which it found in the things that delighted it."[1] "The God of Abraham, the God of Isaac, the God of Jacob, the God of Christians is a God of love and consolation; he is a God who fills the soul and heart of those whom he possesses; he is a God who makes them inwardly conscious of their wretchedness and of his infinite mercy." (17-556). Often a man must be backed into a corner of misery before he realizes his need and will open his being to the Hound of Heaven. So Pascal came to joy. He discovered his destiny in God. He was whole and knew the "greatness of the human soul" when it is redeemed by Jesus Christ.

Pascal knew that his newfound inner joy was born of a new wholeness in God. The night of the Memorial he prayed "Let me never be separated from him" who had become the fountainhead of joy. From that night on, he sought to live in surrendered obedience to Jesus Christ. More and more he immersed his mind in Holy Scripture. In his Memorial he had written, "we can only keep him by the ways taught in the Gospel." He meditated on the Passion of Jesus. He lived in the atmosphere of Holy Writ. The Bible became a channel of God's Word to his life. It was a pipeline of joy to his soul. Gilberte put it: "The whole of the time that was not given up to the charitable work . . . was devoted to prayer and to reading Holy Scripture. It was, so to speak, the core of his existence from which he derived all his joy. . . ."[2] Gilberte also wrote: "He had a marked love for . . . the little hours which are composed from Psalm 118 in which he discovered so many admirable things that he always experienced a fresh joy when he said it; and when he discussed the beauty of the Psalm with his friends he was carried away and communicated the same enthusiasm to all those to whom he happened to be talking."[3] This was no dour, gloomy Pascal. Enthusiasm and joy flowed from God, through His Word, into the life of this son of France.

The Church, even though divided and strife-ridden, was also a channel of joy to Pascal's soul. Following the Apostle's description of the Church as the Body of Christ, Pascal extolled the happiness of those who know the joy of fellowship in the Body of believers. "Our limbs do not feel the happiness of their union. . . . How happy they would be if they felt and knew it." (676-482). "To be a member means to have life, being and movement only through the spirit of the body and for the sake of the body. The severed member, no longer seeing the body to which it belongs, no longer has anything but a wasting, moribund existence." (688-483).

In spite of the sickness of the Church, Pascal felt it was still a channel of God's grace to his life. So, as long as he lived, he worshipped. He resolved never to be separated from it. He loved its members because he saw Christ in the faithful. Particularly, he loved those who shared the poverty of Christ. He donated to the poor his income from the bus service he helped to create. During his last illness he sighed, "How is it that I have never yet done anything for the poor although I have always been so devoted to them?"[4] When Holy Communion was denied him during his last sickness, he said, "Since I cannot have Communion in the Head I should like to do so in the members."[5] Then he pleaded to have some poor, sick person brought in to share the care being given him. His desire even to the end was to be intimately related to Christ through union with those whom Christ loved. So the Body of believers was both a channel of grace and an object of joyous devotion for Pascal.

Following the teachings of the Gospel and the Church, Pascal sought to become more and more obedient to his Lord. Misguided as his more ascetic practices may seem to some, they were his attempts to keep his body and soul subject to the God of grace and joy. He wanted nothing to come between his soul and his God. He began to retreat from the comforts of life. He dispensed with as many servants as possible. He restricted his diet. He wore an iron belt studded with spikes to keep him humble. He shunned human affection. He avoided the pleasures of the world in order to enjoy the pleasures of a higher order. The Christian hedonist, celebrating and enjoying the good things of life, finds this style of life difficult to comprehend. Yet Pascal was a child of seventeenth century Roman Catholicism which understood the process of sanctification as more dependent on man's own works of mortification than on the gracious work of the Holy Spirit. Pascal, following the teachings of his church, was attempting to work his way closer to God. But his very works of mortification tended to short-circuit the joy which the gracious gift of the Holy Spirit brings. Yet he toiled laboriously on, ascetically punishing himself and trying to bring himself into conformity to the holy love of Jesus.

His joy may sometimes have been short-circuited. His attention was somewhat diverted from the Lord of Glory to his own sinfulness and his struggles to overcome his unworthiness. But joy was not cut off. Even in his asceticism, he was happy and blessed. He said in a letter to the Roannez, "We give up pleasures only for other greater pleasures. . . . He who has found a treasure in a field is so filled with joy that for joy thereof, according to Jesus Christ, he selleth all that he hath and buyeth that field."[6]

Yet the joy of that mystic night in 1954 was to be tarnished at times. On that night, he felt totally possessed and accepted by the Lord of Grace. But the teachings of the Roman Catholic Church caused him to retain guilt rather than to release guilt. Though he was assured of God's forgiveness, he could not totally forgive himself. The Roman Catholic teaching on penance would not allow him to release fully his guilt to the God who "remembers our sins no more." Gilberte states: "It was in accordance with these same principles that he displayed such a love of penance because he said that we must punish a sinful body, and punish it unstintingly by continual penance. . . ."[7] Medieval Roman Catholicism, strangely confusing justification and sanctification, taught that man is justified partly on the basis of his own good works. Pascal's mystic joy at being totally accepted by God later was diluted by the teaching that he had to punish himself and to pay part of the price of his sin himself. So, in his "Prayer Asking God to Use Illnesses to a Good End," he revealed a consciousness that the past is not blotted out. He remembered his sins. "Lord, although my past life has been exempt from great crimes . . . nevertheless it has been very odious to Thee by its continual negligence, by my persistent repugnance to Thine inspirations, by ill use of Thy most august Sacraments, by contempt for Thy Word, by the idleness and utter uselessness of all my acts and of my thoughts. . . ."[8] In that same prayer, he indicated an awareness of continuing punishment for his past sins. "I have misused my health, and Thou hast justly punished me for it; do not suffer me to misuse thy punishment."[9] "The ills of the body are both but the outward image and the punishment of the ills of the soul."[10]

The loving sacrifice of Jesus on Calvary was not recognized as final and all-sufficient by his church or by Pascal. So, to the end of his days, Blaise was haunted by a consciousness of guilt. He interpreted his illness, as, in part, punishment from God. He saw his works of mortification as part of his attempt to cleanse and purify his soul. With such an inadequate understanding of the mercy and forgiveness of God, his joy was alloyed by a continuing sense of guilt and punishment.[11] Yet the joy of being loved by God in Christ could not be stifled.

Blaise *did* have a very real happiness and joy in the present moment. Even when persecution and sickness grew acute, he had joy. "I live joyfully either among the good things which it pleases him to bestow upon me, or amid the ills which he sends me for my own good, and has taught me to suffer by his example." (466-737). A continuing certainty and awareness of his Lord's Presence kept him joyful when bitter persecution assaulted him. During his battle with the Jesuits, his niece was cured by the touch of a Holy Thorn. This reassurance of God's approval sent joy surging through his being again. Gilberte Perier put it: "He was more deeply moved by the miracle because God was glorified in it and because it happened at a time when the faith of the majority of people was at a low ebb. His joy was so great that he was entirely absorbed by it."[12] Joy overflowed his life, as persecution raged around him, because he was assured of God's approbation.

Even when the pain of his last disease coursed through his body, deep inner joy seemed to glow even more brightly. Gilberte who nursed him so tenderly described it: "He looked on his state of prostration with joy, and we saw everyday that he blessed God for it out of the fullness of his gratitude."[13] Sickness and pain for Pascal were tokens of God's love, designed for his good. So he rejoiced in affliction believing with the Apostle that "all things work together for good to them that love God, who are called according to His purpose." (Rom. 8:28).

Finally, when death drew near, Pascal believed he was approaching the ultimacy of joy. He had earlier declared "The Old Testament contained symbols of future joy, and the New described the means of reaching it." (527-666). ". . . eternal and essential bliss begins with death." (717-447) In his Memorial experience he had been pointed toward "Eternal joy in return for one day of travail in this life." Compared to the bliss of eternity with God, life on earth seemed fleeting and brief.

Thus, on August nineteenth 1662, at one o'clock in the morning, Blaise Pascal entered into the fullness of joy where faith gave way to glorious sight.

Contrary to the opinion of many, Pascal after his night of surrender to Jesus Christ was not gloomy and sad. He was possessed by a sublime joy.[14] Though his countenance was serious and often screwed in pain, his was the joy unspeakable of Christian mystics through the centuries.[15] His was not a humorless life as Guardini suggests.[16] The *Provincial Letters* abound in humor, though barbed with satire. His was a serious joy which could laugh but more often was serious with a concern for unhappy souls threatened with infinite unhappiness. Though his joy was at times tarnished by the medieval confusion of justification and sanctification, his was a joy that came to his soul from the highest order of reality. It would sustain him through years of pain and testing. At the last it would burst into sheer bliss in the ultimate cleansing, wholeness, certitude and love of eternity. So Pascal had been captured by joy, lived in joy and finally went to joy.

CHAPTER FIFTEEN

PASCAL AND A NEW MORALITY

"INSTEAD of adjusting the life of men to the precepts of Jesus Christ, these new theologians have undertaken to adjust the precepts and rules of Jesus Christ to the interests, passions, and pleasures of men."[1] With these words of Pascal and his Jansenist friends, the age-old tension between the defenders of universal ethical principles and the exponents of accommodation to specific situations comes into focus. How do men in Christ relate the precepts of Jesus to the specific situations of life? Are men to be guided by fixed, absolutist transcendent principles or are they to be guided by the needs and context of each specific situation? For many centuries Christian thinkers have sought to relate the unchanging laws of God to the changing situations of life. In the modern world, the tension has been manifest in the running debate between contextualists who emphasize the specific act and its situation and principialists[2] who tend to stress the transcendent, unchanging rules of moral life. The former, while criticizing the legalism of the latter, have tried to create new secular theologies to justify their accommodation to the situations of contemporary life.[3] And so debate goes on as to whether human history must be continually directed toward righteousness by transcendent precepts and principles or whether these principles can be abandoned for a more existentialist view of life. Transcendence vs secularity is the issue. Parallel to this debate is the discussion whether induction or deduction is the appropriate ethical logic. Underlying all the argumentation is the basic question, "by what authority do we decide in ethical matters?" The present situation remarkably parallels Pascal's day.

The Jesuit-Jansenist controversy of Pascal's time was essentially a clash between two tendencies which have always been present in the history of the Church: the tendency toward accommodation and the tendency toward absolutism. The Jesuits represented the spirit of accommodation. They inductively extracted morality from each specific situation. They sought to relate Christianity to the spirit of a new age. They realized that seventeenth-Century man was out of touch with the historic, orthodox Christian faith. "Honnêteté homme" was "man come of age." He tipped his hat to the Church but Christianity did not really influence his life in any personally meaningful way. In order to keep him in the Church, the Jesuits had devised a system of casuistry which analyzed specific cases seeking to rationalize and to justify a style of life which was essentially at odds with the Gospel. Dueling, lying, stealing and even murder were made acceptable by utilizing such practices as "the direction of intention" and "probabilism." In so doing, they not only changed traditional Christian morality but also introduced basic changes into theology.

Christian ethics and theology are intimately interrelated. When ethical values change, thoughtful men must devise a new theology to undergird a new morality.[4] Thus it was with the Jesuits of the seventeenth century. Pascal recognized that their transformation of ethical values was accompanied by a corresponding deformation of Christian theology.

On the other hand, the Jansenists represented the second tendency toward absolutism and perfectionism. They clung to the ancient Christian heritage. They stressed the essential immutability of Truth in theology and in morality. Morality was to be deduced from Scripture and tradition. Pascal cast his lot with these proponents of an absolutist ethic and entered the lists against the Jesuit innovators.

The Jesuits had been deeply influenced by the renaissance humanism of the new age and so they were essentially optimistic about human nature. According to the Spanish Jesuit, Molina,[5]

Adam's sin had only deprived man of the supernatural gifts which God had bestowed upon him. Man was essentially unchanged by the Fall.

The Jansenists, however, were pessimistic about the nature of man. Following Saint Augustine, they believed Adam's Fall had totally corrupted human nature. The Jansenist saw man's essential selfhood identified with a corrupted human nature while the Jesuits tended to see man's self expressed by a series of transitory acts. Man's essential concupiscence, ever since the Fall, has prompted man to seek his happiness in created things rather than in God. This was Pascal's position.

The Jesuits believed that man is not fundamentally sinful and so a radical change in human nature is neither needed nor sought. Uncorrupted man still possesses free will and therefore is equally capable of doing good or evil. However, to help man to do good. God has given man grace, promptings which are "sufficient" to enable man to do the good. All men possess this grace sufficient to obey God's laws. But how do men obey the laws of God in particular situations of life? Obedience or disobedience to the laws of God in specific cases had to be spelled out. So casuistry, the science of interpreting the commandments as they apply to life-and-blood situations was developed. It was an ancient and honorable art. In its nobler aspects it has had the endorsement of Christians in all ages. But it had received a new direction from the Jesuits. In order to encourage converts to the Church and to hold the unconverted in the Church, they had worked out the minimum requirements for salvation. They had eliminated the scandal and offense of the Gospel. Easy salvation seemed to be their theme in sharp contrast to the Biblical understanding of a salvation which involved total surrender and sacrifice with a personal cross and resurrection.

Into this scene, Pascal had come. He was profoundly stirred by the Jansenist teaching on grace which had been verified in his own experience. The Jansenists believed the sacrifice of Christ was sufficient to have redeemed all men. But the fact is that only certain men actually have been saved by the grace of Christ. Who are they? Those whom God has predestined for salvation; those who have received grace; those who, by grace, have been empowered to obey God's commands. The elect are those whose souls have been transformed by the grace of God. So Jansen, Saint-Cyran and their followers taught that the Christian must experience a total conversion, a renunciation of self-love in favor of love for God. This had happened to Pascal. He had become an ardent champion of the grace of God. The cheap grace and easy morality of the Jesuits was repugnant to him because it prostituted Biblical teaching and saved men from an awareness of their own sin and guilt thus confirming them in their lostness.

Since Christian ethics and theology feed on each other, Pascal focused his critique of the Jesuits on their theology, especially in his fourth and eighteenth "Provincial Letters" and in his "Écrits et fragments sur la grace." In his fourth "Provincial Letter" he had his man from the provinces say to the Jesuit Father, "Certainly, according to Father Bauny, we may be said to behold a redemption of an entirely new description."[6] Pascal discerned a tragic deformation of redemption in the theology of the Jesuit casuists like Father Bauny. Bauny, in "The Summary of Sins," had written, "In order to sin and become culpable in the sight of God, it is necessary to know that the thing we wish to do is not good, or at least to doubt that it is — to fear or to judge that God takes no pleasure in the action which we contemplate, but forbids it; and in spite of this, to commit the deed, leap the fence, and transgress."[7] Man was not a sinner unless he had a clear vision of the wrongness of his act and a full understanding that it was contrary to God's will.

Montalte, Pascal's provincial, responded, "Why, I see more people, beyond all comparison, justified by this ignorance and forgetfulness of God, than by grace and the sacraments."[18] "If one could only succeed in bringing himself not to think upon God at all, everything could be pure with him. . . ."[9]

Against such a warped view of sin, grace and personal responsibility, Pascal had Montalte appeal to Scripture. "In fine, is it not enough that Jesus Christ himself has taught us that there are two kinds of sinners, the one of whom sin with 'knowledge of their masters will,' and the other without knowledge; and that both of them will be 'chastised,' although, indeed, in a different manner?"[10] Ignorance of sin does *not* free man of culpability.

In his eighteenth "Provincial Letter," Blaise probed even more deeply into the question of sin and grace. He placed himself between the extremes of Calvin and the contemporary Thomists.[11] To Calvin, he ascribed the position of "maintaining that the will, when under the influence of grace, has not the power of resisting it." Of the Thomists of that day, he said they affirmed "that efficacious grace of itself governs the will in such a way that it still has the power of resisting it."[12]

Following St. Augustine, Pascal would maintain a dynamic tension between both man's freedom of will and the sovereignty of God's grace. "When it pleases God to visit him (man) with his mercy, he makes the soul do what he wills, and in the manner he wills it to be done, while, at the same time, the infallibility of the divine operation does not in any way destroy the natural liberty of man. . . . For, according to this great saint (Augustine), . . . God transforms the heart of man, by shedding abroad in it a heavenly sweetness, which, surmounting the delights of the flesh . . . makes him conceive a distaste for the pleasures of sin. . . . Finding his chiefest joy in the God who charms him, his soul is drawn towards him infallibly . . . not but that the person has always the power of forsaking his God . . . provided he choose to do it. But how could he choose such a course, seeing that the will always inclines to that which is most agreeable to it. . . ."[13] "Such is the manner on which God regulates the free will of man without encroaching on its freedom, and in which the free will, which always may, but never will resist his grace."[14]

239

In all his exposition of grace, Pascal sees efficacious, saving grace as necessary to enable man to choose and to live the way of salvation. The Jesuits, with their optimistic view of human nature, had eliminated the need for a new birth, for a radical infusion of grace. But Pascal, with his Biblical view of the utter sinfulness of man, stressed the absolute necessity of grace for salvation. Pascal also saw grace as radically changing the nature and morality of man. The grace of God is powerful and dynamic, according to the Bible, Augustine and Pascal. It is not the mild, gentle promptings of his Jesuit adversaries. Grace, as experienced by Pascal, had been the powerful intervention of God into his own life. It had changed his life. It was absolutely necessary and it was absolutely persuasive.

What was man's part in the experience of grace? Pascal repudiated Luther's view that "we cooperate in no way whatever towards our salvation."[15] He equally disavowed the Jesuit Molina "who will not allow that it is by the strength of divine grace that we are enabled to cooperate with it in the work of our salvation."[16] He endorsed Augustine's position that "our actions are ours in respect of the free will which produces them; but that they are also of God, in respect of his grace which enables our free will to produce them."[17] So Pascal asserted the Divine synchronization of free will and grace. But he emphasized the priority of sovereign grace. The power of God's grace to radically change man had been his own experience. "Thou wouldst not be seeking Me, if thou hadst not found Me."[18]

It is not, therefore, difficult to understand why Pascal was so opposed to the casuistry of the Jesuits. It involved the salvation of humanity. Their deformation of morality and theology was establishing men in their lostness. The Jesuits were removing from men their sense of anguish and sin without which salvation is impossible. The Jesuits "render those worthy of enjoying God through eternity who never loved God all their life! Behold the mystery of Iniquity fulfilled.[19] He knew, by experience and from his study of the Bible, that the grace of God in Jesus was not impotent and weak. It prepared a man for eternity. It was radical and explosive. It was given to change human nature and to produce a radical new humanity with an ethic which opposed the morality of natural man.

Through the centuries, a deficient understanding of sin and grace has inevitably produced a deficient morality and vice versa. Modern secular theologians as well as situational and contextual ethicists, busily adapting, adjusting and even discarding the lofty Biblical commandments, need to examine their view of grace. Pascal insists that Christian morality is distorted when one's understanding of the grace of God is anemic. And similarly, one's views of sin and grace are cheapened when one's understanding of God's moral requirements are lowered So he appealed for men of every age to believe the message of the Bible and the Fathers of the Church. "If it relates to a supernatural truth, we must judge of it neither by the senses nor by reason but by Scripture and the decisions of the Church.[20] His appeal for the Jesuits to rediscover the radical grace of God and its corollary, the radical sinfulness of humanity, are essentially appeals to return to the truth of Scripture.

But the Jesuits were not ready to make such revisions. Radical sin, radical grace, radical morality would offend the darlings of society they were courting. So they continued with the use of "probabilism"[21] and the "direction of intention"[22] to justify the ethics of society. By the "probable" opinions of their writers and by directing the intention of man when he violates a commandment of God, they were able to rationalize and to justify most any crime.

Pascal, ever the champion of truth and the defender of the absolutist Biblical Commandments, drafted a "Comparison of The Christians of the Earliest Times With Those of Today." The early Church was distinct from the world. The early Christians under the impact of Divine grace practised a radical Biblical morality which distinguished them from the pagans in society. "Whereas people formerly saw an essential distinction

241

between the two, they now regard them as mingled and blended, so that they are now scarcely distinguishable."[23]

No wonder that Pascal could say "Our cause is the cause of Christian morality."[24] He attacked the new morality of the Jesuits because it not only corrupted moral standards but also degraded the basic mores of society. Pascal was well aware that the destruction of the structures of society begins with laws first being undermined in theory and then abolished in practice. He suspected that this was the intention of the Jesuits as they sought to rule the world. They repudiated the laws of God upon which were based the laws of man. He protested that "we have seen those who pass themselves off as doctors and theologians, substitute for true morality, which should have divine authority alone as its principle, and charity alone as its end and aim, a totally human morality, whose principle is reason alone, and whose aim is merely carnal desire and natural passions."[25]

He followed up by declaring, "If we consider the consequences of this teaching. . . ."[26] Advocates of any new morality, based on corrupted reason probing the situations of life independent of supernatural revelation or grace, always need to ask themselves what will be the consequences of their teaching. Will it sever the Church's ties with Divine Authority? Will it destroy the Church as the Body of Christ and the witness to Divine Truth? Will it lead society down the road into a mystic subjectivism and chaotic relativism? In modern times Daniel Day Williams asks "an ethic without principles sounds free and flexible, but can it answer the question 'What ought we to do?' Certainly we should act justly, out of love. But what is doing justly?"[27] A morality without rules always will lead us from one question to another to another. Men who must live in relationship with one another must have some universal principles upon which to base their actions else there will be chaos. The new moralists must always consider the consequences of their teaching both for the Church and for society.

Blaise asserted the importance of being able to teach "That

it is always a crime to slander one's neighbor; that it is more in keeping with one's conscience to offer the other cheek after having received a blow than to kill the man who flees after having delivered the blow; that duelling is always a crime and that it is a horrible falsehood to say that it is for natural reason to discern when it is permissible or forbidden to kill one's neighbor."[28] Even infidels and savages observe principles of ethical behavior, yet, Pascal observed, only where Jesuits dwell are unchanging moral principles exchanged for a new morality derived from each specific situation by corrupted reason.

Yet Pascal pointed out that the direst consequence of the new morality was the judgment of God. He cited occasions when the prophets and priests of the Old Testament had espoused false teaching. God had visited His wrath upon them and had caused their impieties to turn back upon them. So he pleaded "just as the piety of the saints of the Old Testament consisted in opposing the innovations of the false Prophets who were the Casuists of their times, so the piety of the faithful must now aim to resist the laxity of the Casuists who are the false prophets of today. And we must not cease to make clear to our peoples what the true prophets incessantly cried to their peoples, namely, that the authority of these doctors will not make them pardonable before God if they follow their false doctrines."[29]

Personal accountability to God, surrender to the radical grace of God in Jesus Christ, obedience to God's precepts revealed in Scripture — these were the cornerstones of Pascal's morality. Though he certainly yearned to make these understandable to men of his day, he refused to compromise the truth. He rejected any attempt "to adjust the precepts and rules of Jesus Christ to the interests, passions and pleasures of man." His whole being was intent on "adjusting the life of men to the precepts of Jesus Christ."[30]

Pascal was convinced that the hard claims of the Gospel and the unchanging requirements of the commandments of God could challenge and shake up those who considered religion irrelevant. He was equally convinced that to tone down the Biblical message of sin and grace, for whatever reason, would only pacify sophisticated men and would offer them no confrontation or challenge.[31] He had been confronted and challenged and changed by the lofty claims of the Gospel. So, he saw in Biblical-Augustinian Jansenism an opportunity to confront and challenge and change the sceptics and atheists of his day. This then, was Pascal, evangelist-extraordinaire, contending for the only Gospel which can save men's souls. "All that we need to know is that we are wretched, fallen, separated from God, but redeemed by Jesus Christ" (14-560). "For the Christian faith seeks little more than to establish these two truths: the corruption of nature and its redemption through Jesus Christ" (11-195). "Deum meum et deum vestrum." (737-).

CHAPTER SIXTEEN

PASCAL AND VIOLENCE

BLAISE PASCAL was a violent man who reflected in his personality the violence of a turbulent age. Born in a time of change, he suffered the loss of his mother while still an infant. Step by step through life he was forced to compete with his younger sister, Jacqueline, for their father's approval. As a lad, he saw his father flee for his life to escape the outrage of Chancellor Séguier, and the power of Richelieu. After his father's reinstatement, he journeyed to Rouen where he witnessed the aftermath of a bitter confrontation between the establishment and the rioting Frondeurs. There the agony of physical suffering began its onslaught of his body. There he spawned a violent attack on the theology of the heretical St. Ange. Returning to Paris, where violence filled the atmosphere, Blaise participated in sharp debates with Réné Descartes and the Jesuit scientist, Noel. When his sister, Jacqueline, entered the convent of Port-Royal, he retaliated bitterly, cuttingly and forcefully, in an attempt to withhold her inheritance from her. Even after his night of surrender to Jesus Christ, Pascal was violent in his pursuit of the Jesuits. He attacked the Society of Jesus in a prolonged series of letters in which at first he defended the Port-Royalists. Later, however, he took the offensive, turning his pen sharply against Jesuitical casuistry. Finally, before his death, Pascal became violently ascetic, almost to the point of endangering his life. Pascal was no stranger to violence and strife.

Violence expresses itself in many ways. There is physical violence such as was exhibited by the Frondeurs when they rioted in the streets. There is also mental and moral violence such as some seventeenth century Jesuits demonstrated in their distortions of the truth. Indeed, Pascal pointed out that there is also the violence of silence. "Silence is the greatest of persecutions" (830-920).

Pascal had little sympathy with the rioters of the Fronde. After all, his father was an official of the establishment. He wrote of "the injustice of the Fronde which sets up its pretended justice against power," (175-878). Again he wrote, "the greatest of evils is civil war," (184-313). A sickly Pascal was opposed in principle to physical violence.

Pascal recognized well, though, that many of the injustices of society are maintained by violence. He saw lust for power and dominance rampant at the royal court in Paris. "Tyranny lies in a desire of domination which is universal and out of order," (106-332). He saw fools in silks and brocades, born to wealth and power, misusing their authority over the common man. He stated, therefore, "When we choose the captain of a ship, we should not choose the passenger who came from the best family," (67-320). Neither should those who rule have power simply by the accident of birth.

Pascal saw clearly the foolishness and inequity of human justice, which maintains itself by power and violence. He acknowledged that the power structure had repudiated justice. "Power has repudiated justice and declared that it was unjust, and has maintained that power itself was just," (192-298).

Pascal knew that human laws were frail and subject to distortion. Ugly violence exists in every society. It is often legitimatized by the laws of the state. He still, however, exhorted people to obey the laws of society for folk "are liable to revolt as soon as someone shows them that law and custom are worth nothing," (195-325). Therefore, to prevent insurrection and unlimited physical violence, the laws of the power structure must be obeyed. Violence must be contained even by foolish customs and unjust laws. For Pascal the Christian ought constantly to be seeking to make power just and justice powerful. Yet, he did recognize that if the state were to repudiate the use of force and violence, chaos would result. He, therefore, accepted violence as practiced by the state as necessary in a violent world in order to keep violence within limits.

Nevertheless, the fact acknowledged by Pascal is that the great and powerful of earth often keep their power by foolishness, force and violence. "It is extraordinary: People do not want me to honor a man covered with brocade who is followed by seven or eight servants! Come! He will have me whipped if I do not salute him. His dress is a form of power," (179-315).

Pascal longed to diminish the violence in society. He wished to limit even the violence used by the establishment to maintain law and order. He appealed for a wedding of justice and power. "Justice without power is impotent; power without justice is tyrannical. . . . Justice and power must therefore be brought together," (192-298).

Pascal, though disliking physical violence, nevertheless was caught up in violence of an intellectual sort. He wrote with passion the words, "How I hate all this nonsense, not believing in the Eucharist and that sort of stuff!" (353-224). And again, "attack those who use too many symbols," (488-649). Later he declared, "How I hate those who profess to doubt miracles!" (897-813). Admittedly, it was the practice of disputants in that century to use strong language. Nevertheless, it appears that Pascal was not merely following the custom of the day. He was also expressing a personal intensity of thought which approached violence. His opponents had no doubts about the violence of his attacks and counterattacks. St. Ange, Descartes, Father Noel, Miton, the Jesuits, felt the force of his pen and knew the anger behind his words.

In both "The Pensées" and "The Provincial Letters," Pascal revealed many of his thoughts about violence. He had learned well from Méré the importance of understanding man. Thus, "The Pensées," began with an analysis of the contradictions within man. Man is in a state of blindness and misery. Reason and justice are debased and overwhelmed by imagination and passion. Man is full of contradictions and frustration. "What can man do? . . . he wants to be great and finds that he is small; he wants to be happy and finds that he is unhappy; he wants to be perfect and finds that he is riddled with imperfections; he wants to be the object of man's affections and esteem and sees that his faults deserve only their dislike and contempt," (99-100). Man is a mass of frustrations. Frustration leads to hostility and violence. Pascal pictured man in a state of hostility and violence toward the truth. Truth about reality saturates the relationships of life and permeates all of life. This reluctance to face reality exists in all men. "There are different degrees in this dislike of the truth; but it can be said that it exists to some extent in all of us. . . ." (99-100).

Yet this deep inner hostility toward truth and reality is not to be charged against God. Man is responsible. Man has departed from the innocence in which he was originally created. In his alienation, man hates and resists God and His truth. "We only suffer to the extent that vice, which is natural to us, resists supernatural grace. Our heart feels torn between conflicting impulses; but it would be very unjust to attribute the violence to God, who draws us to Him, instead of to the world which holds us back," (744-498). Alienated man is violent in life because of the inner violence within his own soul. There exists an inner tug-of-war. Man's self is rifted between the pull of the fallen world as over against the pull of the God of holy love. Alienated man is also divided man, torn apart by conflicting loves within his heart. He, therefore, resists reality and struggles violently against facing the truth of his condition.

As Pascal saw it, violent men are constantly exercising violence, especially against the truth of God. He closes his twelfth "Provincial Letter," saying, "It is a strange and tedious war, when violence attempts to vanquish truth, and only serves to give it fresh vigor. All the lights of truth cannot arrest violence and only serve to exasperate it."[1]

Here Pascal suggests a basic law which is that violence begets violence more often than it realizes victory. In his violent struggle with the Jesuits he had learned that the harder he struck out at them, the more exasperating became their resistance. "Violence and verity can make no impression on each other."[2] Violence, even in defense of the truth, only begat more violence. Violence always escalates violence.

However, something in Pascal pressed him to carry on the warfare against the Jesuits. He explained it: "When the enemies of the Faith offend against truth by trying to tear it out of the hearts of the faithful in order to set up error in its place, would it be a service to the Church or a betrayal of her to remain at peace when truth is being attacked. . . . There is, therefore, a time when peace is just and another when it is unjust. . . . Truth is therefore the first rule and the final end of things," (835-949). His Jansenist friends in their Preface to the Port-Royal edition of "The Pensées," described the violence of his attack in these words: "He wishes to declare war on all those who impugned either its (Christianity's) truth or its holiness: that is to say, not merely on atheists, infidels and heretics, who refuse to submit the false enlightenment of their reason to faith and to recognize the truths that religion teaches; but he even wanted to declare war on Christians and Catholics who, being in the body of the true Church, nevertheless do not live according to the precepts of these gospels."[3]

Nevertheless, Pascal was acutely aware that violence was not the way taught in the Gospel. After the twenty-third of November 1654, in the midst of writing his seventh "Provincial Letter," he declared "the Gospel commands us not to render evil for evil, but to leave vengeance to God."[4] Again, in "The Pensées," he said that Jesus Christ came to bring men His grace, "in order to transform them all into one holy Church," (642-783). The God of Jesus Christ is gracious and gentle. Rather than force men into accepting Him, God while revealing Himself, also hides Himself. Pascal understands the Divine example for he puts on the lips of Divine Wisdom the words: "I do not mean to you to submit and believe in me without a reason, and I do not claim the right to reduce you by force," (309-430). God is gracious, not violent in His attempts to redeem man. Thus He reveals but also hides Himself.

Again, in his fourteenth "Provincial Letter," he expressly wrote, "The spirit of the church is diametrically opposite to these seditious maxims, opening the door to insurrections to which the mob is naturally prone enough already. She has invariably taught her children that they ought not to render evil for evil; that they ought to give place unto wrath; to *make no resistance to violence*. . . . She forbids them still more strongly than is done by civil law, to take justice into their own hands. . . ."⁵

If Pascal saw Christ's way as the way of gentle persuasion and love, how did it happen that he could defend that way so violently? Admittedly Pascal addressed "The Provincial Letters" to those Jesuits whom he claimed were endorsing murder when one's honor is affected. Pascal in attacking the Jesuits' use of probablism and of directing the intention, felt he was defending the way of love and peace. The question for Pascal is, "Does the end justify the means? Does a defense of the truth ever justify violent means?"

Apparently Pascal, at one point in his development, would answer in the affirmative. He believed he had Holy Writ for his example. In his eleventh letter he declared, "as Christian truths are worthy of love and respect, the contrary errors must deserve hatred and contempt."⁶ Indeed, the God of the Bible at once "hates and despises sinners."⁷ He cited David, Job, Jeremiah, Daniel, Elias, and even Jesus Christ in their ridicule of error. He quoted Augustine's words, "The wise laugh at the foolish, because they are wise, not after their own wisdom, but after that divine wisdom which shall laugh at the death of the wicked."[8] According to Pascal, at this stage of his life, the Jesuit attacks on the truth of God had to be met by counterattack. To fail in the defense of truth would be to betray the truth. He found in the Scripture his justification for using violent means of defending the truth.

However, he laid down certain guide lines a Christian must follow in his defense of the truth. First, "the spirit of piety always prompts us to speak with sincerity and truthfulness . . ., but we should publish only those things which it is useful to disclose, and not those which can only hurt without doing any good." Secondly, "speak with discretion." Thirdly, "when there is need to employ a little raillery, the spirit of piety will take care to employ it against error only." Then he sums it all up in a fourth rule which is the "essence and end of all the rest: that the spirit of charity prompts us to cherish in the heart a desire for the salvation of those against whom we dispute."[9] Again he cites Augustine: "We ought ever to preserve charity in the heart even while we are obliged to pursue a line of external conduct which to man has the appearance of harshness; we ought to smite them with a sharpness, severe but kindly, remembering that their advantage is more to be studied than their gratification."[10]

Pascal claims to have been thus motivated in his attack on the Jesuits. Charity ought to prompt his readers to accept his assertion that the love of truth, which prompted his sometimes violent defense of truth, had also kindled in his heart a love even for his adversaries. In other words, Pascal claimed that intellectual violence in defense of the truth is legitimate for the Christian so long as it is carried out in love. Love, even for the Christian, sometimes must be so serious and so stern that it may become violent.

Yet one cannot help but wonder at the abrupt cessation of hostilities. Suddenly, in the midst of his nineteenth letter, Pascal stopped the attack. He devoted himself to raising money for the poor. He withdrew from the field of battle and channeled his intensity of spirit into an even more rigorous spiritual discipline. Had the Lord, who opened not His mouth when He was reviled, led his follower into a deeper level of faith and love? Indeed, Pascal had acknowledged that men change. "Time heals sorrows and quarrels because we change. . . ." (206-22). Having spoken the truth in love, as he understood it, he rested his case before the God of all truth. The evidence of his deepening humility, compassion and trust seems to indicate that his abandoning the attack on the Jesuits was due to a deepening experience of faith.[11] Violence seemed to fade as he drew closer and closer to his Lord. In every age, violence can melt away as men draw closer and closer to the Lord who is Love.

Thus Pascal had come on a long pilgrimage. Through those younger years, when ambition drove him to seek fame and perfection, violence had flared whenever his drive was frustrated. In those middle years, after the Christ of love touched him on the night of November 23rd, his love of the truth of the Gospel had channeled the residue of his inner hostility and intensity into a defense of the truth. He legitimatized non-physical violence when it was done in the name of truth and in a spirit of love. He continued to justify some forms of physical violence when executed by the state. Though he preferred the limited violence imposed by foolish and often unjust laws to the unlimited violence of chaotic lawlessness, he pleaded for the power structure to seek justice. Then in the closing years of his life, a higher vision of love and non-violence seemed to grip him. He had journeyed through three orders of reality, analyzing the physical order, fighting valiantly for truth in the order of the mind, but now he had come to the empire of the saints, the highest order of reality which is love. "The infinite distance between bodies and minds symbolizes the infinitely more infinite distance between minds and charity; for charity is supernatural," (585-793). The realm of truth was now subordinated to the realm of love. A deepening experience of the holy love of God seemed to teach him to trust the ambiguous situations of life to the Lord of history. In the radiance of Divine Authority and Love, inner hostility and outward violence seemed to melt away and vanish. Prophetic words penned in the heat of the battle with the Jesuits seemed at last to have come alive for him: "Violence has only a certain course to run, limited by the appointment of Heaven, which overrules its effects to the glory of the truth which it assails; whereas verity endures forever, and eventually triumphs over its enemies, being eternal and almighty as God Himself."[12]

CHAPTER SEVENTEEN

PASCAL AND AUTHORITY

SOME men belong to the ages. Blaise Pascal was one of these. A son of the seventeenth century, Pascal stood in the no-man's land between science and religion; between Protestantism and Roman Catholicism. He, like twentieth century man, sought truth and certainty amidst conflicting authorities. First, he was enthralled by reason; then he was fascinated by the authority of the Bible; finally he was captured by an experience of the heart. All the while the Roman Church was seeking to maintain its authority over its wandering son. Through the maze of authorities competing for his and our souls, he walked. His anguish and confusion, when beset by such conflicting authorities as reason, science, the Bible, the heart and the Church, are ours. His quest for that which is ultimate and authoritative beyond all else is the quest of modern man who is fascinated by the fruit of scientific reason but dumbfounded at the unintelligibility of theological thought. His personal striving for that which was to be most authoritative in his life reveals a struggle for certainty that is our struggle. The answer he found can be our answer.

Born beneath the shadow of the Church at Clermont in 1623, Pascal lived and died in communion with the Church of Rome. Yet the authority of sheer size and age, which was the Church's inheritance, could not satisfy the soul of one who was searching for that which was ultimate and personal.

Tutored by his father, Pascal's brilliant mind explored the

255

world of science. His father's teaching method was to hold the lad a little ahead of his work. So the restless mind of the brilliant young Pascal discovered the 32nd proposition of Euclid, wrestled with the proportions of conic sections and invented the adding machine. In his more mature years, his research on the vacuum, in hydraulics and mathematics led a contemporary to say, "Vous esgalez les plus fameoux du siecle." Yet reason merely led him to contradictions and antinomies. Reason left him unsatisfied because it offered him more and more questions but never the answers which could fill an infinite void within him.

Then came those years when under the influence of the teachings of Cornelius Jansen, a controversial Augustinian of that day, he discovered the Bible. For awhile the Church and scientific reason faded into the background of his life. He explored the facts, dogmas, propositions and principles of the written Word of God. The Bible was the authority with which he challenged those who seemed to have deviated from the pristine faith of the early Church. One of his victims, the admittedly heretic St. Ange, was driven into obscurity as Pascal wielded the Sword of the Spirit. The Bible during these years was authoritative as an objective source book to be analyzed by reason. He quotes from it matter of factly after his father's death. His understanding of the Bible, however, lacked the passionate inwardness which characterizes the man to whom that which is ultimate has become personally authoritative.

So Pascal, having given his allegiance in turn to the Church, scientific reason and then to the Bible and theological reason, next turned to the social whirl. He joined with the sophisticates of Paris in their more worldly pursuits. He detected strange stirrings in his heart when a young lady entered his life. Though his love apparently was not returned, he discovered that the intuitions of the heart often reveal more about life than other authorities which had previously dominated his life. Finding that the deceit of the world could not satisfy his yearning for the peace that comes with the assurance that one has been touched by the ultimate, he seemed to wilt in despair. The authorities of the age had failed to meet his need.

Then came the night of November 23rd, 1654. In the solitude of evening, Pascal, bowed over Scripture, was confronted with the personal Presence of God. He surrendered himself. He described this flaming experience: "Renunciation, total and sweet . . . total submission to Jesus Christ. . . ." Jesus Christ, the incarnation and condensation of Holy Love, the personalization of the highest order of reality which is love, became the authority over all and in all other authorities to Pascal. "Certitude," even that certainty with which God is certain of Himself flooded his life.

From this point of viewing, Pascal's eyes were opened to see the whole landscape of reality diffused with Transcendent Authority. The Bible, the Church, the heart of man and human reason now became channels of the personal Authority of Jesus Christ.

The Bible now was the primary witness to Jesus Christ. Through its pages God spoke to him not merely of facts and propositions penned hundreds of years before, but more — of submission to the Lord who lived and loved him in every moment of his days. The Bible seen as a channel of the Authority of its Lord was seen to belong to the dimension of personal encounter. Seen from a Christological perspective seeming contradictions were reconciled. "In Jesus Christ all the contradictions are reconciled," (491-684). Following his night of encounter with Jesus, he learned to enter the Biblical dimension where he escaped time and space to relive sacred scenes from the past. In his "Life of Christ," he passionately joins the disciples of old in following the Master. Scripture was alive to this man who had surrendered to the Authority of the Scripture's Lord.

The Church, too, was seen in a new light. Now it was subject to judgment by the authority of Jesus Christ mediated

257

through the Bible. Gallican elements in the Roman Church had long recognized that the Church was not the ultimate authority. Now Pascal came to a new love for the Church, especially the Church of Jansenist (Augustinian) persuasion, as the arena of God's saving grace. Yet he realized that the Church must bow to the Authority of Jesus as mediated by the Scriptures. Thus, when his "Provincial Letters" were condemned by the Church, he called upon a higher authority: "Ad tuum Domine Jesu, tribunal appello." Throughout his days he remained one who knew that the Church divorced from the Word of Jesus Christ destroys men. He sought both by taunting and pleading to turn the Church back to the sovereign authority of its Lord.

The mind of Pascal before his mystic night of revelation had led him to frustration in contradictions and antinomies. Reason had led him to the horns of many a dilemma. For example, on one hand sceptical philosophers had led him to see man as a confused brute. Others, Stoics, had opened his eyes to view man as a clever angel. The reconciliation was to be found in the Scriptural account telling how man, nobly created in the image of his Creator, had fallen into sin which no beast has ever known. Pascal saw clearly that reason without revelation to guide it leads to seemingly irreconcilable dilemmas. Pascal came to realize that an infinite gulf separates the arena of reason with its multitude of questions and the arena of Transcendent Wisdom which contains Divine answers. Brunschvicg described Pascal's insight as a "Dialectic founded upon antinomies . . . only more consistent than Hegel, Pascal has clearly seen what Kant recognizes that if reason itself establishes the thesis and the antithesis, it declares by this contradiction its own essential relativity, and prohibits itself from establishing the synthesis by itself alone. . . . The contradiction (in reason) being of a natural order, the solution will be supernatural."[1] Pascal had come to realize that reason needed revelation to furnish Divine answers. Reason was humbled in the face of its own results which was a learned ignorance. "The last proceeding of reason is to recognize that there is an infinity of things which are beyond it," (373-267).

Pascal's encounter with the Divine Authority of Jesus led him into the very depths of reason where he became sublimely aware of the authority of the heart. The heart was seen as the center of personality, transcending, yet enfolding thought, feeling and will. The heart was an instrument of knowledge. It initiated the deepest of all knowledge, and was the ground of reason. "Heart, instincts, principles," (331-281). The heart could be called reasoning in depth. Thought was a precipitation of the heart. "We know truth not only by the reason but also by the heart, and it is in this last way that we know first principles . . ." (214-282). For Pascal the heart is indeed the ground of feeling and reason. The heart became the arena in which the Authority of Jesus, mediated through His Word and the Church produced certainty and assurance in the soul of man.

In later times, Cardinal Newman in his Grammar of Assent[2] spoke of the "illative sense" which resembled Pascal's understanding of the heart. Certainty for Newman was arrived at when "convergent probabilities" unite in the "illative sense." Pascal was aware of the heart as the locus in which the witnesses to Jesus Christ (Scripture, the Church, reason) unite under Divine Grace. In the surrendered heart, where thought, feeling and will bow in humility, the witnesses to Christ, these "probabilities," become united and are transformed into living assurances of the Authority of Him to whom they point. The heart was seen as possessing a creative, personal function apprehending objective witnesses and finding in them the personal Authority of Jesus. Objective witnesses to His grace, meeting God in the human heart, become catalysts producing profound assurance of Divine Grace and Authority.

To Pascal, the Sovereign Authority of the highest order of reality was incarnate in the Jesus of Holy Love. Lesser authorities ought to be channels of the One Supreme Authority of Jesus. Therefore, all channels of Authority are to be reconciled in the unity of His Authority as it is primarily mediated by Scripture to the Church and the mind of man. Only as the Church and reasoning men bring themselves into accord with the Authority of God shining through Scripture do they too share in that authority. As men study the Scripture, the proclamations of the Church, the questionings of humble reason, Divine Authority draws near bringing assurance and that profound certitude with which God is certain of Himself. If a man's heart is yielded and submissive, he will be gripped by the Holy Love and Authority of the Sovereign God and will be held in a grip that is as firm and certain and eternal as God Himself. Then violence and all crises of identity vanish away in the fire of Divine Love, Authority and Certitude.

This then is the Authority for all men and civilizations. Without it, all is darkness and despair. With it, there is peace and faith that is sure. Gripped by Divine Authority, men can be eternally united with God in the upbuilding of the universe. With such a faith, men can march forward triumphantly out of anguish into joy.

SELECT BIBLIOGRAPHY

THIS present work has grown out of twenty years of reading in the vast literature on Pascal, his life, his period, his thought and his influence. The works listed below represent just a few of these but they are those upon which the author has leaned most heavily.

Brehier, E. *The Seventeenth Century,* University of Chicago Press, 1966.

Brunschvicg, Leon. *Oeuvres de Blaise Pascal,* Hachette, Paris, 14v.

―――. *Descartes et Pascal, Lecteurs de Montaigne,* Cahiers de Philosophie, Neuchatel, 1945.

―――. *Le Genie de Pascal,* Rieder, Paris, 1937.

Cailliet, Emile. *The Clue to Pascal,* S.C.M. Press, 1944.

―――. *Pascal, Genius in the Light of Scripture,* Westminster Press, Philadelphia, 1945.

――― and Blankenagel, J. *Great Shorter Works of Pascal,* Westminster Press, Philadelphia, 1948.

Chevalier, Jacques. *Pascal,* Plon, Paris, 1922.

Chinard, Gilbert. *En Lisant Pascal,* Lille et Geneve, 1948.

Clark, William. *Pascal and the Port Royalists,* T. T. Clark, Edinburgh, 1902.

Cousin, V. *Jacqueline Pascal,* Didier, Paris, 1861.

Daniel-Rops, *Pascal et notre coeur,* Roux, Strasbourg, 1949.

Droz, E. *Etude sur le scepticisme de Pascal,* Alcan, Paris, 1886.

Ducas, A. *La Pensée et la connaissance de Pascal,* Mediterranee Vivante, 1952.

Eastwood, D. M. *The Revival of Pascal,* Oxford Univ. Press, 1936.

Etudes sur Pascal, Pascal Tercentenary number of the Revue de Metaphysique et de Morale, Avril-Juin, 1923.

Fletcher, F. T. H. *Pascal and the mystical tradition,* Blackwell, Oxford, 1954.

Giraud, Victor. *Pascal, L'homme, L'oeuvre, L'influence,* Paris, 1905.

————. *La vie heroique de Blaise Pascal,* G. Cres, Paris, 1923.

Guardini, Romano. *Pascal for our time,* Herder and Herder, New York, 1966.

Guitton, Jean. *Entretien avec M. de Saci,* Aix, 1946.

Hubert, M. L. *Pascal's finished apology,* Yale Univ. Press, New Haven, 1952.

Humbert, P. *L'oeuvre scientifique de Blaise Pascal,* Paris, 1947.

Jovy, E. *Etudes Pascaliennes,* Vrin, Paris, 1936.

Lafuma, Louis, *Recherches Pascaliennes,* Delmas, Paris, 1949.

Lhermet, J. *Pascal et la Bible,* J. Vrin, Paris, 1930.

Lowenthal, M. *The autobiography of Michel de Montaigne,* Vintage Books, New York, 1956.

Mauriac, F. *Blaise Pascal et sa soeur Jacqueline, Hachette,* Paris, 1931.

Mesnard, Jean. *Pascal his life and works,* Philosophical Library, New York, 1952.

————. *Pascal et les Roannez,* Desclee de Brouwer, Paris, 1965, 2v.

Montaigne, M. *Montaigne: Selected essays,* Modern Library, New York, 1949.

Mortimer, Ernest. *Blaise Pascal,* Harper and Bros., New York, 1959.

Pascal, B. *Oeuvres completes,* Editions du Seuil, Paris, 1963.

————. *Pensées, the provincial letters,* Modern Library, New York, 1941.

Patrick, D. G. M. *Pascal and Kierkegaard,* Lutterworth Press, London, 1947. 2v.

Romanes, E. *The story of Port-Royal,* John Murray, London, 1907.

Ronnet, G. *Pascal et L'homme moderne,* Nizet, Paris, 1963.

Sainte-Beuve. *Port Royal,* Hachette, Paris, 1878.

Steinmann, Jean. *Pascal* (translated by Turnell), Harcourt, Brace and World, New York, 1966.

Stewart, H. F. *The holiness of Pascal,* Cambridge Univ. Press, 1915.

———. *The secret of Pascal,* Cambridge Univ. Press, 1941.

———. *Pascal's apology for religion,* Cambridge Univ. Press. 1942.

Strowski, Fortunat. *Pascal et son temps,* Plon-Nourrit, Paris, 1921.

Turnell, Martin. *Pascal's Pensées,* (tr. by Turnell), Harper and Bros., New York, 1962.

Vinet, A. *Etudes sur Blaise Pascal,* Payot, Lausanne, 1936.

Waterman, M. *Voltaire, Pascal and human destiny,* Kings Crown Press, New York, 1942.

Webb, C. C. J. *Pascal's philosophy of religion,* Oxford Univ. Press, 1929.

Wells, A. N. *Pascal's recovery of man's wholeness,* John Knox Press, Richmond, 1965.

FOOTNOTES

CHAPTER ONE

1. For details of Pascal's ancestry, including data concerning Martin Pascal's Calvinism, see Ernest Jovy, *Etudes Pascaliennes*, VII, pp. 217-224. Paris: J. Vrin, 1930.
2. Etienne's fortune has been variously estimated at six hundred thousand gold francs, three hundred thousand gold francs, etc. All we can be sure of is that Etienne was solidly middle class.
3. Mersenne's academy would one day become the French Academy of Science.
4. Tallemont des Reaux suggests that actually Etienne merely found Blaise studying a volume of Euclid. Leon Brunschvicg favored this interpretation but it does not account for Etienne's outburst of amazement. Moreover, would not Blaise have called circles and lines by their correct names if he had been reading Euclid?
5. Gilberte Perier in her *Vie de Blaise Pascal* observed, "As soon as my brother was old enough for talk he gave tokens of an extraordinary mind by the extremely apt little replies he made to questions, and still more by his own questions on the nature of things, which surprised everyone."
6. Etienne may have implanted in the fertile mind of his young son the seed which would develop into Pascal's famous three orders (cf. *Pensées*, Fragment 585-793).

CHAPTER THREE

1. Ernest Mortimer in his *Blaise Pascal* has observed that Msgr. Knox in *Enthusiasm* pointed out the flair for histrionics amongst the Arnaulds. Mortimer declared that Arnauldism came to mean singularity or "the itch to be different," Cf. Mortimer, E., *Blaise Pascal*, Harper Bros., New York, 1959, p. 52.

265

CHAPTER FOUR

1. The seeds of his doctrine of the three orders (585-793) are evident here.
2. When the clockmaker stole Blaise's idea and tried to steal the glory by constructing his own machine, which would not work, young Pascal was so crushed that he nearly abandoned this endeavor. Only the encouragement of the Lord Chancellor and the securing of a special license for the project caused him to continue his efforts.
3. Gilberte records that "from this time he renounced every other subject of knowledge to apply himself solely to the one thing that Jesus Christ calls necessary." Obviously, she was mistaken since he made many significant scientific researches from 1648-54.
4. At the same time, Forton may have impressed Blaise with his theory that men are correct in what they affirm and only incorrect in what they deny. Later Pascal would say, "All heresies spring from the exclusion of these truths. . . ." (462-862).
5. Various diagnoses have been offered of Pascal's illness. It has been variously described as hereditary tuberculosis, arteriosclerosis, neurosis, syphilis, cancer, opthalmic headaches, etc. For references, see Peyre, Henri, "Pascal et la Critique Contemporaine," *The Romanic Review,* v. 21, No. 4, October-December, 1930, pp. 325-340, and also Onfray, R., *L'abime de Pascal, Alencon,* 1949.

CHAPTER FIVE

1. In that same letter we can discern the faint outline of the three orders. He recalled that "corporeal objects are only an image of spiritual objects." Cf. Cailliet, E. and Blankenagel, J., *Great Shorter Works of Pascal,* Westminster Press, Philadelphia, 1948, p. 77.

CHAPTER SIX

1. Clermont was proud of its intellectual heritage. Four or five hundred students were enrolled in its college.
2. A bishop was paid 100,000 livres a year.
3. Again, we see evidence of the emerging idea of the three orders. (cf. 585-793).
4. Cf. Cailliet and Blankenagel, op. cit., p. 92.
5. Since no name is given in the existing manuscript, scholars have conjectured that Jacqueline was refering either to Gilberte or Louise

Default. The former is more likely since it is unlikely that a servant would have presumed to oppose her former mistress.

CHAPTER SEVEN

1. There has been difference of opinion regarding the date of this trip to Poitou. Morris Bishop suggested the spring of 1651. Yet the records indicate that the Duke visited Poitou from October to December in 1651. During that period it is unlikely that Pascal who had just lost his father and had to settle his father's estate would absent himself from Paris. July 1652 has been widely accepted by others, but Ch. H. Boudhors in his "La date du voyage en Poitou (Pascal et Méré)," Revue d'histoire litteraire de la France, xxix (1922), 338, concludes that there were no periods in 1652 when both he and his friends were free to take such an extended trip. Autumn 1653 seems to be the best dating for his journey.

2. It is likely that it was during this period that Blaise composed his *Espirit de Geometrie* while he was pondering how beliefs are communicated from one mind to another. The role of the heart and esprit de finesse in human experience were clarified for Pascal during this period.

3. Fragment 269-139 may reflect this period. "Dancing: We must consider rightly where to place our feet."

4. The argument of the wager was not new with Pascal. cf. Arnobe (*Adversus nationes,* I, 53; II, 4); Augustine (*De Utilitate credenti,* 12, 26); Raimonde Sebonde (*Theologie naturelle,* trans. by Montaigne, ch. 68); Lachelier, J. *Du fondement de l'induction,* 7th ed., Alcan, Paris, 1916, p. 199; Eastwood, D. M., *The Revival of Pascal,* Oxford University Press, 1936, pp. 84-86.

5. Marguerite Perier wrote of Pascal's plans for marriage as did Racine cf. Brunschvicg, "Oeuvres," I, 130. n.l. Pascal's secret emotions of love are probably reflected in the "Discours sur les Passions de l'Amour" which lay for years among his unpublished works in the library of Saint-Germain-des-Pres. It was discovered by Victor Cousin in the nineteenth century and contained the words written under the title, 'On l'atribua a M. Pascal." cf. Gustave Lanson, "Le 'Discours sur les passions de l'amour' est-il de Pascal?" (French Quarterly, II, March 1920), 7-26. Most scholars attribute it to Pascal since there exists no compelling argument against his authorship.

6. In the facsimile of the *Memorial* these last lines of Pascal's handwriting are so illegible that the words cannot be made out clearly. Louis Perier in his copy of the *Memorial* deciphered the words as

they stand above. They certainly express the direction of Pascal's later years when he sought a spiritual director.

7. Augustin Gazier listed the Solitaries and gentlemen between 1637 and 1660 as given by Besoigne. The list is in Gazier's *Histoire générale du mouvement Janséniste depuis ses origines jusqu'a nos jours*, Champion, Paris, 1923, v. 1, 72, 73. With the exception of sixtyish d'Andilly, the others were between 30 and 45 years of age.

8. The Port-Royalists' suspicion of Pascal's intellectuality and worldiness never seemed quite overcome. A gulf always seemed to separate Pascal and Port-Royal even though he defended it so passionately. Indeed, his sixteenth *Provincial Letter* he would explicitly declare, "I have never had the honor to belong to their establishment."

9. In October, 1655, the orphan Jean Racine, became one of the students.

10. For a reconstruction of the scene, see Hallays, Andre, *Le Souvenir de Pascal a Port-Royal-de-Paris et a Port-Royal-des-champs*, in *L'Illustration*, No. 4189, 81st year, June 16, 1923, p. 610. For a reconstruction of the conversation see Cailliet, E. and Blankenagel, J. *Great Shorter Works of Pascal*, Westminster Press, Philadelphia, 1948, pp. 121-133.

11. Blaise had spent years reading Epictetus. It is probable that his study of Epictetus, Guillaume du Vair, Charron and other Stoics had begun during his years in Rouen. In a time of civil war when all order was being shaken, many found support in the Stoic teaching on order and restraint.

CHAPTER EIGHT

1. Mons was a family name. Pascal's maternal grandmother was Marguerite Pascal de Mons. Jacqueline closed her letter dated October 25, 1655, with a P. S.: "Let me know, please, if you are still Monsieur de Mons," (Oeuvres, V, 4, 80).

2. Strowski, *Pascal et Son temps*, III, p. 80, note shows that a comparison of the *Provincial Letters* with Arnauld's earlier works, the *Apologie pour les Saint Peres* and the *Theologie Morale des Jesuites* show how extensively Blaise relied on Arnauld.

3. On March 30th, the police confiscated some type at Langlois' print shop and the lieutenant of police at Aubray searched Port-Royal des Champs but found nothing. Reaction to the letters was rising.

4. At first the Abbess declined saying, "It was not a time for amusing

ourselves by looking at a holy relic, that we should think only of prayer and lamentation before God," (Oeuvres, IV, p. 328).

5. Professor Morris Bishop in his *Pascal, The Life of Genius,* N. Y., 1936, Reynal and Hitchcock, quotes Dr. Gifford, Professor of Opthalmology at Northwestern University, who diagnosed this condition as dacryocystitis. He has cured this in children by pressure on the swelling. This ruptures the membrane which has grown to keep the naso-lacrymal duct from perforating into the nose. If this diagnosis is correct, the "miracle" would consist in its happening just at the time that Port-Royal needed a sign. Cf. n. 19, p. 376 of Bishop's work.

6. Henceforth Blaise took as his motto, "Scio Cui Credidi." Cf. II Timothy 1:12, "I know whom I have believed."

7. For an admirable translation of this correspondence see Cailliet, E. and Blankenagel, J. *Great Shorter Works of Pascal,* Westminster Press, Philadelphia, 1048.

8. These views were not new, having been expressed often by the Gallican wing of the Roman Catholic Church. Pierre d'Ailly, Gerson, the University of Paris and the Assembly of Bourges (1439) had declared that by natural, divine and canonical law the Pope is subject to the General Council which has the right to judge and to condemn him. In 1682, the Assembly of the Clergy of France put it more moderately in its fourth declaration: "Though the Pope have the principal part in questions of faith . . . yet is his judgement not incontrovertible, unless the consent of the church have been given," cf. Sabatier, Auguste, "Religions of Authority and the Religion of the Spirit," trans. L. S. Houghton, New York, McClure, Phillips and Co., 1904, pp. 382-383. Papal infallibility was not made a doctrine of the Roman Catholic Church until 1871.

9. Lafuma has shown that during 1658 Pascal wrote hundreds of pages in preparation for the Apologetic he hoped would win some the unbelieving to Christianity. Mersenne estimated that there were 20,000 atheists in Paris (cf. Lafuma, *Histoire des Pensées de Pascal,* Paris, 1954, pp. 11-28).

CHAPTER NINE

1. Another pain to be borne in 1659 was the death of his housekeeper, faithful Louise Default.

2. The date and even the occurrence of the episode at the Bridge of Neuilly has been questioned by some scholars. This writer, however,

sees no convincing reason for not considering it to be factual.

3. Sainte Beuve said, "This death enlightened Pascal. She explains Pascal, completes him, in some respects surpasses him, and now for the last time she converts him."

CHAPTER TEN

1. Cf. Guardini, R. *Pascal For Our Time,* Herder and Herder, New York, 1966, p. 220. Guardini suggests that this was a "third conversion". If so, it was a withdrawal from the battle but not a repudiation of the cause. Guardini sees this as a conversion of Pascal's "obstinate will to be right".

2. After Pascal's death Father Beurrier reported to the Archbishop of Paris that Pascal had died as an orthodox Roman Catholic "in perfect submission to the Church and Our Holy Father the Pope." This raised something of a controversy as to whether Blaise had repudiated the Jansenism of Port-Royal. Evidence of Pascal's intellectual evolution was given in 1680 when Nicole wrote that twenty-five years earlier he had begun to think that Jansen's interpretation of Augustine was too rigid and that the Dominicans and Thomists were closer to. the truth. He added that "the late M. Pascal . . . helped me not a little in encouraging that inclination." (Cf. Jovy, *Pascal Inedit,* Tome III, p. 362). Beurrier also reported that Pascal felt that Port-Royal was "going too far in the matter of grace and it seemed they were showing less submission to the Church and to Our Holy Father the Pope" (Oeuvres X, 338-339). However, Blaise and the Port-Royalists had always been submissive to the Pope. His basic quarrel was with the Jesuits and the French hierarchy. There seems to be no disavowal of basic Jansenism in his dying statements. Beurrier admitted this when he later said to Gilberte, "I have well recognized that his words might have another sense than the one I gave them, as also I believe they did have. . . " (Oeuvres, X, 360). In 1673, he repeated this in a letter to Etienne. M. Jovy's contention of a deathbed disavowal of Port-Royal has little evidence to substantiate it. It is apparent that there was no retraction of Pascal's Jansenism though there had been a withdrawal from the battle.

3. After his death, Pascal's family decided to have the now familiar death mask made. They also allowed the doctors to conduct a post-mortem.

CHAPTER ELEVEN

1. Throughout this volume, whenever a fragment is cited, the number given first is the enumeration given by Lafuma and the second that of Brunschvicg. The author is persuaded that the ordering of Lafuma is closer to the intention of Pascal.
2. Cf. Wells, A. N., *Pascal's Recovery of Man's Wholeness,* John Knox Press, Richmond, 1965, p. 104-105. "In these unforgettable thoughts the dominant theme is that of discontinuity, and this discontinuity is absolute in the ascending direction. . . . But in the direction of descent the reverse is true. Here it is possible to proceed from one order to another. In fact, from the perspective of the summit, reality in all its expressions can be comprehended as wholeness. . . . What distinguishes the Christian thinker from other men is that he is able to discern the meaning of the orders of reality and the meaning of his activities in them."

CHAPTER TWELVE

1. Albert Camus, *The Fall,* p. 143, New York, N. Y.: Vintage Books, a division of Random House, 1956.

CHAPTER THIRTEEN

1. *The Christian Scholar,* Spring 1965.
2. Turnell, M., *Pascal's Pensées,* page 79. New York, N. Y.: Harper and Brothers, 1962.
3. Cailliet, E., and Blankenagel, J. C., *Great Shorter Works of Pascal,* Westminster Press, Philadelphia, 1948, p. 140.
4. *Ibid.,* page 147.
5. *Ibid.,* page 146.
6. *Ibid.,* page 140.
7. *Ibid.,* page 135

CHAPTER FOURTEEN

1. Cailliet, E. and Blankenagel, J., *Great Shorter Works of Pascal,* Westminster Press, Philadelphia, 1948, p. 118.
2. Turnell, M., *Pascal's Pensées,* Harper & Bros., New York, 1962, p. 45. Turnell's translation of "Life of Monsieur Pascal by Madame Perier."

271

3. *Ibid.,* p. 68.
4. Ibid., page 70.
5. Ibid., page 72.
6. Cailliet, E. and Blankenagel, J., Op. Cit., p. 152.
7. Turnell, M., Op. Cit., p. 56.
8. Cailliet, E. and Blankenagel, J., *Great Shorter Works of Pascal,* Westminster Press, Philadelphia, p. 224.
9. Ibid., p. 221.
10. Ibid., p. 224.
11. Cf. Cailliet, E., *Pascal, Genius in the Light of Scripture,* Westminster Press, Philadelphia, 1945, pp. 118-119. Professor Cailliet put it: "He (Pascal) had yet to learn the full meaning of the Epistles to the Galatians and to the Romans, and particularly of that central feature of the Gospel which Saint Paul, having learned it from Christ, undertook to preach and to set down in writing: the utterly free character of man's salvation. The dramatic tension of Blaise Pascal's inner life arose from this fact: he had been serving two masters, plumbing the depths of Scripture on the one hand, while on the other he trusted in the infallibility of an authority which was charged to interpret this same Scripture, but which often forgot the central point therein contained, and which even went so far as to contradict this central truth."
12. Turnell, M., Op. Cit., p. 47.
13. Turnell, M., Op. Cit., p. 55.
14. Cf. Brémond, H., *Histoire Litteraire du sentiment religieux en France,* Paris, 1916-1936, 4, 332.336. Brémond characterized Pascal's joy as egotistical. Yet it came from outside Pascal (i.e., from God). It expressed itself in love toward others. Is this egotism?
15. Cf. Augustine: "The soul in contemplation will arrive at that most high and sacred reward for sake of which it has so laboured; and in which are such joys, such a full enjoyment of the highest and truest good, such a breath of serenity and eternity, as are indescribable." (*DeQuant, Anim.* 74, 76).
16. Guardini, Romano, *Pascal for Our Time,* Herder and Herder, New York 1966, p. 212.

CHAPTER FIFTEEN

1. Cailliet, E. and Blankenagel, J., Op. Cit., p. 174.
2. Cf. Gustafson, James., *New Theology No.* 3, MacMillan, N. Y., 1966, pp. 69 ff.
3. Gabriel Fackre analyzes the contemporary effort to accommodate

theology to modern man in his excellent article in *New Theology No. 4*, MacMillan, New York, 1967. On p. 181 he says "The phrase, 'The new theology,' is of course a slippery one. . . . By it, we mean the contemporary point of view in the church which seeks to interpret Christian faith without reference to a divine Other."

4. It is significant that William Hamilton, responding to a new secular morality, entitled his important book, "The New Essence of Christianity," New York, Association Press, 1961.

5. Seventeenth Century Jesuits relied upon Molina. But the popular Molinism was much different from Molina's own complex teaching which in some ways was closer to Jansenism.

6. Pascal, Blaise. *Pensées. Provincial Letters,* The Modern Library. New York, 1941, p. 360.

7. Ibid., p. 360.

8. Ibid., p. 361.

9. Ibid., p. 362.

10. Ibid., p. 365.

11. Pascal clearly differentiated between the deficiencies of the contemporary Thomists and the teachings of St. Thomas, the Doctor of Grace.

12. Ibid., p. 597.

13. Ibid., p. 599.

14. Ibid., p. 600.

15. Ibid., p. 600.

16. Ibid., p. 600.

17. Ibid., p. 601.

18. Cailliet, E. and Blankenagel, J., Op. Cit., p. 135.

19. Pascal, B., *Pensées, Provincial Letters,* Modern Library, New York. 1941, p. 465.

20. Ibid., pp. 612-613.

21. Pascal would not object to a legitimate usage of probabilism in matters not clearly defined by Scripture. But he did object to accepting *any* of many probable opinions in favor of a single, reasoned, probably opinion.

22. "The direction of intention" allows man to will a bad deed if it is considered the means to a good end.

23. Cailliet, E. and Blankenagel, J., Op. Cit. p. 157.

24. Ibid., p. 173 "Factum for the Priests of Paris."

25. Ibid., p. 174.

26. Ibid., p. 180.

27. Williams, Daniel. *What Present Day Theologians Are Thinking,*

Harper Bros., New York, 1967, p. 146.

28. Cailliet, E. and Blankenagel, J., Op. Cit., pp. 181-182.
29. Ibid., pp. 186-187.
30. Ibid., p. 174.
31. Admittedly some Jesuits of that day did present the severity of Christianity to those desirous of an austere life, but others offered an easy Christianity which is not Biblical Christianity. Obviously, men will always incline to the easy road when such an option is presented.

CHAPTER SIXTEEN

1. Pascal, Blaise, *Pensées, The Provincial Letters,* page 498. The Modern Library, Random House, N. Y., 1941.
2. *Ibid.,* page 498.
3. *Ibid.,* page 403.
4. *Ibid.,* page 403.
5. *Ibid.,* page 526.
6. *Ibid.,* page 468.
7. *Ibid.,* page 469.
8. *Ibid.,* page 470.
9. *Ibid.,* pages 475-477.
10. *Ibid.,* page 477.
11. Guardini, R., *Pascal For Our Time,* Herder and Herder, New York, 1964, p. 220, calls this Pascal's third conversion in which he surrendered "the compulsion of rational consistency, the compulsion to be right, the will to power through knowledge, the spirit of combat."
12. Pascal, Blaise. *Pensées, The Provincial Letters,* page 498.

CHAPTER SEVENTEEN

1. Pascal, Blaise, ed. L. Brunschvicg, *Pensées et Opuscules* (15th ed.), page 298. Hachette, Paris, 1928.
2. Cf. Newman, J. H., *An Essay in Aid of Grammar of Assent,* page xvii. Longmans, Green and Co., New York, 1947.